GW01454140

THE INFRASTRUCTURAL CITY

NETWORKED ECOLOGIES IN LOS ANGELES

EDITED BY KAZYS VARNELIS

MAPS BY LEAH MEISTERLIN

A PUBLICATION OF

Actar Barcelona/New York

The Los Angeles Forum for Architecture and Urban Design

The Network Architecture Lab
Graduate School of Architecture, Planning and Preservation
Columbia University

Kazys Varnelis

INTRODUCTION
NETWORKED ECOLOGIES

Submerged a little over a mile off the coast of Will Rogers State Beach in Pacific Palisades, an array of twenty-four silicon-iron alloy electrodes hangs suspended in concrete enclosures. Acting as a grounding device, this structure is paired with 1,067 cast iron anodes laid out in a 3,400-foot-wide ring, buried in a two-foot-deep trench of petroleum coke some eight hundred fifty miles away on the Oregon-Washington border. Together, these two structures serve the Pacific Intertie, North America's longest, highest voltage direct current transmission line. Capable of delivering some 3,100 megawatts, the Pacific Intertie brings current from the Bonneville Power Administration in the Pacific Northwest to Los Angeles, providing nearly half of the Los Angeles Department of Water and Power's capacity in the summer. In the winter, when cooling needs in the south decline and electricity demands in the north climb, Los Angeles returns the favor, sending electricity back up the lines.

The Pacific Intertie's transmission towers each carry only two wires. Normally, in what is called bipolar mode, one transmits current while the other acts as a ground. When a wire needs to be taken off-line for repairs, the remaining one is dedicated to transmitting current. To provide the ground, the two electrodes are activated, giving electricity a return path through the ocean and earth itself. Conveying an invisible force between them, these two megalithic structures power an entire city.

Pacific Direct
Current and Alternating
Current Interties

Source: Bonneville
Power Administration, Celilo
Modernization
Project Fact Sheet, http://
www.transmission.bpa.gov/
PlanProj/Transmission_
Projects/ Completed-TransP/
Celilo/4-15-03FactSheet.pdf

Ground   ⏚
Pacific Direct Current Intertie   ——
Pacific Alternating Current Intertie   – – –
Interstate Highways   ·······

0   50 100   200
Miles

John Wesley, the founder of Methodism and eighteenth-century electrotherapist called electricity "the Soul of the Universe."[1] But even Wesley had little inkling of just how electrification would transform life. Captured from the wild rivers of the American West as they rushed down mountainous slopes, the Soul of the Universe fueled the growth of the region.

With its promise to harness untamable nature and transform it into paradise for man so appealing to the inhabitants of the frontier, infrastructure is the only theology that really took hold in the American West. Facing the vast and unknown American continent, its awesome terrain unprecedented in Europe, colonists confronted the sublime. Through such wonders as Death Valley, Niagara Falls, the Grand Canyon, and Yosemite Valley, North America was capable of overwhelming the senses. The European mind swiftly set out to dominate this wild nature. By overpowering the wilderness mentally through exploration and mapping, then taming it physically, reshaping the sublime terrain for production, settlers created a justification for their own existence. On the basis of this capacity to exploit the land, Americans held to the doctrine of "Manifest Destiny." They assumed it their divine mission to expand westward and bend the continent to their will.[2] If farming turned the great vastness of the plains into geometric regularity, infrastructure reshaped the West. The building of bridges, the damming of rivers, the harnessing of electricity, even the construction of long-distance telecommunications lines proved the legitimacy of man to God by showing his ability to make use of the land.

But the frontier is only the most dramatic place that infrastructure and theology came together. As Colin Rowe observes in *The Architecture of Good Intentions,* modern architecture understood itself as a religion, promising that "the Good Works" would result in the establishment of Paradise on Earth. Modernists believed in the virtues of the plan, the capacity of a clear idea to bring order to the chaos of the metropolis.[3] In implementing the plan, modern architecture relied on infrastructure above all else. A city's modernity was dependent on its infrastructure, something we can see in the Haussmannization of Paris, the technological landscapes of Tony Garnier's *Cité Industrielle,* or the wild, electric fantasies of Antonio Sant'Elia's *Città Nuova.* Modern architecture would be mere pastiche without the infrastructure to support it, nothing but new clothes for an old body. The engineer, Le Corbusier concluded, "puts us in accord with natural law." It was necessary for the engineer to lay down infrastructure in order for the architect to realize his visions above.[4]

Infrastructure also captured the popular imagination. Americans came to accept modernism through bridges and dams before they accepted it in buildings. Only once the massive burst of infrastructure building under the New deal accustomed Americans to the idea that structures based on functionalism and technology would lead the country to economic prosperity could modern architecture spread in the United States.

---

[1] John Wesley, *The Desideratum: Or, Electricity Made Plain and Useful By a Lover of Man and Common Sense* (London: Ballière, Tindall, and Cox, 1759), 9.

[2] On the role of the sublime in America and the technological sublime see David E. Nye, *American Technological Sublime,* (Cambridge, MA: The MIT Press, 1994). For a discussion of infrastructure as theology in the American West see Marc Reisner, *Cadillac Desert: the American West and its Disappearing Water,* (New York: Penguin Books, 1993).

[3] Colin Rowe, *The Architecture of Good Intentions. Towards a Possible Retrospect* (London: Academy Editions, 1994). In modernist texts the plan is often written as the Plan, indicating its divine nature.

[4] Le Corbusier, *Towards a New Architecture,* trans. Frederick Etchells (1931; New York: Dover, 1986), 1. Corbusier repeats the passage for emphasis on 11.

Infrastructural City Founded in 1850, Los Angeles is the epitome of the modern city, a planned metropolis supported by infrastructure. Whereas New York's grid is for pedestrians and horses, Los Angeles is laid out according to the progressive ideals of the decongested metropolis, planned for the efficient movement of trolleys cars and, later, automobiles.

If the West was dominated by the theology of infrastructure, Los Angeles was its Rome. Cobbled together out of swamp, floodplain, desert, and mountains, short of water and painfully dependent on far-away resources to survive, Los Angeles is sited on inhospitable terrain, located where the continent runs out of land. No city should be here. Its ecological footprint greater than the expansive state it resides in, Los Angeles exists by grace of infrastructure, a life-support system that has transformed this wasteland into the second largest metropolis in the country.[5] Nor was this lost on Angelenos. They understood that their city's growth depended on infrastructure and celebrated that fact. After all, what other city would name its most romantic road after a water-services engineer?

Los Angeles, then, provides an ideal case study for a book on infrastructure. To be sure, it is a unique condition, but it is also a modern city par excellence now undergoing significant changes. As Ed Soja has observed, Los Angeles is both an exception and the rule, a singular instance that reveals generic conditions.[6] This is our point of departure for this book.

[5] Worldwatch Institute, "What is your Ecological Footprint?" *World Watch* (April 2000), http://www.nwf.org/nwfWebAdmin/binaryVault/CoC_ecofootprint.pdf, 1.

[6] Edward W. Soja, *Postmodern Geographies: The Reassertion of Space in Critical Social Theory* (New York: Verso, 1989), 191.

We do not claim to focus on the historical development of infrastructure in Los Angeles. That has been covered elsewhere.[7] Rather, our concern is with the transition taking place today. Understanding it allows us to make sense not only of this city but of all cities.

The plan has long been exhausted. Infrastructure—in Los Angeles as well as other cities—regularly breaks down or produces undesirable feedback effects. This, by itself, is nothing new. Historically, Los Angeles's rapid growth has led to an exacerbated rate of failure. At the turn of the century, the city was running out of water.[8] In the 1920s, downtown was jammed to a degree unimaginable today. By the 1950s, the city's air pollution was probably the worst in the world.[9] What makes our moment distinct is that the remedy of creating a new infrastructure or using new technologies to surmount breakdowns is no longer an option.

In Los Angeles, new infrastructures have become difficult, if not impossible, to build due to the staunch individualism of the city's residents. Settled by self-sufficient loners—often having fled Eastern cities—the West has always been individualistic. Its citizens' obsession with their private lives is a key factor toward the city's antipathy toward the civic. Communal places to gather have always been lacking: there are few parks, squares, or plazas in Los Angeles. Open space is the province of the lawn, not a yard to occupy but a buffer against the street and adjoining neighbors (this is changing in neighborhoods like East Los Angeles as Mexican families fence off their yards, turning them into extended living areas).[10] Trees are less for shade and more to demarcate subdivisions, giving identity to real estate schemes.

Thus, although Los Angeles is noted for its architecture, that architecture is almost exclusively single-family homes. If in Chicago and New York capital expressed itself on the skyline, Los Angeles's skyscrapers are generic, its downtown void of any interest except for the fact that it is there. Downtown's recent redevelopment serves only to make it more generic: run-down buildings remodelled into run-of-the-mill lofts. Recent attempts to give the city the illusion of a civic architecture also ring hollow. Take the two most celebrated recent examples, Frank Gehry's Disney Concert Hall and Renzo Piano's addition to the Los Angeles County Museum of Art. Both are products of billionaire Eli Broad's vision. Once known as the "King of Sprawl," Broad founded KB (Kaufmann Broad) Homes, a company responsible for building more suburban sprawl than any other in the country. As Broad describes it, his shift toward civic architecture is by no means a renunciation of his past activities or penance, it is simply the Bilbao-effect, the use of high-design architecture as a means of boosting property values.[11] Architecture, in Los Angeles, becomes less art than infrastructure.

Hollenbeck Park, in Boyle Heights, was given to the city in the 1880s. The I-5 freeway bisected it in the 1960s.

Caught between the needs of jet airplanes and blue butterflies, the beachfront development of Surfridge is permanently abandoned.

[7] See Catherine Mulholland, *William Mulholland and the Rise of Los Angeles* (Berkeley: University of California Press, 2000), Blake Gumprecht, *The Los Angeles River: Its Life, Death, and Possible Rebirth*, Creating the North American Landscape (Baltimore: Johns Hopkins University Press, 1999), David Brodsly, *L. A. Freeway*, an *Appreciative Essay* (Berkeley: University of California Press, 1981), William L. Kahrl, *Water and Power: The Conflict over Los Angeles' Water Supply in the Owens Valley* (Berkeley: University of California Press, 1982), Richard W. Longstreth, *City Center to Regional Mall: Architecture, the Automobile, and Retailing in Los Angeles, 1920-1950* (Cambridge, MA: MIT Press, 1997) as well as Kevin Starr's series: *Americans and the California Dream, 1850-1915* (New York: Oxford University Press, 1973), *Inventing the Dream: California through the Progressive Era* (New York: Oxford University Press, 1985), *Endangered Dreams: The Great Depression in California* (New York: Oxford University Press, 1996), *The Dream Endures: California Enters the 1940s* (New York: Oxford University Press, 1997), *Embattled Dreams: California in War and Peace, 1940-1950* (New York: Oxford University Press, 2002), *Coast of Dreams: California on the Edge, 1990-2003* (New York: Knopf: Distributed by Random House, 2004).

[8] Gumprecht, 88.

[9] Mark Z. Jacobson, *Atmospheric Pollution: History, Science, and Regulation* (Cambridge: University of Cambridge, 2002), 225.

[10] Margaret Crawford and Adobe LA, "Mi casa es sua casa," *Assemblage* 24 (1994): 12-19.

[11] Mark Arax, "Convention is Just an Introduction to Eli Broad's vision of Downtown; Once the King of Sprawl, Billionaire Turns his Sights to Reviving the City's Heart," *The Los Angeles Times*, August 6, 2000 and Kazys Varnelis, "Cathedrals of the Culture Industry," *Forum Annual* (2004), 35-40, http://www.varnelis.net/articles/cathedrals

If Los Angeles was founded on the primacy of the individual, as the city has densified and wealth has accumulated, this has led to an impasse. Angelenos understand their homes to be their castles, prime investment opportunities to be defended at all costs against any possible actions that might lower real estate values, be they new developments within view, densification of neighboring properties, increasing traffic, or any infrastructural or industrial interventions that could be seen, heard, or smelt. By the 1960s, encroaching sprawl and the construction of freeways led to unrest and the emergence of widespread NIMBY (Not In My Back Yard) politics. Fearing the effects on their properties, the city's citizens became experts in cancelling or delaying new proposals. Compounding this, the passage of Proposition 13 in 1978 cut property taxes by two-thirds and capped further increases, effectively preventing the funding of new infrastructural initiatives, which in any event would have become exponentially more expensive as construction costs have risen.[12]

The result has been a halt to nearly all new initiatives. Without money or public will, infrastructure, at least as we have known it, was finished in Los Angeles by the 1980s. A few minor projects such as the subway have been built, but the era of heroic infrastructure is past us. The end of the plan comes at the hands of millions of individuals, all banding together to protect their fiefdoms. Although the particularities of this narrative are specific to Los Angeles, most city governments in the United States—and increasingly abroad—are hamstrung by similar combinations of NIBMYism, rising costs, and depleted finances.

Angelenos had good reason for protecting their environment. By the 1960s, the city was becoming known as a hopeless mess, the product of a century of infrastructure employed for the bottom-line, of real estate development gone awry, of *nouveau riche* lack of taste.

In the face of such criticism, British historian Reyner Banham suggested that this anti-aesthetic landscape was something that architects and planners could learn from. Fed up with the modernist plan, Banham advocated spontaneous urbanism. In his 1971 *Los Angeles: The Architecture of Four Ecologies*, he produced an homage to the city after attempts to plan it had failed:

> Conventional standards of planning do not work in Los Angeles it feels more natural (I put it no stronger than that) to leave the effective planning of the area to the mechanisms that have already given the city its present character: the infrastructure to giant agencies like the Division of Highways and the Metropolitan Water District and their like; the intermediate levels of management to the subdivision and zoning ordinances; the detail decisions to local and private initiatives; with ad hoc interventions by city, State, and pressure-groups formed to agitate over matters of clear and present need.[13]

Instead of a comprehensive urban vision, Banham's Los Angeles was driven by competitive interests, government agencies, pressure groups, and above all, individuals. In Los Angeles, Banham saw a new society emerging and, along with it a new way of making buildings. He was attracted to "the convulsions in building style that follow when traditional cultural and social restraints have been overthrown and replaced by the preferences of a mobile, affluent, consumer-oriented society, in which 'cultural values' and ancient symbols are handled primarily as methods of claiming or establishing status."[14] Banham valorized this bottom-up action, which he called "Non-Plan," as a critical counter to modernism.

[12] William B. Fulton, *The Reluctant Metropolis: The Politics of Urban Growth in Los Angeles* (Point Arena, CA: Solano Press Books, 1997).

[13] Reyner Banham, *Los Angeles: The Architecture of Four Ecologies* (London: Allen Lane, 1971), 121.

[14] Banham, 106.

Shipping containers at the Port of Los Angeles

But Non-Plan ultimately paved the way for neo-liberalist urban planning.[15] Left unfettered, the competing interests of individuals, government bureaucracies, and private corporations have lead to a vicious stalemate, an urban trench warfare that effectively undoes the city's ability to fix its problems. This new landscape offers little hope for solutions through new infrastructural interventions, at least not of the conventional sort.

Still, Banham gave us a new reading of the city, situating built forms within the environment and understanding that those aspects of the metropolis that seemed banal or discordant were essential parts of its function. Banham divided Los Angeles into four ecologies, each with its own particular flora and fauna. Three of these were distinctly geographical: Surfurbia encompassed the beach communities and was where the laid-back life ruled the residents and their architecture; the Foothills were dominated by privileged communities such as Bel Air or the Hollywood Hills; the Plains of Id consisted of the vast stretches of the city that were a pure product of Non-Plan, a landscape of exuberant self-expression coupled with cheerful banality. These three ecologies allowed Banham to go beyond the traditional stylistic methodology of the architectural historian and understand the city's landscape as a totality. Tying these geographic zones together was the fourth ecology, Autopia, the freeways. These vast concrete bands were the final great infrastructure that gave shape to the city, the last and most audacious effort to implement the plan and the very thing that ultimately killed it by producing massive homeowner backlash.

[15] Jonathan Hughes and Simon Sadler, *Non-Plan: Essays on Freedom Participation and Change in Modern Architecture and Urbanism* (Boston: Architectural Press, 2000).

Today, reading Banham on the freeways, it is almost unimaginable to see them as he did. His freeways still worked. They flowed, infrastructure at its purest, allowing individuals the freedom to pursue their dreams.[16] Today's freeways are clogged in perpetual gridlock. Fixing them is impossible. Any new freeways would be fought by NIMBYist homeowners, but more than that, traffic planners recognize that if new freeways were built, motorists would choose to live further out. After a brief period of time, the freeways would, once again, be jammed hopelessly.

Networked Ecologies Much has changed since Banham's day. Infrastructure is no longer a solution, but the California dream seems to have expired too. After a decade of delirious growth, real estate has collapsed while, confounding logic, remaining unaffordable to almost anyone. After a period of depopulation, people are once again coming to Los Angeles and massive growth is predicted for the city, but without new land to sprawl into, where these new citizens will go or how the city can sustain them is uncertain. The city's coffers are exhausted. Pollution, which seemed to be getting better for a time, has returned. The city has changed in other ways too. It is a polyglot metropolis, home to no majority, only many minorities. Going to the beach, you are more likely to be surrounded by a club of Mexican-American youths with souped-up low-rider Hondas or a group of Korean motorcyclists than by white-bread surfers.

This book can only offer a partial insight into Los Angeles. In this immensely complex landscape, we cannot hope for a total approach the way that Banham did. Instead we set out to paint a picture of a particularly crucial aspect of the city, its dominance by an out-of-control infrastructure. To accomplish this, we can still turn to Banham's idea of ecologies as well as to the method of geographer Anton Wagner in his 1935 analysis of Los Angeles, a work profoundly influential on Banham. Wagner set out to understand the city on its own terms, taking the city as a *städtische Landschaft*, an urban landscape, the product of Americans confronting the forces of nature. Writing evocatively of the "drilling tower forests" and the "façade landscapes" that began as Hollywood's stage-sets and spread, like weeds, throughout the city, Wagner saw Angelenos as just one species, playing out its role in the landscape.[17] Banham drew on this idea of urban landscape to understand how ecologies formed distinct communities in Los Angeles.

If we begin with Wagner's idea of looking at the city as landscape and Banham's notion of ecologies, we need to be more critical. Ecologies were still innocent in the 1960s. By now, today they are much more complicated. Contemporary nature has been thoroughly reshaped by human activities. Brought from around the world by accident or by design, non-native plants and animals have settled in the area, providing some of the city's most well-known

---

[16] Banham's description of how the distributed structure of the freeways supported individualism prefigures the 1990s "Californian Ideology," a melding of techno-utopian beliefs, libertarian social ideals, and neo-liberal economic thinking in venues like *Wired* magazine. See Richard Barbrook and Alan Cameron, "The Californian Ideology," Hypermedia Research Centre, http://www.hrc.wmin.ac.uk/theory-californianideology-main.html, published in Peter Ludlow, ed., *Crypto Anarchy, Cyberstates and Pirate Utopias* (Cambridge, MA: MIT Press, 2001), 363-388.

[17] Anton Wagner, *Los Angeles. Werden, leben und gestalt der zweimillionenstadt In Südkalifornien* (Leipzig: Bibliographisches Institut, 1935), translated by Gavriel D. Rosenfeld as *Los Angeles: The Development, Life and Form of the Southern California Metropolis*, unpublished typescript (Los Angeles: Getty Research Institute for the History of Art and the Humanities, 1997), 185. Such an approach resonates with the much more recent work of philosopher of science Bruno Latour, who suggests that agency emerges within networks of people, things, and concepts (for example, regulations and laws). See Bruno Latour, "On Actor Network Theory: A Few Clarifications," *Soziale Welt* 47 (1998): 360-81,translated version posted to nettime mailing list, archived at http://www.nettime.org/Lists-Archives/nettime-l-9801/msg00019.html.

features, from the iconic palm tree to the fragrance of eucalyptus that pervades the mountains. But if the landscape has been tamed, our interventions—intentional or not—have altered it into something unfamiliar and, in its own way uncontrollable. As Mike Davis pointed out in his *Ecology of Fear,* the massive fires that rage through the surrounding hills are the result of Angelenos' continued attempts to suppress smaller blazes. Other "disasters," such as mudslides and floods, are the result of developers building in places in which nobody should build. Attempts to remedy these conditions only breed further complexity as those who seek to mitigate such conditions or, alternatively, dream of restoring the landscape, turn to legislation or to complex infrastructural systems for some degree of mitigation. Infrastructure's only possible future, it seems, is to restore what it had previously destroyed. These efforts only compound the condition of the urban landscape today. Before us we see a second nature, a wild and untamable terrain that undoes our attempts to control it or even understand it fully.

Setting out to understand this city, and by extension all contemporary cities, we treat it in terms of *networked ecologies,* a series of codependent systems of environmental mitigation, land-use organization, communication and service delivery. In our analysis, these infrastructures form the basis of the contemporary city, but they are vastly different from the infrastructures of old.[18] Rather than being executed in conformance with the outline of a plan, they are networked, hypercomplex systems produced by technology, laws, political pressures, disciplinary desires, environmental constraints and a myriad other pressures, tied together with feedback mechanisms. Networked ecologies embody the dominant form of organization today, the network, but these networks can be telematic, physical, or even social. What matters is that we do not think of these ecologies as discrete terrains as Banham did, but rather as the sort of networks that artist Mark Lombardi drew—inextricable and impossible, like balls of yarn after visitation by a litter of kittens.[19]

If contemporary Los Angeles is an object of study for us, we hope to avoid the traditions of either positive or negative boosterism. For us Los Angeles is neither the progressive, decongested metropolis nor the potential-filled neo-liberal conurbation of the non-plan. Nor is Los Angeles any longer the imploding postmetropolitan region described so eloquently by Mike Davis, Ed Soja, and the Los Angeles School of Urbanism.[20] Instead, we set out to see the city as a local manifestation of global conditions. If this book addresses Los Angeles, the conditions here are in play everywhere else. Like Los Angeles, cities throughout the world are confronted by the problems wrought by an aging modernity and a spreading sameness caused by capital seeking a profitable, homogeneous field. As Los Angeles densifies, New York accepts Home Depot. The Grove and Soho become, little by little, indistinguishable, urban infrastructures supporting Banana Republic, the Apple Store, and Anthropologie.[21] In addressing one city this book is likely a transitional object; future books may well treat global networks rather than cities.[22]

[18] Our intents in extending Banham are similar to those that Stan Allen set out in "Los Angeles: 4 (Artificial) Ecologies," *Hunch* (1999), no. 1, 18-23.

[19] Robert Hobbs and Independent Curators International, *Mark Lombardi: Global Networks* (New York: Independent Curators International, 2003).

[20] Mike Davis, *City of Quartz: Excavating the Future in Los Angeles* (New York: Verso, 1990), Edward W. Soja, *Postmodern Geographies: The Reassertion of Space in Critical Social Theory* (New York: Verso, 1989), Allen John Scott and Edward W. Soja, *The City: Los Angeles and Urban Theory at the End of the Twentieth Century* (Los Angeles: University of California Press, 1996).

[21] Paul Goldberger, "The Malling of Manhattan." *Metropolis* (March 2001), [134]-139, 179.

[22] For an example of such a project, see Reinhold Martin and Kadambari Baxi, *Multi-National City: Architectural Itineraries* (Barcelona: ACTAR, 2007).

This book began from two trajectories. The first was as a course I taught at the Southern California Institute of Architecture starting in 1999. The second, also begun at roughly the same time, was a project to gather and present data on the Los Angeles River watershed started at the Los Angeles Forum for Architecture and Urban Design. The spread of easily accessible watershed data on city Web sites powered by GIS (Geographic Information Systems) made the Forum's initial project obsolete. When I became Forum President in 2004, I proposed that we rethink the project as a group exploration of the impact of infrastructure on the city. Given the scale of a book on contemporary infrastructure in Los Angeles, it was clear to me that this project needed not one but many authors. To this end, I commissioned essays from researchers—many of them architects—to explore different infrastructural ecologies. Beginning on site in Los Angeles, this book has been finished far away, at the Network Architecture Lab at Columbia University's Graduate School of Architecture, Planning, and Preservation.

I replaced Banham's four geographic ecologies with three scales of networks that operate throughout the basin, indeed throughout the world. Punctuated by Lane Barden's aerial photographs of the channelized Los Angeles River, the linear Wilshire Boulevard, and the Alameda Corridor cargo expressway, these scales comprise the landscape (Owens Lake, the Los Angeles River watershed, the oil extraction industry, and the gravel pits of Irwindale), the urban fabric (traffic management, telecommunication, trees, and mobile phones), and the object (super-distribution centers, property, and prop houses).

Tying together the essays are maps produced by Leah Meisterlin, a student researcher at the Network Architecture Lab. Beyond geographically relating each chapter, they allow comparisons of place and location. The maps help to transform the book into an atlas of the unseen infrastructural systems in Los Angeles, depicting ecologies that help make up the city. Singularly, they annotate or elaborate on their respective essays. Together, they describe coexisting, overlapping networks of infrastructure, spanning industries and scales, that have driven and continue to drive the city.

This book is an atlas, but it is also a manual, something that might be found on the floor of a yellow pick-up truck parked next to the Los Angeles River channel, next to some rubber boots. As such, it could be used as a guide to the city, however incomplete, but it also also might be for another audience, for a future kind of urban planner, designer, architect, or resident. This new kind of urbanist might very well resemble a hacker, in the best sense, re-imagining how to appropriate the codes, rules, and systems that make up the contemporary city and manipulate them so as to create not a plan but a new kind of urban intervention more appropriate for this century.

LANDSCAPE

Barry Lehrman

RECONSTRUCTING THE VOID

OWENS LAKE

Two hundred miles due north of Los Angeles lies a 108-square-mile playa, the abandoned corpse of Owens Lake, a silent victim of the city's destructive thirst. Almost a century ago, Los Angeles became dependent on this distant watershed, funneling its life-giving liquid into a vast aqueduct to nurture its delirious growth. But this history of water, politics, and exploitation has grown ever more complicated and inextricable, reshaped by networks of negotiation, litigation, and politics. As much artificial as natural, the result is a second nature, a wild, uncontrollable condition created by social, infrastructural, and organic ecologies interacting with the environment and with each other.

Los Angeles is now a thoroughly urbanized landscape while the Owens Valley faces stagnation, drought, and vast dust storms. But in taking the water from the Owens Valley, Los Angeles ensured that agribusiness and exurban sprawl would never take over, thus preserving a unique fragment of the American frontier as a permanent rural antipode to the sprawling metropolis to the south.

The Owens Valley is a land of extremes. Running north-south for some seventy-five miles, the valley sits at an elevation of 4,000 feet. Lining it on the west, the Sierra Nevada Mountains rise to 14,000 feet while to the east the Inyo and White Mountains reach the same height. This is one of the deepest valleys in the world. Mount Whitney, the tallest peak in the continental United States, looms above in the Sierra Nevadas. The Methuselah tree, the world's oldest living thing, lives in the White Mountains.

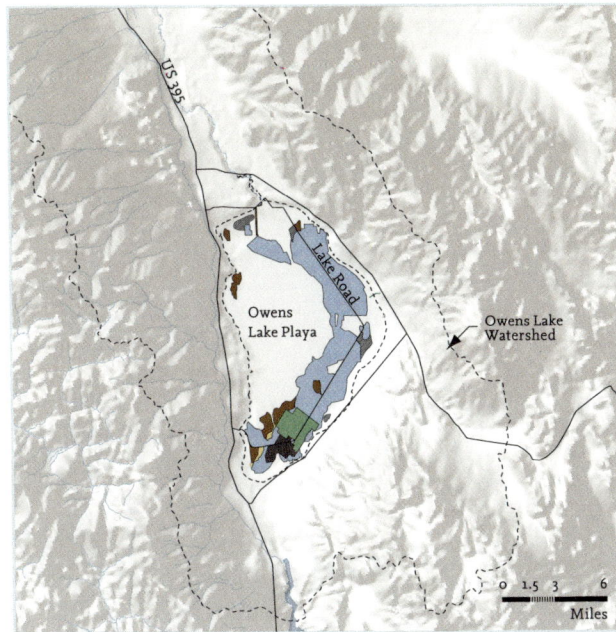

Owens Lake Dust Control Project Zones

Sources: author, with information provided by Los Angeles Department of Water and Power, CH2M Hill, the United States Geological Survey, and the Great Basin Unified Air Pollution Control District

Shallow Flooding
Habitat Flooding
Moat & Row
Managed Vegetation
Channel Area
2008 Study Area

US 395
Lake Road
Owens Lake Playa
Owens Lake Watershed

0 1.5 3   6
Miles

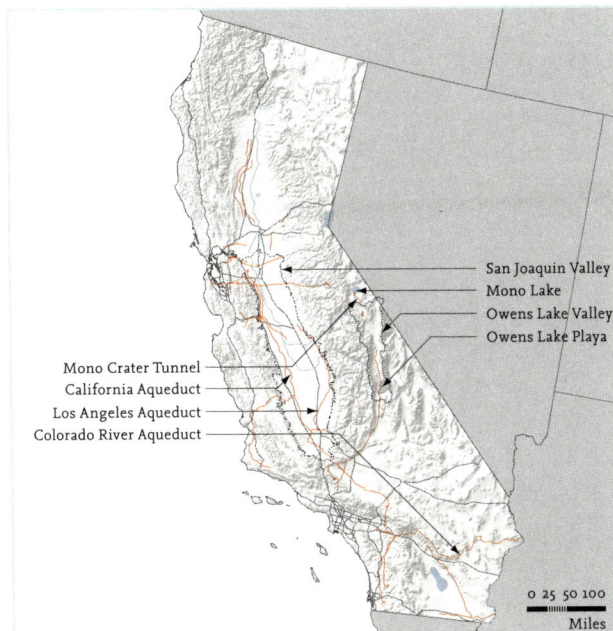

Aqueducts in California

Sources: author, with information from Department of Water Resources, State of California. Preparing for California's Next Drought: Changes since 1987-1992 (Sacramento: California Department of Natural Resources, 2000).

Aqueducts
Major Rivers and Lakes
Interstate Highways

San Joaquin Valley
Mono Lake
Owens Lake Valley
Owens Lake Playa

Mono Crater Tunnel
California Aqueduct
Los Angeles Aqueduct
Colorado River Aqueduct

0 25 50 100
Miles

Relic Landscape This relic landscape stands in stark contrast to the San Joaquin Valley, a mere twenty miles to the west across the Sierras (even if the distance is short, there is no drivable pass between the two valleys). There, farmers turned once-verdant wetlands and sloughs into farmland, creating the nation's vegetable garden only to see it become one of the most rapidly growing regions in the country in the mid-2000s.

First Los Angeles
Aqueduct,
Jaw Bone Siphon

The tangled relationship between the desiccated valley and the city that drained it first emerged a century and a half ago. Long before water, the Owens Valley aided Los Angeles's rise from a sleepy cattle town into a vibrant global metropolis. The discovery of silver at the Cerro Gordo mine above Owens Lake in 1865 funneled the first flush of wealth through Los Angeles.[1] That silver helped bring the Southern Pacific Railroad to the city in 1876, in turn ensuring the success and growth of San Pedro harbor and contributing to the initial real estate boom of the 1890s. This first significant wave of growth was sustained until Los Angeles started running out of water at the end of the nineteenth century.[2]

By diverting the Owens River two hundred miles south to slake Los Angeles's thirst, chief city engineer William Mulholland promoted urban growth over rural agriculture, thereby changing the future of the West. With the Los Angeles Aqueduct complete in 1913, a second wave of growth followed, creating the city we recognize today. The aqueduct could deliver ten times as much water as was available from local resources in the city, yet the phenomenal growth that ensued meant that within a decade, Southern California was once again searching for even more water—a quest that continues today. The aqueduct became the new Los Angeles River, extending the city's watershed some three hundred fifty miles north to the Mono Lake Basin while making the original river superfluous, allowing its unpredictable flows to be funneled from the San Fernando Valley to the ocean as rapidly as possible through a system of channels not unlike that which straitjackets the Owens River on its epic journey south to the same San Fernando Valley.

But the aqueduct also preserved the rural character of Owens Valley. To protect the city's water rights and the purity of the watershed, a series of legislative acts at the local, state, and federal levels effectively prevented development in the area, the political clout of the young city steamrolling over the sparsely populated countryside.[3] Adding to this regulatory oversight, Washington created Inyo National Forest at the city's behest to preserve the watershed in the mountains surrounding the valley while the Los Angeles Department of Water and Power (LADWP) became the second largest landholder in the county. As a result of these external limits, the Owens Valley and surrounding Inyo County have remained rural, one of the few places in California with no projected growth.[4]

Owens River, just
north of lake

[1] Jeff Putnam and Ginny Smith, *Deepest Valley: A Guide to Owens Valley, Its Roadside and Mountain Trails,* 2nd ed. (Palo Alto: Genny Smith Books/Live Oak Press, 1995), 245-249. Cerro Gordo produced $17 million of silver and lead between 1865 and 1879. While this seems small compared to other bonanzas, it was enough to catapult Los Angeles from being a town of less then 2,000 people in 1850 to over 50,000 in 1890. Between 1880 and 1890 alone, the city experienced 450% growth.

[2] Remi Nadeau, *The Water Seekers* (Santa Barbara: Crest Publishers 1997), 11-15. Based on the precipitation in the Los Angeles River watershed, the city can sustain a population below the 1904 total of 200,000 people.

[3] See Norris Hundley, *The Great Thirst—California and Water: A History* (Berkeley: University of California Press, 2001), 141-166, on the politics behind the Los Angeles Aqueduct. For an economic analysis, see Gary Libecap, "Chinatown: Transaction Costs in Water Rights Exchanges the Owens Valley Transfer to Los Angeles," (working paper, University of Arizona, Tucson, 2004), http:// www.international.ucla.edu/cms/files/Libecap.pdf.

[4] Owens Valley/Inyo County has projected population growth at less then 10% over the next 50 years and may even lose population. State of California, Department of Finance, *Population Projections for California and Its Counties 2000-2050, by Age, Gender and Race/Ethnicity* (Sacramento, 2007).

The development of the irrigation network that crisscrosses Southern California goes back to its indigenous tribes and the Spanish colonists. Long before California was home to Europeans, the Tongva tribes established a village by the river on a raised site that didn't flood during the winter monsoons. They created a modest network of ditches to irrigate some crops that supplemented their hunting and gathering. The Spanish took over the network, expanding the ditches and instituting rules and regulations for access to the water of the *Zanja Madre* or "mother ditch." The colonists moved the diversion point up into the Elysian Valley, and the city of Los Angeles was officially born.

Once California became an American territory, the growing population and thirst for water continued to drive ditches further from the Los Angeles River. Eventually the diversion points reached nine miles north of the small city to what is now Griffith Park at the southern edge of Burbank. By 1886, so little water flowed in the river below the ditch's intakes that the city dug tunnels below the riverbed to tap the remnant subsurface flow to provide water for drinking and irrigation.[5] With such a precedent, looking north to the Owens Valley for more water was not such a great leap of faith for William Mulholland in 1904. All the chief city engineer needed to do was extend the ditch digging by an order of magnitude.

When the Los Angeles Aqueduct diverted the Owens River's water to the city, the draining of Owens Lake was only a matter of time.[6] After the 1913 opening of the aqueduct, the lake's water level started to drop drastically, and its saline content increased as water evaporated. A new industry harvesting the precipitating salt was born, taking advantage of the ideal arid conditions and harvesting the valuable minerals. Salt works sprung up on the eastern and western shores, but soon the falling water level left the lagoons on the east dry. After an effort to pump the brine into saltpans failed, they were abandoned. By 1923, only a dusty brine pool covered the lowest part of the once-mighty lake. In 1926, the dust storms began.[7]

But Owens Lake could hardly have avoided this fate if it had stayed independent of the city's thirst. Water, a scarce commodity in the American West, is subject to the "Colorado Doctrine," which states that the first person to divert and use a water source acquires future rights to it. Well aware of this, farmers dug irrigation ditches along the Owens River in 1872, causing the lake's level to decline. Thirty years later, the Federal Bureau of Reclamation proposed to divert water to a vast irrigation network to serve the area's agricultural interests. Such a scheme would have been just as effective at desiccating the lake as Mulholland's diversion of the river to feed Los Angeles was.[8]

---

[5] Blake Gumbrecht, *The Los Angeles River: Its Life, Death, and Possible Rebirth* (Baltimore: Johns Hopkins University Press, 1999).

[6] Marith C. Reheis, "Owens (Dry) Lake, California: A Human-Induced Dust Problem," United States Geological Survey, http://geochange.er.usgs.gov/sw/impacts/geology/owen.

[7] At the end of Pleistocene Ice Age, a 270' foot deep Owens Lake was part of a chain of lakes, flowing through Haiwee Pass into China Lake, filling Death Valley with Lake Manley and cascading into Lake Lahontan north of Lake Tahoe. In 1872, the lake was 49' in depth; by 1876 it had dropped to 38'. In 1913 it was only about 29' deep. Hoyt S. Gale and F. L. Ransome; "Salines in the Owens, Searles, and Panamint Basins, Southeast-ern California," *United States Geological Survey Bulletin 580* (1913). See also the 1888 map reproduction in Jeff Putnam and Ginny Smith, *Deepest Valley*, 247.

[8] A. S. Jayko and C. I. Miller, "Impact of Climate Change on the Landscapes of the Eastern Sierra Nevada and Western Great Basin—Workshop Summary," *Open-File Report 01-202* (United States Geological Survey, 2000) have found that Owens Lake may have been dry a few times over the past 1,000 years during prolonged droughts. George I. Smith and James Bischoff, eds., *An 800,000-Year Paleoclimatic Record From Core OL-92, Owens Lake, Southeast California* (Boulder, CO: Geologic Society of America, 1997), claim that Owens Lake continuously existed for at least 800,000 years.

With Los Angeles's rapidly growing population exceeding projections and the city facing drought in the 1930s,[9] the LADWP began drilling hundreds of wells to tap the Owens Valley's ground water to bolster its supply. Until the 1970s, these wells had a relatively minor impact on life in the valley, at least compared to the draining of the river, but with the completion of a second aqueduct in 1970, Los Angeles greatly increased its rate of pumping and the groundwater level dropped. As a result, lush meadows, sparkling lakes, and the rolling river were replaced by the current basin-and-range landscape of sagebrush and sand dunes.

Contested Landscape The Owens Valley is a contested landscape, its residents chafing against the infrastructure imposed on their land to serve the distant metropolis. The groundwater pumping of the 1970s sparked the "Second Owens Valley Water War," as the inhabitants of the area protested the death of their land. But unlike the infamous water war of the 1920s and 1930s, when valley residents dynamited the aqueduct to little avail, this time residents had a new weapon to fight the annexation of their ground water—the California Environmental Quality Act (CEQA). CEQA provided the citizens of Inyo County a process and the legal leverage to challenge impact of the Second Aqueduct. Already in 1925, the state legislature had passed a law requiring compensation of all business and property owners for financial losses due to water diversions. This was finally enforced in 1929 when the California Supreme Court ordered Los Angeles to comply, but this injunction only compensated direct financial losses and did not require any remedy of the environmental costs. Only with CEQA, half a century later, did these get considered. When the original Los Angeles Aqueduct was built, there were no environmental review laws on the books anywhere in the country. In contrast, by the time of the Second Aqueduct, the country was in the midst of the burgeoning environmental movement. In response to legal pressure, Los Angeles was forced to create an Environmental Impact Report (EIR) and to mitigate the reported impacts. This process leveled the battlefield and, at least to a degree, made it possible to assess the environmental costs of the city's vast infrastructure. The EIR process discovered several conditions caused by the Los Angeles Aqueduct that required immediate mitigation: the dropping water table from the increased pumping, the death of Owens River below the Aqueduct intake, the lowering of Mono Lake's water level, and the dust storms from Owens Lake playa.

Litigation against the city to rectify the environmental damages in Owens Valley started in 1970 with the first successful case being a 1972 Inyo County suit to limit groundwater pumping. Only in 1990, once extensive scientific studies and ground water modeling defined a sustainable level of pumping that would preserve plant life above, was this lawsuit completely settled.[10]

[9] California droughts over the past 150 years include: 1863-64, 1887-88, 1912-13, 1922-24, 1928-34, 1947-50, 1959-61, 1976-77, and 1987-92. 1977 was the driest year on record with only 20% of average precipitation. A. S. Jayko & C. I. Miller, *Preparing for California's Next Drought—Changes Since 1987-92* (Sacramento: Department of Water Resources, State of California, 2000).

[10] Greg James et al, *Green Book For The Long-Term Groundwater Management Plan For The Owens Valley And Inyo County* (Los Angeles: City of Los Angeles & Inyo County 2000). Additional Technical Memorandums have been issued as addenda to the Green Book, to address specific subjects and refine the management and monitoring of the pumping. The City of Los Angeles and Inyo County have recently started work on a major revision of the Green Book for completion in 2009.

The second successful fight under CEQA was over Mono Lake, just north of the Owens Valley, a unique ecology of two million migratory water birds nesting among dramatic tufa towers formed by the lake's unique, saline chemistry. In 1940, the LADWP bored eleven miles through solid rock to create the Mono Craters Tunnel, diverting water that would otherwise sustain Mono Lake to the aqueduct system. As at Owens Lake, the water level dropped, but this time local residents and scientists were able to get the courts to help. With the lowered water level, coyotes and raccoons could walk across the lakebed to reach the formerly isolated island on which endangered California Gulls made their nests. In 1979, with the leadership of biologist David Gaines, the Mono Lake Committee launched lawsuits against the LADWP to protect the bird nesting sites. The 1994 Mono Lake Accord established a minimum water level for Mono Lake to protect the rookery and established a schedule of allowable water diversions that would gradually increase water in the lake to a sustainable level.

Even with these reforms upstream, Owens Lake was left an ecological disaster. Wind gusts above twenty miles an hour lifted over fifty tons per second of "Keeler Fog" off the lakebed. Often reaching over two miles high, these dust storms sent 130 times the United States Environmental Protection Agency's limit for particulate matter into the atmosphere, blowing the dust over 250 miles from the lake. Such storms occurred two dozen or more times each year, generally in the spring and fall. Composed of microscopic particles smaller than ten microns (PM10), the dust contains significant levels of toxic metals like selenium, arsenic, and lead along with efflorescent salts. The largest single source of PM10 pollution in the country, these dust storms were a clear threat to the 40,000 people in the immediate region. Even the feds suffered: the dust reduced visibility so badly that nearby China Lake Naval Air Station to the south had to stop flight operations five to ten days each year—costing the Navy over $5 million annually. Physicians at China Lake linked the dust to significant health problems in the region, including higher rates of cancer, lung disease, and eye problems.

Finally in 1998, the City of Los Angeles and the Great Basin Unified Air Pollution Control District reached a third major court-negotiated settlement to abate the dust blowing off the lakebed.[11] The dust mitigation process initiated by the Memorandum of Agreement (MOA) focused on a few specific and tangible results: the reduction of dust being blown off the dry lake and the preservation of the nesting habitat of the Snowy Plover, an endangered wading bird.[12] As a result of the MOA, Los Angeles installed over 300 miles of pipe (some as large as five feet in diameter), more than 5,000 irrigation bubblers, and hundreds of miles of fiber optic control cables and valves, all to irrigate the thirty square miles of the Playa from which most of the dust would originate.

Trucks that spray water onto the playa to control construction dust refill their tanks at this filling station on the lake access road offshore from Keeler.

Bubblers produce shallow flooding on the playa.

[11] The 1998 mitigation Memorandum of Agreement is administered by the Great Basin Unified Air Pollution Control District/Inyo Water District and was enacted as a "fix-it" agreement to prevent future lawsuits and liability claims against the Los Angles Department of Water and Power who have funded the entire project.

[12] There are three strategies for dust reduction legally specified in the MOA: shallow flooding, planting, and gravel cover. It is also specified that all berms have "snowy plover crossings incorporated every 500 feet."

Control Mechanism The scale of the dust control project on Owens Lake is roughly equivalent to that of a waterworks for a city of over 220,000 people. Construction of the first five phases, treating the worst thirty square miles of dust-emitting soils on the playa, has cost the City of Los Angeles $425 million dollars to build.[13] But that sum doesn't factor in the lost revenue from the water being appropriated for the project (around $15 million/year) or the operations and maintenance budget, some $10 million per year.[14] Instead of continuing with the MOA's open-ended mandate for additional construction until the dust-emission goals are met, the city negotiated a final phase for the construction of an additional 12.7 square miles of shallow flooding amidst "moat and row" landforms. Projected to cost another $100 million and to be completed by 2010, moat and row is a promising alternative compared to the already deployed shallow flooding. It will have many fewer pipes to leak, valves to stick, or controls to break, while using less water and requiring almost no energy to operate. The future of dust control on Owens will be a zigzagging wet corduroy of low berms, sheltering water-filled ditches instead of the sparkling braids of water over bright red salt flats that the bubblers create.

51,000 acre-feet of water, once bound for Los Angeles, are now being diverted back onto Owens Lake each year. But this amount will never refill the lake. For that to happen, it would take at least seven years of the entire Owens River flowing unimpeded back into the basin. Still, this bounty of water has been the genesis for a new ecosystem, with brine flies and microbes flourishing in the shallow pools. The acres of mudflats and brine pools have become the dreamed-of habitat for the migratory shore birds that inspired the MOA. Birds and birdwatchers are visiting Owens Valley in increasing numbers, enhancing the local ecology and economy.[15] The sky may never be completely darkened by millions of ducks as reported by early pioneers, but the Pacific Flyway has restored an oasis that balances some of the needs of nature with the needs of the city.

Los Angeles is just starting to adjust to the imposed reductions of water from the Owens River Valley and the Mono Basin. In the days of unlimited water exports, the Los Angeles Aqueduct provided 70% of the water for the city. Currently, one-third of the aqueduct's flow remains in the Owens River Valley and the Mono Basin. At best, the aqueduct can provide half the water the City's needs. But with the prospect of climate change, the future of Los Angeles is starting to look dry. Best-case climate models predict that California should expect a 30-60% loss in the Sierra snow pack, a decline that would be reflected in the amount of available water.[16]

There are no unclaimed or unutilized water basins left for the city to tap. Around the country, a myriad of different interest groups and water users fight for their share of the scarce resource. To the east, the over-allocated Colorado River is fought over by the states along its banks as well as by Mexico. Moreover, that river's water quality is threatened by pollution from farms and mines as well as piles of radioactive tailing. To the west and north,

Surface mining on Owens Lake

Surface mining on Owens Lake

[13] Up to 54,000 acre-feet may be diverted from the Aqueduct for the dust mitigation project. This amount can support a population of between 220,000 and 440,000 people. On the other hand, if the dust control project's area were settled at the population density as the city of Los Angeles, then the lake would have 31,000 residents.

[14] Wayne Bamossy, Senior Project Manager, Los Angeles Department of Water and Power, e-mail correspondence with the author June 22, 2007.

[15] Wayne Bamossy, conversations with author, January 5, 2005. Richard Cervantes, Inyo County Supervisor, conversation with author January 7, 2005. LADWP, *Policy for Public Access to LADWP Facilities at Owens Lake* (Los Angeles, May 20, 2004).

[16] Dan Cayan et al, *Climate Change Scenarios for California: An Overview* (Sacramento: California Climate Change Center 2006), http://www.energy.ca.gov/2005publications/CEC-500-2005-186/CEC-500-2005-186-SF.pdf.

the massive California Aqueduct faces the possible extinction of several species of fish, saltwater infiltration into the delta, collapsing dikes, and competing economic interests over that water. It appears unavoidable that there will be less water for metropolitan Southern California in the future.

The days of building massive aqueducts are over and most alternative sources of drinking water are not viable. Desalination doesn't create high-quality potable water, is very energy intensive (even with the high-efficiency membranes being developed by the Metropolitan Water District), and is very expensive. Icebergs from Alaska or giant bags of fresh water floated down from the Columbia River are just pipe dreams, since those places need the water too, and the cost of these enterprises appears to be prohibitive.

But Los Angeles has a long tradition of pursuing efficiency and conservation of water, something it can trace back to the days of Mulholland, who installed the first water meters in the city prior to turning to the Owens Valley. Even with the rapidly growing population, the amount of water used in Southern California has stayed almost steady, near the 1990 level. Indeed, the entire state of California has struggled to use less water, and postsuburban California is beginning to shift from its earlier ideal of a verdant, irrigated Eden of swimming pools and lush lawns, to a native xeriscape of chaparral and oak savannahs. Within the culture of conservation lies the new water source for continued urban growth. Water recycling, off-stream reservoirs and in-ground storage are a few proven solutions to creating more available water with the existing supply.

The city's main wastewater facility, Hyperion Sewage Treatment Plant in El Segundo sends over 362 million gallons of secondarily treated water out into the Santa Monica Bay every day. Reclaiming this discharged water through tertiary treatment and additional filtration could provide for the needs of at least another 1.6 million people. The biggest hurdle to recycling water is the psychological factor of drinking fluid that once flowed in toilets. The accepted method of mentally "sanitizing" this connection is to recharge groundwater with the treated effluent, then pump it out at a later date for use.[17] For now, however, most of this valuable water is dumped into the Los Angeles River or Santa Monica Bay, and only a small fraction gets reused for irrigation or industrial uses. Negative press and public opinion have defeated other water-recycling projects in the region, but the area has little choice except to turn in this direction in the future.

As the antipode to sprawling Los Angeles, the artificial emptiness of Owens Lake simulates the conditions of the frontier. As you stand at the edge of the lake, the stark flatness of the playa recedes into the distance, the monumental dust control project barely visible, comprising only a subtle shading of grays, reds, and greens against the white salt. Only as you get into the project itself, do you see the bubblers, rising like alien plants on the terraformed lakebed. This vast infrastructure, dedicated to preserving the integrity of the void, undoes any notion that this is a pristine wilderness. Looking back out towards the surrounding mountains, the other subtle traces of human activity jump into stark relief—the road snaking up the sheer wall of the mountains, the gossamer threads of the power lines, and the absolute horizontal trace of the aqueduct cutting into the foothills.

Once natural, California is now thoroughly artificial. Perversely, only in places as heavily regulated and mechanized as Owens Lake is there any semblance of what the territory might have been like before settlers arrived. In a strange gift, Los Angeles has preserved the open rural landscape of Owens Valley, re-creating the void where by all rights we shouldn't expect to find it.

Irrigation pipes lead out of a reservoir at Owens Lake, part of the LADWP's dust mitigation efforts

Pipes from the LADWP's dust mitigation project, reminiscent of the Fountain in Robert Smithson's Tour of the Monuments of Passaic, New Jersey

---

[17] City of Los Angeles Department of Public Works, Bureau of Sanitation, "About Wastewater," http://www.lacity.org/san/wastewater/factsfigures.htm.

David Fletcher

FLOOD CONTROL FREAKOLOGY
LOS ANGELES RIVER WATERSHED

The Los Angeles River runs through one of the most complex urban watersheds in the world. From its headwaters in the Santa Monica and San Gabriel Mountains, it flows fifty-one miles through the San Fernando Valley, past downtown Los Angeles to the Pacific Ocean just east of the nation's busiest seaport. As it does so, the river channel weaves its way through thirteen municipalities and crosses over forty-seven political boundaries. Once a meshwork of meandering rivers, streams, arroyos, and washes, the river is a fully engineered flood-control system. No longer a natural, aqueous phenomenon, it is now a man-made web of vascular networks, many of which channel other flows besides water: freeways, streets, bridges, railways, power lines, cell towers, as well as sewage infrastructures. Embedded within the fabric of the watershed are political structures and bureaucracies, environmental conditions, economic organizations, and cultural relations. These fluid systems are more evident in their political and social operations than physical form: rivers of energy, streams of revenue and resources, movement of goods and services.

In the 1954 film *THEM!* the city's massive stormdrain networks hosted a colony of radio-active ants. Long Hollywood's favorite local symbol of dystopia, the Los Angeles River is perceived by many residents as unnatural or non-existent. This "narrative of loss" has dominated river discourse for the last quarter-century and is used by many to promote visions of bucolic transformations, irrespective of existing land uses and the need for flood control. If freakish, the river is a living ecology. In spite of many voices that suggest it is an ecological disaster, it contains a vibrant mix of varied ecologies, vegetable, animal, and human. To be sure, these are not the Arcadian ideals of bucolic and pure nature. Instead, this is an

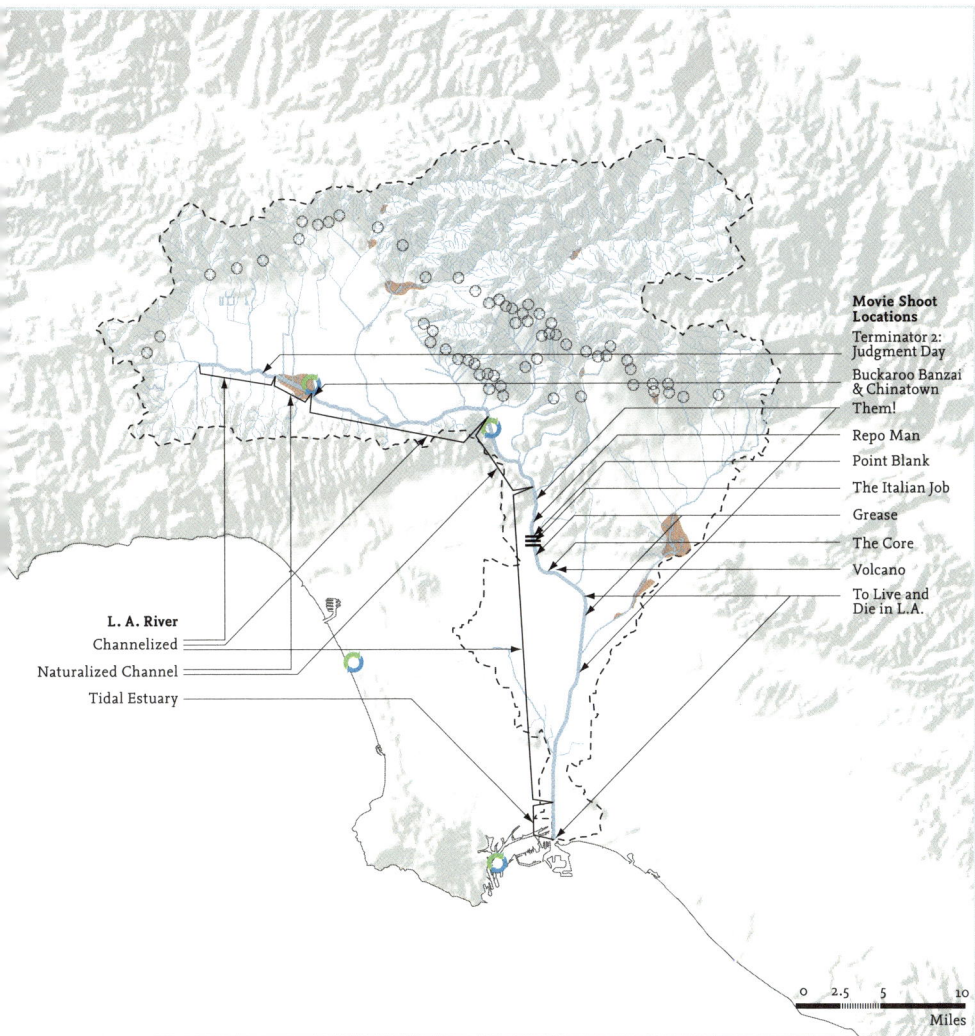

Movie Shoot Locations

Terminator 2: Judgment Day

Buckaroo Banzai & Chinatown

Them!

Repo Man

Point Blank

The Italian Job

Grease

The Core

Volcano

To Live and Die in L.A.

L. A. River

Channelized

Naturalized Channel

Tidal Estuary

0   2.5   5   10

Miles

Points of Interest in
the Los Angeles River
Watershed

Sources: author,
Los Angeles Department
of Public Works and
Bureau of Sanitation

L. A. River Watershed ····

Tributaries ⎯

Dams & Flood Control ▬

Debris Basins ○

Sludge Mat ≡

Wastewater Treatment
Plants ◎

infrastructural ecology, opportunistic and emergent, one that lives off human excess, with many of its values and functions unknown or misunderstood. We need to develop new narratives to understand and appreciate urban watersheds and how they function: where the water flows, what flows in them, who uses, owns, and manages them, how they function, what they are connected to, and what ecologies exist within them.

Technocratic Flow Embracing freakology rather than bucology is the key to understanding the contemporary river, its watershed, and our place within it. The Los Angeles river offers an extreme example of how an urban river becomes enmeshed in infrastructure and urbanism and generates new life. Combining nature and infrastructure while tying together— even defining—the basin, the Los Angeles River is the single most powerful space in Southern California: our Golden Gate Bridge, our Yosemite.

Historically, as the river flooded and meandered across the floodplain, the watershed boundary constantly redefined itself. Originally, the river ran through a broad alluvial floodplain, the result of meandering dendritic flows that constantly redefined and disturbed the landscape and its ecologies. These natural disturbances produced a great diversity of habitats including riparian woodlands, coastal dunes, and freshwater and brackish wetlands. Vast forests of oak and walnut, along with dense willow thickets, dominated the riparian environment. The river would join with springs from surrounding hills to form shallow lakes, ponds, and vast marshes. Sedges, cattails, and bulrush thrived in open wetlands and sloughs. As late as 1872, a Coast Guard survey shows a continuous series of tidal estuaries, lagoons, mudflats, and salt marshes from the mouth of the Los Angeles River east to the San Gabriel River.

Today, that boundary encompasses an 834-square-mile drainage area defined not only by topography but also by wastewater and stormwater infrastructure. The river begins at the confluence of two tributaries, the Arroyo Calabasas and Bell Creek, and absorbs eleven other tributaries as it flows to the Pacific Ocean at Queensway Bay in Long Beach. As reconstructed by the United States Army Corps of Engineers, the County Flood Control District, and the Works Progress Administration, the river and its tributaries are largely channelized and lined with concrete. The resulting landscape is an exercise in the oblique, composed of graceful patterns of flumes—vertical, trapezoidal, and transitional structures—that craze throughout the basin. This technocratic flood-control system was designed to serve a projected population of three million; today, Los Angeles's population is 10.4 million and expected to increase 15% by 2020.

The present-day river functions mainly as a flood-control system consisting of tributary debris basins that capture sediment from the mountains, dams and reservoirs that regulate and detain water, and a concrete riverbed engineered to conduct water to the ocean as quickly as possible. Urbanization, oil extraction, port activities, agriculture, coastal development and channelization have virtually eliminated the historic ecologies. Overall, this has resulted in the loss of all of the original riparian habitats, the dry arroyos, and 98% of the lakes and ponds.[1]

The river itself has ceased to exist as a single entity. Rather it is a jurisdictional matrix of boundaries, rights-of-way, easements, and liabilities. More even than a physical thing, it is a zone comprised of an invisible pattern of ownership and maintenance jurisdictions, railroad lands, and utility easements. Through its many reaches, the river channel is a shattered mosaic of public and private ownerships, with parcels going into and through the channel. Often these federal, state, county, city, and private territories overlap, as air rights, water rights, and mineral rights, are superimposed on rights to movement, maintenance, and law

---

[1] Sean Woods, *Wetlands of the Los Angeles River Watershed* (Oakland: California Coastal Conservancy, 2000), 78.

L. A. River Watershed

Political jurisdictions
in the Los Angeles River
Watershed

Sources: author,
County of Los Angeles
Department of Regional
Planning

L. A. River Maintenance
L. A. County
Army Corps of Engineers

Major Jurisdictions
Incorporated Cities
City Council Districts
County Supervisor Districts
California Senate Districts
California Assembly Districts

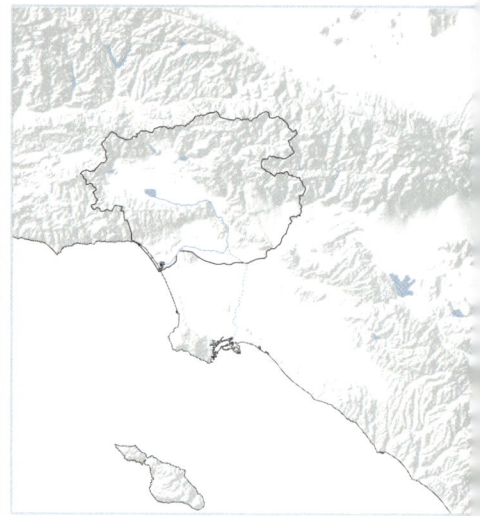

Pre-1815

1815-1825

Historical Extent of
the Los Angeles River
Watershed

Source: author

enforcement. No single agency controls the river: the City of Los Angeles owns the water that flows within the city boundary, the Water Master manages groundwater, the County of Los Angeles Department of Public Works maintains the channel for flood safety, and the Army Corps of Engineers ensures the structural integrity and capacity of the channel to "effectively convey flows." Together, the Corps and the County are responsible for maintenance and operations in the channel right-of-way. Finally, the State of California certifies that the water meets the requirements of the Clean Water Act. Standing under a bridge, in the river, you might be on private property, in city-owned water, in a channel built and maintained by the federal government within a county easement, and in the air rights of the California Department of Transportation. Railways and utility easements will flow on either side of you, conducting goods from the port and power to adjacent municipalities.

The river is also a place of illicit boundaries, with gang territories crisscrossing its pathways and spaces, and human encampments within stormdrains and under bridges. Bisecting the Los Angeles basin, it serves to define the "other side of the tracks."

In the unurbanized past, the river did not exist in the summers. Its flow was seasonal, dry in the summer and flooded during winter storms, but now effluent and urban runoff allow it to flow more consistently, year round. Such extremes inspired settlers to view the river as a violent flood machine, something to be restrained.[2] Today, there is no distinct seasonal change in flows. With increased irrigation, the summer flows increase while winter rains still occasionally result in flash floods. Throughout any given year, Los Angeles averages 15.4 inches of rainfall, but more than 85% of the total precipitation occurs through high intensity storms between January and March.[3] River flows can rise and fall rapidly during storms, reaching flow levels of 36 billion gallons per day. Within a five-hour period,

[2] Jared Orsi, *Hazardous Metropolis: Flooding and Urban Ecology in Los Angeles* (Berkeley and Los Angeles, University of California Press, 2004), 11.

[3] City of Los Angeles Department of Public Works. "Rainfall Indices: For the Period October 1, 2002-September 30, 2003", http://dpw.lacounty.gov/wrd/report/0203/precip/indices.cfm.

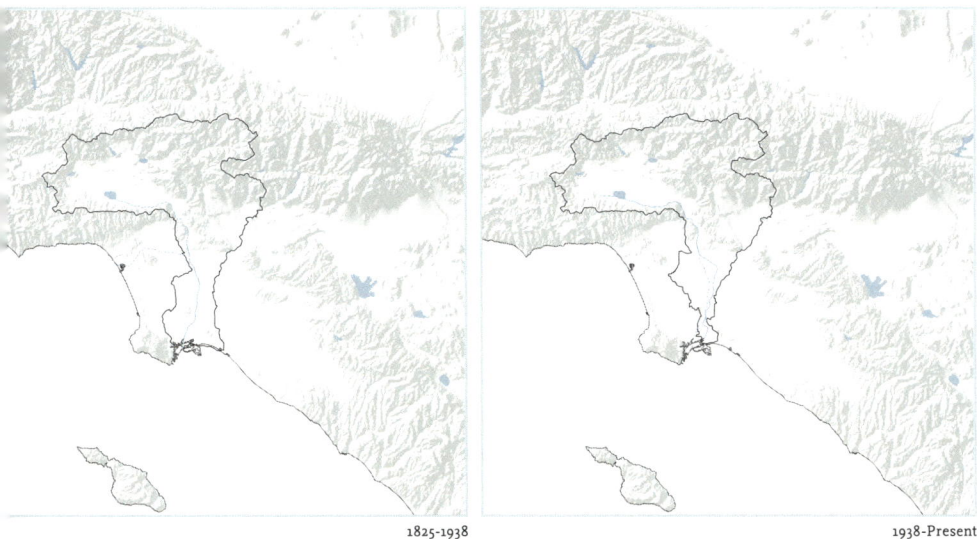

1825-1938   1938-Present

the water level in the channel can rise from three inches to twenty-five feet. Because of the great volume of water entering the system, adjacent urban areas would flood every time it rained, if not for the coordinated choreography of stormwater control. During storm events, Corps and County dam commanders are in constant communication to coordinate their responses to specific storm event and downstream conditions, releasing water before their individual flood basins overflow. Storm events result in a massive flow of not only water but also debris in the riverbed. While the County is mobilized to remove debris from the channel, the Los Angeles City Fire Department's Swift Water Rescue Teams remove people.

Between rain events, flows are considerably lower, between 64 and 99 million gallons per day (mgd). Over the past seventy years, urbanization, channelization, and discharge within the watershed dramatically altered flow conditions. The river's present baseline water flow of 88 mgd, equating to a depth of 4 inches, is a relatively new phenomenon, the product of increased urbanization, water use, and water waste. From the 1930s to the late 1970s, when municipal sewage treatment plants began discharging into the river, the average flow was 10 mgd. Today, flow in the river is dictated by the amount of wastewater discharged from the Tillman, Burbank, and Los Angeles/Glendale sewage treatment plants, which contribute 55 mgd collectively. The next greatest quantity is the 30 mgd of dry-weather urban runoff introduced through over 2,200 stormdrain outlets collecting water from excess irrigation, car washing, as well as sidewalk and street cleaning. The remaining flow is 3 mgd of upwelling groundwater, which is contaminated in many areas. With new sewage discharges, the average daily flow increased 25 mgd during the early 1980s. In the sense that the river has more continually running water than it has had in its post-colonial history, it is by many definitions more a "river" today than it ever was.[4]

[4] CH:CDM, A Joint Venture. Phase II City of Los Angeles Integrated Wastewater Resources Plan for the Wastewater Program (Los Angeles: Department of Water and Power, 2005), ES-1.

Freakology The government considers the river and most of its tributaries to be "impaired water bodies." Development, over the past century, along with the use of fertilizers, pesticides, and household chemicals, has resulted in the degradation of surface and ground water within the region. The most recent report lists trash, fecal coliform bacteria, lead, ammonia, scum, pesticides, fertilizer, and last but not least, odors as key factors impacting the river.[5]

The most significant visual blight on the river is the omnipresent urban trash from illegal dumping, wind deposition, and malicious action. Stolen or junk cars are driven into the riverbed, shopping carts rolled off bridges, and pit bulls that have lost fights are dumped into the channels. Many recent investigators are astounded by the amount of trash in the river, but also mention its unlikely role in creating riparian structure.[6] After winter storms, thousands of multicolored bags—known as "Los Angeles moss"—hang from trees, often as high as thirty feet in the air. Bedframes and automobile fenders can be seen stacked and wedged in trees and wrapped around bridge supports. Shopping carts are remarkably common; one study counted twenty-five within a sixty-foot diameter circle.[7] The remaining trash is a mix of clothing, paper, and spray cans from the multitude of "graffiti universities" that exist under bridges. Three of the naturalized reaches are termed "soft-bottom," because strong groundwater pressure and tidal activity made them impossible to line with concrete.

Every year, the river is purged at the ocean's expense, as winter storms wash out the man-made debris and all but the largest stones in the riverbed, eliminating most of the fine sediments vital to life such as silts and organic materials. Recent studies suggest that, although trash obviously has its own set of hazards for ecology, it has become a vital component to the riparian ecosystems; loose debris gets incorporated into the vegetative community, binding and forming a structural substrate that holds organic nutrients and silts.[8]
Some of the most vigorous stands of new vegetation have been observed growing through and around dense stands of inorganic trash and debris.

The river has many elaborate and well-furnished human encampments, which have become established in the channel stormdrains, riverbeds, and under bridges and freeways. The inhabitants harvest aluminum and plastics daily from its flows and redeem them for cash at local recycling centers. On any given day, individuals and groups, some of whom have made the river a home, may be seen washing and socializing in the low-flow channel. Fires can be seen in the channel at night, with smoke emanating from well-furnished stormdrain apartments.

The present river ecology is a churning soup of exotic and native vegetative communities that have been introduced since the nineteenth century, some by design, others by accident. Tourism, shipping, rail, industry, agriculture, and ornamental vegetation have brought humans, animals, insects and seeds, from around the globe to colonize the river's naturalized reaches. These reaches have established a curious equilibrium with their ecologies, depending on nutrient-rich flows from sewage treatment and urban runoff.[9] 82% of the river is lined with concrete channels, with the remainder divided among five "naturalized" reaches. Three of the naturalized reaches are termed "soft-bottom", because strong ground-

[5] California Regional Water Quality Control Board. *Water Quality Control Plan for the Los Angeles Region* (Sacramento: EPA and California Regional Water Quality Control Board, 1998).

[6] Bureau of Reclamation, Natural Resources Group, *Los Angeles River Physical and Biological Habitat Assessment* (Los Angeles: Bureau of Reclamation, 2004).

[7] Bureau of Reclamation, *Los Angeles River*, 18.

[8] Bureau of Reclamation, *Los Angeles River*, 18.

[9] Brown and Caldwell, *Greater Los Angeles County Integrated Regional Water Management Plan* (Los Angeles: Leadership Committee of Greater Los Angeles County IRWMP, 2006).

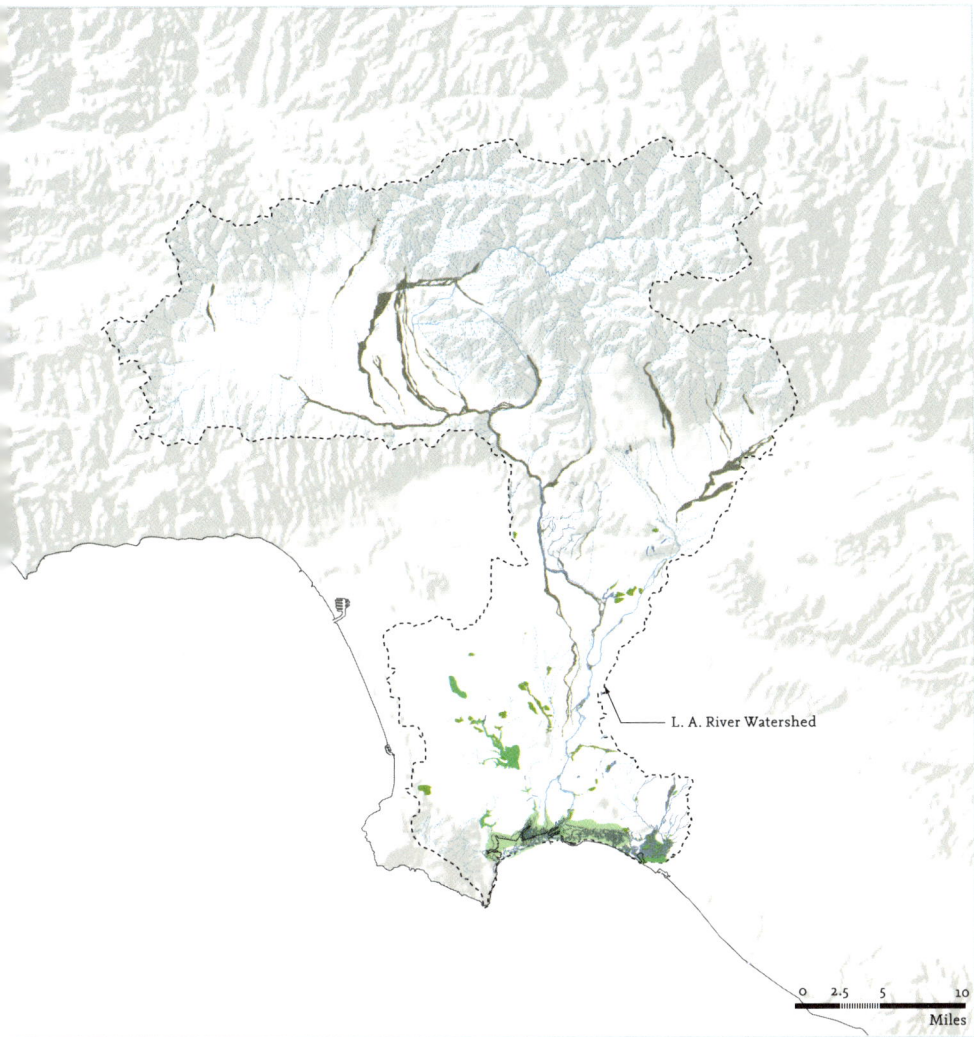

L. A. River Watershed

0   2.5   5   10
                    Miles

Historic Features of
the Los Angeles
Watershed, 1904

Source: author

Intermittent Streams ⋯
Perennial Streams —
Arroyo /Dry Marsh ■
Ephemeral Lake or Pond ■
Freshwater Wetland ■
Tidal Marsh ■

water pressure and tidal activity made them impossible to line with concrete. The Sepulveda Basin, the Glendale Narrows, and the Willow Street tidal estuary are all ecologies rooted in soft sediment, cobbles, and boulders. With their riparian willow woodlands and wetland habitats of bulrush and cattails, these reaches appear to be the healthiest of the river's habitats. Such ecologies provide for a variety of native and endangered species, including Swainson's thrushes, night herons, ospreys, wood ducks, and many reptile and amphibian species, otherwise rare or non-existent in the lower reaches.[10] They also serve as conduits for many mammals, including deer and coyotes that use the channels to connect to ecological patches and habitats across the basin. Many of the river's bridges house bat colonies and swallow nests. These species are critical to urban disease vector control, feeding on the mosquito populations that emerge from pools and standing water.

These reaches have also become habitat for thriving parrot colonies, ragtag teams of birds that escaped private homes as well as from the old Busch Gardens amusement park, closed in the early 1980s. Vegetated islands emerge throughout these channel segments, composed of a ruderal mixture of agricultural and ornamental landscape plants with origins in all of the world's continents, except Antarctica. These islands are populated with tree-of-heaven from China, eucalyptus from Australia, the castor bean plant from Ethiopia, the ubiquitous Mexican fan palm, passion flower vine from Brazil, and the extremely aggressive giant reed from Nepal, the latter growing to 30 feet at a rate of 3 feet per week.[11] New invasive species and biomass are constantly introduced to the river through wind and through storm drains. The County regularly clears vegetation from the channel to maintain flood capacity, which is considered to be at 50% in most of the naturalized reaches, due to the maturity of existing stands.

The Willow Street tidal estuary runs two miles from Willow Street to the river mouth, at Long Beach. Here, the banks are covered with rock riprap, and the area absorbs significant sediment deposit from upstream zones.[12] Most of the sediment load is dropped at the river mouth or beyond, at Queensway Bay. As a result, the port must be dredged annually to maintain navigability. Tidally influenced, this zone supports a great diversity of estuarine invertebrates such as barnacles, mussels, annelid worms, and small crustaceans. These ecologies are not federally protected, yet have a powerful and vocal constituency among the many naturalists and birders, who visit and study them regularly.

The Lower Los Angeles River, which runs six miles to the tidal estuary zone, is perhaps one of the most interesting ecologies. In this reach, the increased nutrient-rich waters spill out of the low-flow channel, a 1-foot-deep by 20-feet-wide channel running through most of the river. This channel was originally designed to concentrate and conduct silt-laden water out to sea and to allow Steelhead Trout up the river to spawn. But the original design did not anticipate the increased flows from the sewage treatment plants. This effluent-enriched water spreads out across the concrete sills, forming a thriving and vast algal zone, the "Sludge Mat." Invertebrates have extensively colonized this zone, creating the most biologically productive stopover for migrating shorebirds in Southern California. It has the largest concentration of black-necked stilts in the United States.[13]

The Headwaters of the Los Angeles River, Arroyo Calabasas (left) and Bell Creek (right)

The Glendale Narrows, Elysian Park

---

[10] Peter Bloom, *Avifauna Along Portions of the Los Angeles River* (Los Angeles: FoLAR Riverwatch Biological Monitoring Program, 2002), 7-9.

[11] Bill Neill, *Survey of Invasive Non-Native Plants, Primarily Arundo Donax, Along the Los Angeles River and Tributaries* (Los Angeles, California Coastal Conservancy, 2002), 8-11.

[12] Hampik Dekermenjian, *Technical Memorandum 2: Los Angeles River Flow Evaluation Phase 2: Estuary Reach Literature Review* (Los Angeles: Department of Water and Power, 2004), 2-5.

[13] Bureau of Reclamation, *Los Angeles River*, 16.

As an artificial ecology, the Los Angeles River is by no means unique in the Golden State. Large-scale artificial ecologies have replaced many of the historic ecologies in Southern California. One example is the Salton Sea, an enormous brackish lake in the Imperial Valley resulting from the failure of a water canal. Serving as a waste sump for adjacent agriculture and unprotected by environmental regulations, the Salton Sea is nevertheless the second most biologically productive body of water in the state. These infrastructural ecologies are systems in uneasy equilibrium, and their uncertain futures depend on water supply, policy, and demand. Called the "Salton Stink" by local residents, this water body has become undesirable for recreation and development. It is this relative isolation, born of "undesirability," that strengthens its ecological viability. It should be noted that all of the water on which these riparian freakologies depend is imported at great expense to the environmental health of watersheds across the West. The diversion of water to the Salton Sea has resulted in ecological devastation at the former outlet in Baja California. Despite the very real regional consequences of such accidental ecologies, and their negative perceptions, we need to come to terms with their benefits, so that they may be better understood, protected, and enhanced.

Naturalized Channel at Willow Street

The widespread perception that native is good and that exotic is bad has a corollary in the river itself, whereby the engineered solution is perceived as an eyesore and a travesty. The waterway has many names, each revealing an ideological stance: to engineers it is "the invert," to managers a "storm channel," to politicians and activists it is simply "the river."

Succession The naïve desire to return the river to a "natural" state amidst an asphalt metropolis is, in fact, a threat to the urban ecologies that have emerged in response to the river's modifications. Recent guidelines call for the total removal of exotic species and the planting of vegetation that was historically native to the watershed. But this narrow agenda does not take into account the many thriving species, native or otherwise, that are now dependent on the existing condition and the exotic species that occupy it. Many of these infrastructural freakologies serve as green infrastructures, cleansing and processing excess nutrients, controlling erosion, and providing habitat which survives independent of human agency. Certainly many invasive species are damaging and should be removed, but a blanket eugenic response fails to respect how non-native landscapes perform significant ecological functions. Nor is eradication safe: exotic plant eradication is presently performed by volunteer groups using herbicides of various types or by government agencies with bulldozers. The proposals that call for eradication assume that native vegetation will return to dominance, restoring the balance of nature.[14] Yet often, new invaders replace the old ones, or the offending plants simply return. Moreover, because soil and hydrologic conditions have so radically changed, native vegetation would require careful maintenance to survive.

Channel below the Arroyo Seco confluence

Central to understanding the river's ecology is the concept of ecological succession, the changes due to the disturbance of animal and plant communities over time. Recent approaches to ecology put forth the theory that "natural" disturbances—fire, flood, tornado, earthquake—are integral to ecological processes. Stability in nature is an illusion; moreover, non-natural factors such as urbanization, global warming, and the heat-island effect all have to be included in the ecological equation.[15] Thus the native versus exotic debate is oversimplified: the landscape assemblages should not be mistaken as the cause of environmental degradation, when they are actually an ecologically appropriate result.

[14] Los Angeles and San Gabriel Rivers Watershed Council, *Los Angeles River Master Plan: Landscaping Guidelines and Plant Palettes* (Los Angeles: County of Los Angeles Department of Public Works, 2004), 24.

[15] Peter Del Tredici, "Neocreationism and the Illusion of Ecological Restoration" *Harvard Design Magazine* 20 (Spring/Summer 2004), 87-89.

Nor can we imagine that the river will stay in its current form. The future of the river and its infrastructural ecologies depends on water availability and flood-control policy. With prolonged drought conditions and growing pressure on water supplies in the American West, Los Angeles will have to become more self-reliant, turning to conservation and grey-water reuse as major sources of water savings. Los Angeles uses more fresh water than any other American city. But the way that water is used is unusual: 22% is for non-agricultural irrigation and only 2% is for human consumption.[16]

Both the city and county have plans for greater wastewater reuse, water recycling, and groundwater infiltration on an urban scale.[17] As water becomes more expensive, wastewater storage and reuse will also be a lucrative source of income for the city's Department of Water and Power (LADWP). As the city grows rapidly over the next decades—primarily through sprawl and infill densification—and as wastewater is re-appropriated for that growth, the city forecasts that the amount of water reaching the river will drastically decrease. Decreased water supplies due to climate change and increasing water demand for recycled water means that soon there will not be enough water to sustain the river's ecologies and landscapes. To put the problem in perspective, a LADWP study recently determined that merely topping off its two river-adjacent artificial lakes—Balboa and Wildlife Lakes—and irrigating its Japanese gardens alone requires 27 mgd, while the amount of water needed to maintain all of the currently existing effluent-dependant ecologies along the river is approximately 35 mgd.[18] Studies suggest that the reduction in water supply will concentrate pollutants and salts in the river, resulting in the degradation of freshwater habitats, while marine species downstream will thrive, thereby extending their habitats up the river.[19]

The LADWP recently funded a team of engineers and landscape architects to produce the Los Angeles River Revitalization Master Plan.[20] This study proposes to extensively retrofit the existing channel with new multi-objective parks, open-space networks, habitat enhancements, channel modifications, as well as constructed scenarios for urban and economic responses.

The Plan promotes a vision of the river as a ligamentous void, a 221-mile connective system of channels, offering an unparalleled alternative transportation and wildlife corridor network, linking commuters and connecting ecological patches throughout the basin. Yet, many of the channel modification scenarios and major transformations are predicated on wholesale changes in the way the city deals with water. Realization of much of the plan depends on watershed management, property acquisition, transformation of existing detention basins, and the establishment of new water detention infrastructures on a gigantic scale. The study also recommends an integrative governance structure, combining the forces of the Corps, the county, and the city, into an entity that can implement projects and guide new

Near the 105 freeway, a resident of the channel built this ingenious solution to keep cool in the summer heat.

Industrial facilities, such as this dust-collection unit for Drees Wood Products, line the river channel.

[16] United States Census Bureau, *Statistical Abstract of the United States 2004-2005* (Washington: United States Census Bureau, 2005), http://www.census.gov/prod/2004pubs/04statab/geo.pdf.

[17] City of Los Angeles Department of Public Works, Bureau of Sanitation, *Department of Water and Power. Recycled Water Evaluation Study Phase I Baseline Study* (Los Angeles: City of Los Angeles Department of Public Works,1995), NP.

[18] Hampik Dekermenjian, *Technical Memorandum 1 Los Angeles River Flow Evaluation Phase 2: Projected Dry Season Flow in the Los Angeles River based IRP Alternatives* (Los Angeles: Department of Water and Power, 2005) and Jeff Friesen, *Technical Memorandum 8: Los Angeles River Flow Evaluation Phase 2 Low-Flow Channel Effects for a Range of Flow Alternatives* (Los Angeles: Department of Water and Power, 2005).

[19] Hampik Dekermenjian, *Technical Memorandum 7 Los Angeles River Flow Evaluation Phase 2: Projected Dry Season flow in the Los Angeles River based IRP Alternatives* (Los Angeles: Department of Water and Power, 2005), 5-7.

[20] The author was a project manager and designer on the Master Plan team. The full Master Plan may be found at http://www.lariverrmp.org/.

development. Unprecedented in its scope, this plan will result in many benefits for Los Angeles and its watershed. But if the plan is broad in its ambition, ultimately it is doubtful that there will be enough water to support these new landscapes and ecologies, let alone those that already exist. Public expectation, rooted in an unsustainable, Arcadian image of "the river" has shaped public desires and has influenced revitalization efforts.

Freeways cross the river channel.

The term "revitalization" implies regrowth as a recuperative agent for societal wrongdoings and suggests that it is desirable to correct the freakological conditions in which virtually any invader can thrive. During the past twenty years, there has been an explosion of interest and of new constituents for the river, with causes ranging from complete floodplain restoration to the creation of waterfront development, parks, and habitats. Though there is strong advocacy for the river's renewal and restoration, there is as yet little constituency for understanding the river as it is and as it will be in the future, for the infrastructural sublime, for the freakological, for the river as artifact.[21] Certainly, it is unfair to compare our river to the popular Edenic conception of "river," with all its associated expectations and tidy bourgeois sentimentalities. Rather, we must reassess the very definition of "river," expanding our idea of "nature" to include the parrot, the shopping cart, the weed, the sludge mat, and the stormdrain apartment. We must develop new narratives and vocabularies for our vital urban freakologies for these are the ecologies of the future. If not, the river will never be truly understood or integrated into the ongoing urban project. Only by integrating the river's complexities into planning efforts, can we move forward realistically.

Imported as ornamental plants, these feral specimens inhabit the Los Angeles River channel. The tall plant is Umbrella Plant (Cyperus papyrus) from Africa, the small one to the left is Sea Lavender (Limonium perezii) from the Canary Islands. The small one to the right is Perennial Pepperweed (Lepidium latifolium) from India and Eurasia.

[21] FOVICKS-Friends Of Vast Industrial Concrete Kafkaesque Structures http://seriss.com/people/erco/fovicks/. See the FOVICKS Web site for a comprehensive photo essay of the river from the headwaters to the Rio Hondo confluence.

Preceding pages: Camouflaged oil rigs grace Island White, one of four artificial islands built in the ocean off Long Beach. The islands are named after the first four astronauts who perished while on duty at NASA.

Frank Ruchala

CRUDE CITY

OIL

In 1892, a down-on-his-luck miner named Edward Doheny began drilling for oil on a residential lot to the northeast of the then-small town of Los Angeles. He succeeded with the region's first commercially viable well, tapping what would become known as the "Los Angeles City Field," thereby sparking one of the largest oil booms in the country's history. It was a star-crossed meeting. Doheny would go on to become one of the most powerful men in the United States, and the area would become one of the most productive oil regions in the world. Over the next seventy years, more than sixty additional oil fields were discovered throughout the basin. Los Angeles soon earned the nickname "Oildorado," its oil fields supplying a fifth of the United State's oil demands, as much as Saudi Arabia does today.[1]

Thanks to the geology of Los Angeles, oil deposits are found across the area, from Long Beach to Los Angeles, from El Segundo to Yorba Linda. In total, over thirty percent of the area sits atop underground pools of oil. The basin's small but hyper-dense oil fields have produced over 8.5 billion barrels of oil since 1892, many still producing after nearly a hundred years. Today, over 3,000 oil wells still extract around 30 million barrels per year. While the city's output pales compared to worldwide yearly production of 3 billion barrels, its fields still meet about fourteen percent of the region's oil needs. The land devoted to oil production, refinement, and storage in the Los Angeles basin totaled over 11,500 acres in 2001.[2]

[1] Sam Hall Kaplan, *Los Angeles Lost and Found: An Architectural History of Los Angeles* (Los Angeles: Hennessey and Ingalls, 1993), 75.

[2] For oil production figures see California Department of Conservation, Division of Oil, Gas, and Geothermal Resources, *Annual Report of the State Oil & Gas Supervisor 2005*, publication PR06, ftp://ftp.consrv.ca.gov/pub/

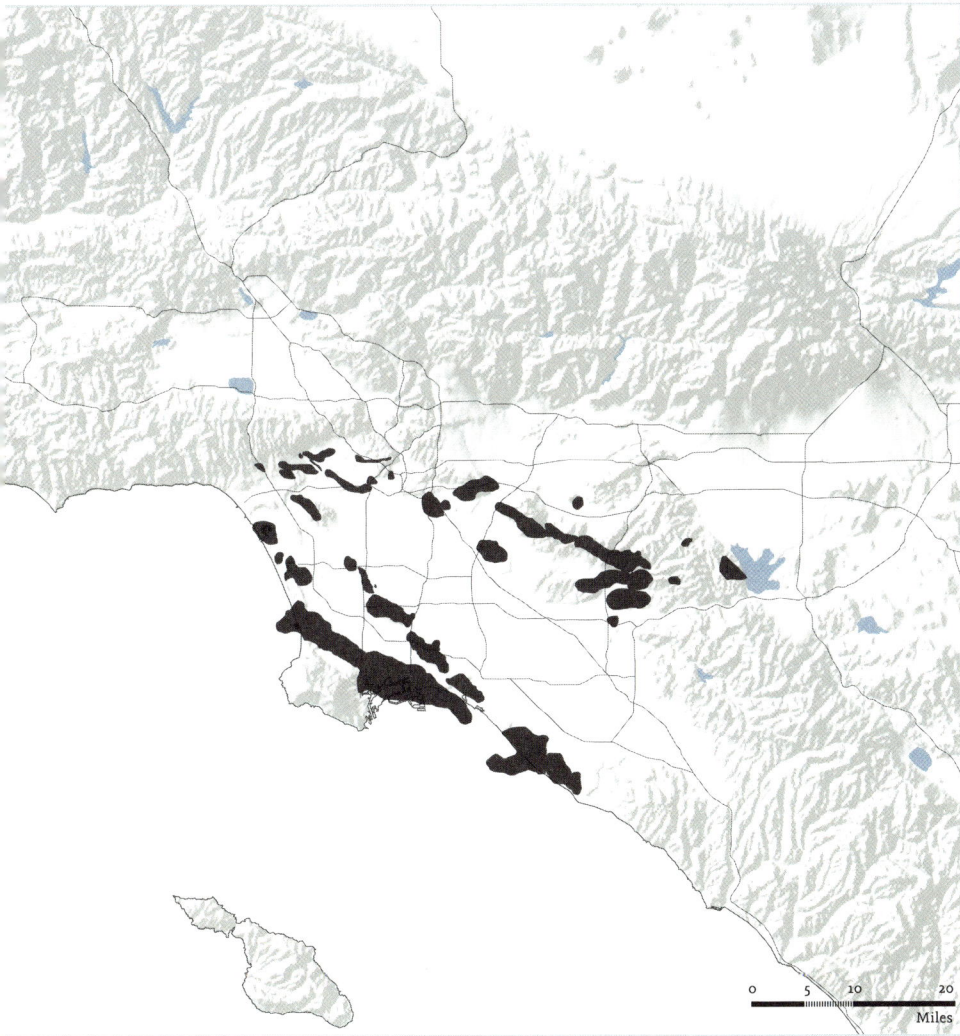

Existing oil fields
in Los Angeles

Source: author

Oil Fields ■
Major Water Bodies ▬
Interstate Highways —

But while the Los Angeles aqueduct and the freeways are well documented and have become part of the city's history, the region's oil story remains relatively unknown. Although Los Angeles named what is arguably its most famous road, Mulholland Drive, after its chief water engineer, almost none of the region's hydrocarbon history has been commemorated, much less remembered, even though Los Angeles is so identified with its consumption of petroleum products. The only indication of where Doheny first drilled for oil is on the maps of California's Department of Oil, Gas, and Geothermal Resources.[3] The site is now the parking lot for a city-owned swimming pool, and the lack of any monument there testifies to how oil is regarded in the region.

Throughout its development, Los Angeles has always told stories about itself and its infrastructure, casting the region as an Arcadian paradise coaxed from the desert by water. Though crucial for the city's expansion, the region's oil infrastructure never fit into this narrative comfortably. Today is no different, as Los Angeles seeks to re-imagine itself as a global city driven by media, high-tech service industries, and fast-moving flows of trade. As Norman Klein points out, the city has a remarkable propensity to "forget" those portions of its history it finds inconvenient or undesirable. Thus, in 2004, the County of Los Angeles removed the three oil wells that had adorned its official seal since 1957 and symbolized the region's oil production. Facing an ACLU lawsuit regarding the inclusion of a cross on the seal, county officials decided to substitute it with a rendering of a historic mission building. The religious symbol had previously hovered above the Hollywood Bowl but, given the graphic impossibility of putting the Bowl and the mission together legibly, something else had to go. The oil wells, it seems, were the easiest target.[4]

In the future this symbolic erasure will be compounded by oil's physical disappearance. Already between 1990 and 2001, spurred by increasing urbanization and decreasing oil reserves, the land area devoted to oil production dropped by twenty-seven percent, almost 3,500 acres. From a peak of 133 million barrels in 1969, production has dropped to 27 million barrels. Given the estimated recoverable oil in the various fields and the ravenous desire for land in the Los Angeles region, a conservative estimate suggests that more than half of the forty-four operating oil fields will go out of production in the next fifteen years. The remaining fields will most likely stop producing in the fifteen years after that.[5] Extrapolating current trends, by 2040 oil production will be completely erased from the Los Angeles basin.

If the history of oil—and its disappearance—is unique to Los Angeles, the history of infrastructures vanishing is not. Infrastructural systems once integral to their urban regions and celebrated as beacons of modernity are forgotten as they age and begin to symbolize outmoded economic orders.[6] Los Angeles's oil infrastructure fits into this historical arc, erased as the region refigures itself. But as this essay suggests, this erasure erases Los Angeles as well. Without oil, the region would have turned out to be a far different place.

The Echo Park Pool is the site of the first oil well in Los Angeles.

Pumps extract oil in the Baldwin Hills.

oil/annual_reports/2005/0101summary1_05.pdf. For land use information see Southern California Association of Governments, *2001 Land Use Data*, http://scag.ca.gov/wags/index.htm.

[3] Patricia Reid, "Pasadena Freeway Becomes National Landmark," *Inside Seven-CalTrans District 7 Newsletter*, (August 1999), http://www.dot.ca.gov/dist07/aboutdist7/pubs/inside_seven/pdf/Aug99.pdf, 1.

[4] Nancy Wride, "Oilmen Upset About New County Seal," *Los Angeles Times*, September 13, 2004, B1. Norman Klein, *History of Forgetting* (New York: Verso, 1997).

[5] California Department of Conservation, *Annual Report of the State Oil & Gas Supervisor* 2005 and William M. Welch, "Record Oil Prices Bring Fresh Interest in L. A.'s Wells," *USA Today*, May 8, 2008, http://www.usatoday.com/money/industries/energy/2008-05-08-laoil_N.htm. United States oil production peaked in 1971.

[6] Maria Kaika, *City of Flows: Modernity, Nature and the City* (New York: Routledge, 2005), 28.

The Machine in the Garden Oil has a particularly uncomfortable relationship with Los Angeles since it literally transformed the city, undoing its first Eden. Apart from agriculture, there was barely any industry to speak of in the area when the first well was drilled. However, over the next few decades the region's oil—cheap and close at hand—would help turn a Los Angeles of orange farms and bungalows into the largest manufacturing center in the United States, a position it still holds today. To utilize Leo Marx's famous image, Los Angeles's oil infrastructure drove the machine into the garden, and oil fueled that machine for over a century.[7]

Before oil was discovered, the region suffered from a dearth of traditional energy sources. Coal, the great fuel of the nineteenth century, was absent. Given the high transportation costs to import outside energy from the east or overseas, industry was loath to set up in the region. It was only with the discovery of viable sources of oil in the Los Angeles basin and elsewhere that the area could free itself from relying on prohibitively costly imported fuel sources and grow.[8]

Railroads soon took advantage of the oil and, starting in 1894, the Santa Fe railway fueled its engines with local oil as they headed over the mountains that line the basin's perimeter. By 1895, both the Southern California and the Southern Pacific railroads had locomotives running on oil. Six years later, the Southern Pacific's entire Los Angeles division discontinued using coal. Henry Huntington's Pacific Electric system ran its power plants on local oil. At the turn of the century, California's per capita coal consumption fell to less than one-half ton, a fraction of the nation's 5.3 ton average. California was fueled by oil. Between 1900 and 1910 per capita oil consumption in the state climbed from three to twenty-eight barrels, compared with one-half to two barrels nationally. With its underground fuel source, Los Angeles was able to achieve energy independence and begin to position itself as a manufacturing center.[9]

Bringing the first industrial activity to the region, oil also demanded equipment to extract and store the fuel source, spurring the development of small manufacturing firms throughout the region. By 1930, oil and its subsidiary industries accounted for the third largest industrial sector in Los Angeles, trailing housing construction and agriculture, but besting movie, automobile, and aircraft production. By 1936, the metal industry—integral to oil production—was the largest industry in the region in terms of employment.[10] Small manufacturers who had their start in the oil industry soon branched out, forming the basis for the region's continued strength in the machinery and metallurgical industries. The industry's refineries were keys to further industrial growth, spurring on a number of related enterprises, of which the most important was the petrochemical industry, itself later spinning off the region's highly important plastics industry. The hula hoop—that most Californian of inventions—was invented by a Los Angeles plastic company, its raw materials produced in a nearby refinery from oil pumped from beneath the city.[11]

A camouflaged oil derrick at Pico and Doheny, at the edge of Beverly Hills, won an award for its contribution to the urban environment.

Tar seeps from the sidewalk at the corner of Wilshire Boulevard and Curson Avenue.

[7] Leo Marx, *The Machine in the Garden; Technology and the Pastoral Ideal in America* (New York: Oxford University Press, 1964).

[8] James C. Williams, *Energy and the Making of Modern California* (Akron: University of Akron Press, 1997), 127.

[9] Williams, *Energy and the Making of Modern California*, 117.

[10] John Jepson, *The Oil Century: The History of the Oil Fields of Los Angeles* (Unpublished Manuscript, 1999), 2. Roger Keil, *Los Angeles: Globalization, Urbanization, and Social Struggles* (London: Academic Press, 1998), 64. Anton Wagner, *Los Angeles. Werden, leben und gestalt der zweimillionenstadt In Südkalifornien* (Leipzig: Bibliographisches Institut, 1935), translated by Gavriel D. Rosenfeld as *Los Angeles: The Development, Life and Form of the Southern California Metropolis*, unpublished typescript (Los Angeles: Getty Research Institute for the History of Art and the Humanities, 1997), 185.

[11] William Kidston, *The Oil Fields of Southern California: a History of the Los Angeles Oil Basin* (UCLA

With the region producing a surplus of oil, the harbor was repeatedly expanded through-out the 1920s, mostly to handle the increased tonnage of oil shipped. From 1923 through the first years of the Depression, Los Angeles was the largest oil exporting region in the world. Soon the port became the largest tonnage-handling harbor on the West Coast. Lumber-handling facilities, the other major segment of the port, grew to serve the industry as well. To take just one year, in 1921 the oil industry imported over 38 million linear feet of lumber to build the forest of derricks that would soon cover great swaths of the region.[12]

The shell of the Packard drillsite on Pico hides dozens of oil drills.

Above all, oil was fuel. Inexpensive and easily available, it generated electricity, allowing Los Angeles to become the first city in the world to be entirely lit incandescently. In the early twentieth century, power in Los Angeles was considerably cheaper than in other American industrial cities. Many of the industries that opened up branch plants in the Los Angeles area, beginning in 1919 with the arrival of the Goodyear Tire and Rubber Company, listed easy accessibility to oil and natural gas as a major reason they moved to the region.[13]

The city's most rapid period of growth, decentralization and automobile acquisition took place in the first decade after World War I, its greatest oil boom. The region's rate of automo-bile ownership grew from one for every eight residents in 1915, to one for every two in 1924. In comparison, nationwide ownership was one in forty-three in 1915, and one in six in 1924. Historians who have looked at these statistics argue these changes were spurred on by oil production. For example, one study showed that gasoline prices in the region were less than half the national average in 1923, prompting increased automobile usage. In addition, oil was easily turned into asphalt. Well before road paving became common in most American cities, Los Angeles was paved. By 1940, Los Angeles was the most decentralized large city in the nation, with more than half its residents living in single-family dwellings, compared to only sixteen percent for Chicago.[14] But until the 1970s, when the city was producing enough oil to meet nearly all its needs, Los Angeles could be considered the most natural city on earth.

A Rogue Infrastructure Powered by its subterranean fuel source, the Los Angeles of the 1920s was well on its way to taking its place as the exemplary twentieth-century metropo-lis. Yet, even as Arcadia was bulldozed to create more and more tract homes and factories, the industrial Los Angeles brought about by the region's oil could not supply a comparable mythos for the place. Oil was passed over for its far more glamorous competitor, Hollywood, which is commonly called the Industry in the area, thereby suggesting that the production of the city is immaterial, though the region still makes almost twice as much money from manufacturing as it does from movies and television. So while cities like Chicago (City of Big Shoulders) and Pittsburgh (Steel City) remain tied to their industrial history, Los Angeles's manufacturing industry remains out of the picture, despite dwarfing both of those other cities' industries for some time.

Oil flows across lawns of homes worth in excess of $1.5 mil-lion. In this case, the owner has installed a wishing well and filled it with sacrifi-cial plants in an effort to distract the eye.

Special Collections, 1936) cited in Robert M. Fogelson, *The Fragmented Metropolis* (Berkeley: Univer-sity of California Press, 1967), 127. Wham-O, History of Wham-O, Inc. http://wham-o.com/default.cfm?page=AboutUsHistory.

[12] W. H. Hutchinson, "The Genie of Yang-Na," *California History* 60 (1981): 47. Keil, 64. Nancy Quam-Wickham, "Work, Home and Autonomy in Blue-Collar Suburbs," in *Metropolis in the Making: Los Angeles in the 1920s*, ed. Tom Sitton and William Deverell (Berkeley: University of California Press, 2001), 129. Wagner, *Los Angeles*, 108.

[13] Wagner, Los Angeles, 186. Fred W. Viehe, "Black Gold Suburbs: The Influence of the Extractive Industry on the Suburbanization of Los Angeles, 1880-1930," *Journal of Urban History* 8 (1981): 14.

[14] Scott Bottles, *Los Angeles and the Automobile* (Berkeley: University of California Press, 1987), 192. Viehe, "Black Gold Suburbs," 8. Martin Wachs, "Autos, Transit and the Sprawl of Los Angeles: the 1920s," *Journal of the American Planning Association* 50 (1984): 302.

Oil is not only hidden in the city's self-image, its full extent is hidden from sight. Unlike the freeways, the infrastructure that pumps, moves, and refines the region's oil is hidden underground or deliberately camouflaged and balkanized amidst the hundreds of private companies that operate the oil network. Like the oil fields themselves, the network sprawls across urban Los Angeles. While there are places of intensity, such as the oil field at Baldwin Hills, to fully grasp the system requires systematic travel across the region.

Oil is deliberately hidden in the city. The most elusive aspect of the network are the numerous underground pipelines that move oil throughout the basin and beyond. Between the refineries, the port, and thousands of continuously pumping wells, Los Angeles contains one of the most intense concentrations of pipelines in the world. Some extend as far out as Texas or the California coast, but most of the network is limited to the basin itself. Some lines have a dedicated use, like those that run from the port to LAX transporting jet fuel. Others run from the region's various oil fields to the system of refineries that are found in the southern portions of the basin. Almost none of this network is above ground. Instead, it lies buried a few feet below streets, homes, and parks, completely out of public view. The only markers of this network are the shut-off valves that can be found sprouting out of the ground every so often along boulevard medians and highways.

In the area in which oil production would be most conspicuous, the dense urban district heading west from downtown toward Santa Monica, measures have been taken to camouflage the oil infrastructure to allow it to better blend into its urban surroundings. After banning oil production within the urbanized area for the previous thirty years, in 1950 the city created new guidelines permitting a limited number of sites from which new oil wells could be drilled—basically onshore off-shore drilling rigs.[15] The city ordered these sites enclosed, landscaped, and sound-proofed. The result is some the most unique oil wells in the world. Fourteen drill sites of one to two acres each have been built, with many still in operation on golf courses, commercial boulevards and residential neighborhoods throughout central Los Angeles. Most of these operations sit behind ten foot high walls that are meant to be inconspicuous from the street. Hunting these sites down takes a trained eye as well as a trained sense of smell—for it is only the sulfurous smell of oil that makes many of these sites stand out from their urban context.

Some facilities are designed to look like regular buildings, such as the thirteen-story Packard drillsite that completely overwhelms its surroundings on Pico Boulevard. Designed in the 1960s to look like a modern office building, the drillsite has done a remarkable job of remaining hidden. Supposedly, two vice presidents of a rival oil company once drove by the building three times before a police officer convinced them it was really an oil site.[16] The entire structure is made up of steel sound-proof panels. All drilling operations take place indoors, including truck loading and unloading. The massive height of the complex is used to mask the height of the drilling rig which completes the individual wells. The oil wells themselves are found in the basement level of the complex.

Unlike the freeway and water networks, oil's infrastructure is privatized, built out by numerous private companies of various sizes throughout the years. This single difference makes this privatized infrastructure a forensic model for more contemporary privatized infrastructures such as mobile phone or fiber optic networks. But this atomization stems not from ideology but from geology. Instead of a single enormous oil pool that could be controlled by one company, Los Angeles's oil is parsed out into more than sixty individual fields. Compounding this, the pattern of land ownership in the region, with millions of individual

[15] William Rintoul, *Drilling Through Time* (California Division of Oil and Gas Publication, 1990), 138.

[16] Rintoul, *Drilling Through Time,* 143.

property owners, has created another layer of complexity. Each homeowner could (and sometimes did) start their own oil company by simply drilling an oil well. As a result, over a hundred companies drain oil from underneath the city. One of these, reportedly, consists of two wells in the backyard of a house owned by a ninety-year-old lady who inherited the pumps from her husband and operates them herself.[17] This situation has been exacerbated recently, as most of the largest players in the global oil industry vacated the region, fearing bad publicity and costly lawsuits from nearby homeowners. The result is that even with oil underlying the city, it actually costs more to recover oil locally than it does to have it shipped from Saudi Arabia.

Los Angeles's oil network is far more sensitive to the machinations of the marketplace than its publicly controlled infrastructures are. This is most apparent in the battle between oil and real estate. Oil production in the region must follow a simple calculus based on land and oil costs. When oil is selling at a price that makes production profitable, the oil wells continue to pump. However, the minute land becomes more valuable or oil production becomes unprofitable, the oil wells are shut down and removed and the land is quickly put on the market for other uses. Imagine this happening to a freeway. As land values in the region have exploded over the last decade and fuel costs have been unable to maintain parity, more and more of Los Angeles's oil wells have been closed forever. As one oil expert put it, "oil men are actually in the real estate business."[18] This means that most of the remaining oil wells in the region are found in relatively undesirable locations. Most of the easily developable oil land has already been transformed into housing tracts or industrial parks. So what remains are drillsites in Signal Hill's residential backyards, on the challenging mountainous topography of the region's eastern stretches, or the remaining camouflaged sites in central Los Angeles.

Fossil Fuels As Los Angeles reshapes its image into that of a post-industrial city, it seeks to erase the traces of its industrial past. But infrastructures, when outmoded, do not just disappear. Forced underground, they undergo metamorphic transformations, the resulting strata propping up the world above.

A geological feature that the city harnessed to fuel its growth, oil sits between infrastructure and landscape. Thus it is fitting that this city's greatest natural wonder is the Rancho La Brea Tar Pits. Here, oil lies precariously close to the surface, and asphalt—the lowest grade of crude oil—seeps out of the ground to fill pools. Over tens of thousands of years, animals wandered into the pits where they became stuck in the asphalt and died. Once their remains drifted to the bottom, they became encased in an oily matrix and fossilized, creating a rich record of North American ice age mammals. After researchers realized the significance of the bones found within the oil, they excavated the tar pits and enshrined the remains of the animals in an on-site museum. The area was turned into a park by a former resident, G. Allen Hancock, who had profited from the oil wells that operated in the area in the first decades of the twentieth century. Closing down the wells and subdividing the property gave Hancock the excuse to preserve the tar pits in perpetuity.

[17] William L. Fox, "Tracking Tar," *Orion Magazine* (January/February 2007), http://www.orionmagazine.org/index.php/articles/article/93/.

[18] Author's interview with Donald D. Clarke, Division Engineer City of Long Beach Department of Oil Properties. Esther Schader, "Land Is New Black Gold for Oil Firms," *Los Angeles Times*, June 2, 1997, 1.

In the years since, the area surrounding Hancock Park has developed into an upscale residential district and the Tar Pits have developed into one of the city's top tourist attractions. But the legacy of the oil fields remains. Asphalt seeps bubble up into the park, ruining the landscaping. Hapless visitors step in the tar and track it across sidewalks. Leaking into nearby basements, it forces owners to undertake costly remediation procedures.

More ominously, however, methane gas, which causes the bubbles in the lake pit by the museum, percolates from the ground. This odorless and colorless gas is highly explosive and poses a constant threat to the surrounding community. In 1985, gas that had accumulated within a Ross Dress-for-Less on Third Street detonated, causing the store's roof to collapse and sending two dozen people to the hospital. Methane-fueled fires spouted from cracks in the earth near the store for days afterward, lending an air of Hollywood apocalypse to the area. The explosion's cause is controversial. Some suggest that it is simply a natural accumulation of methane. Others believe it to be the result of ongoing drilling practices in which waste is forced underground in order to extract more oil.[19]

In other areas, the effects of the oil industry on the city may be more indirect but no less real. To take another example, Charles Canfield, Doheny's partner in his 1892 drilling experiment went on to have a quite successful career in the region's oil development. In 1905, Canfield and his partners sold the Chanslor–Canfield Midway Oil Company to the Santa Fe Railroad. With money from the sale, he purchased the Rancho la Rodeo de Agua in 1907, believing the land offered possibilities much like the Rancho La Brea just to the east, then just peaking as an oil field.

After drilling thirty test wells, Canfield and his partners found no sign of oil. Having paid too much to let the land continue to be agricultural until the sprawling Los Angeles region could reach it and they could subdivide the land for residential use, they looked for a way to recoup their investment, eventually deciding to develop their property as a fashionable garden city. Walter Cook, who had assisted Frederick Law Olmsted with plans in Chicago and Washington, was brought in to design the plan, which called for a variety of housing types, a commercial center and extensive landscaping. Perversely, Canfield added one last touch, an ordinance banning oil drilling within city limits. The syndicate named their city Beverly Hills. Still, Canfield was correct. There was oil below the Beverly Hills. Unfortunately, the oil was much deeper than drilling equipment could reach at the time. It would take over fifty years and the construction of a series of urban drill sites before the oil under the city could ever be recovered.[20] The irony is that Beverly Hills became Beverly Hills because Canfield believed it had oil under the ground but no one could reach that oil, in a region that only existed because it had oil under the ground that someone could reach.

Even as the oil industry disappears from view in Los Angeles, it will never truly vanish, but will always remain just under the surface, a toxic pillow of liquid unsettling the city. In its refusal to obey our wishes, oil reminds us that our actions on the land have created a second nature.

Island Freeman is another of the four artificial islands off the coast of Long Beach. An oil tanker is visible behind it.

A methane gas release pipe on Wilshire Boulevard disguises itself by mimicking a nearby lamp post.

[19] George Ramos and Ted Thackery Jr. "Fairfax Fires Die as Gas Pressure Dips Sharply :[Home Edition]." *Los Angeles Times*, March 27, 1985, 1, Dave Perera, "Fresh Produce and Streets of Fire," *L. A. Weekly* (May 2, 2001), http://www.laweekly.com/news/features/fresh-produce-and-streets-of-fire/11074/, G. V. Chilingar and B. Endres, "Environmental Hazards Posed by the Los Angeles Basin Urban Oilfields: An Historical Perspective of Lessons Learned," *Environmental Geology* (2005) 47: 302-317.

[20] Jepson, *The Oil Century*, 13. Kaplan, *Los Angeles Lost and Found*, 77.

Matthew Coolidge, The Center for Land Use Interpretation

MARGINS IN OUR MIDST
GRAVEL

In Los Angeles, nearly all of our time is spent—whether we are standing, sitting, sleeping, or driving—on concrete or asphalt. This manufactured ground has its origins in the earth, at specific locations around the city. The aggregate that makes up the bulk of these bulk materials tends to be found in the river valleys, where the disintegration of the mountains spills into channels and falls downslope, forming deep deposits in the ground. The material sorts itself out, based on the distance from the mountains, with heavier, coarser material near the base of the slope, and progressively finer material further away.

The city of Irwindale lies at the base of the San Gabriel Mountains, and straddles the San Gabriel River, one of the major alluvial fans bringing marginal material from the mountains into the Los Angeles basin. Here, the margins literally flow into the city's midst. Furthermore, as the largest aggregate mining area in the state, if not the nation, so much sand and gravel comes out of Irwindale that pieces of it can be found around all of Los Angeles in the form of the aggregate in the asphalt that is spread on the city's roads, the aggregate in the concrete of the city's major construction projects, and even the city's land mass itself.

The new terminals at the Port of Los Angeles, piers 300 and 400, are one of the largest land creation projects in American history, and most of their 600 acres of asphalt came from Irwindale. They were made over a ten-year period starting in the early 1990s. When they were completed, the nation was larger by more than a square mile, and extended a bit closer to our largest trading partner, China. Irwindale helped to narrow the Pacific gap. One result of the city continuously giving of itself in this way is that Irwindale is so full of holes that more of the land in the city is a pit than not.

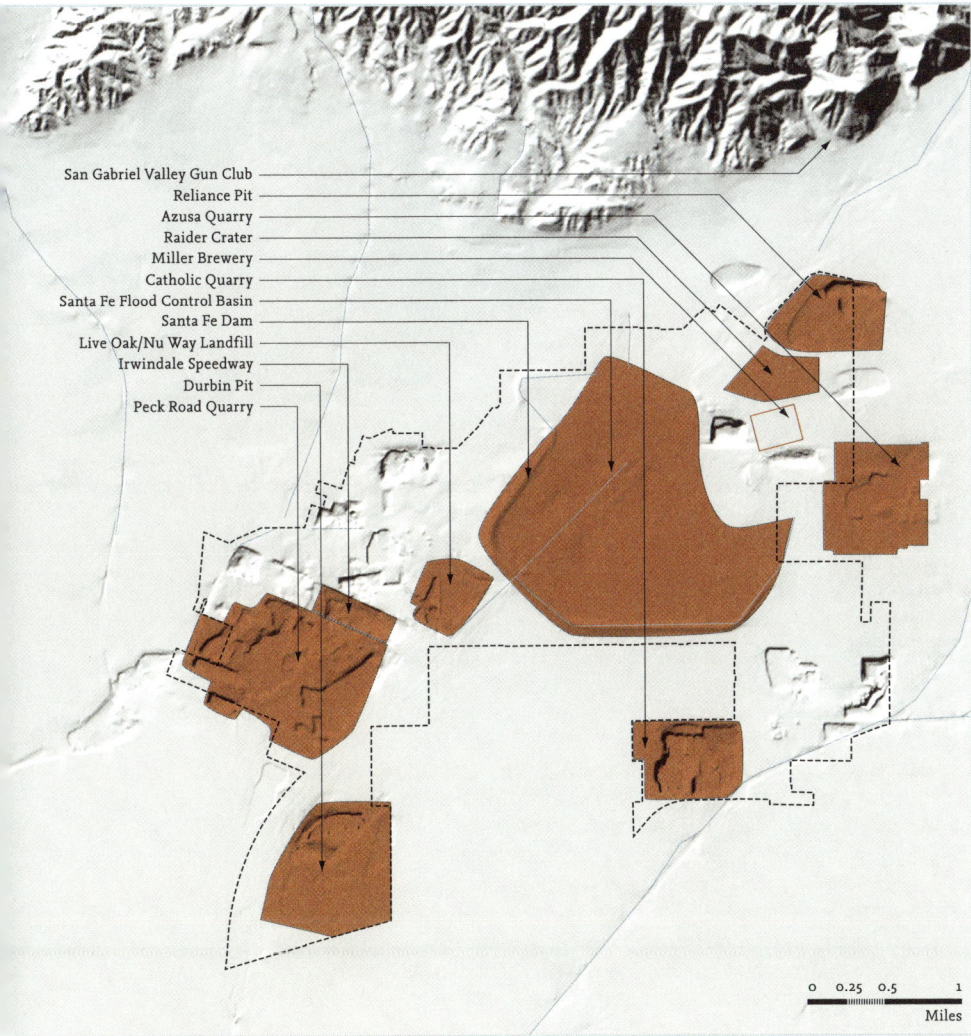

San Gabriel Valley Gun Club
Reliance Pit
Azusa Quarry
Raider Crater
Miller Brewery
Catholic Quarry
Santa Fe Flood Control Basin
Santa Fe Dam
Live Oak/Nu Way Landfill
Irwindale Speedway
Durbin Pit
Peck Road Quarry

0   0.25   0.5   1

Miles

Excavation, Irwindale

Source: Center for Land
Use Interpretation

Irwindale Boundary
The Pits of Irwindale
Rivers

The Durbin Pit is near a rock-studded landscaped cloverleaf at the intersection of the I-10 and the I-605 freeways. The pit is a maze of engineered plateaus, causeways, ordered mounds of material, and extraction machinery. Durbin is one of three pits in the area operated by the Vulcan Materials Company, the nation's largest construction aggregates company. Vulcan started off as Birmingham Slag, mining and marketing the slagpiles from the steel industry in Birmingham, Alabama. Business began to take off in 1951, as demand grew for aggregates for the new interstate highway system (to this day, possibly the largest complex construction project that the world has ever seen). Still headquartered in Alabama, Vulcan now has 10,000 employees working at 162 stone quarries, 33 sand and gravel plants and 43 asphalt plants, all over the country, generating $2.5 billion in annual sales (as well as a chemicals division, making chlorine and hydrochloric acid, based elsewhere).

The Irwindale Speedway

To put this in a national perspective, the aggregate industry overall has around 120,000 employees, and 10,000 quarries, making it easily the largest mining industry in the country. The primary use of aggregates—officially defined as crushed rock, gravel (naturally broken rock), and sand—is in construction projects: 20% home construction; 20% commercial construction; and 20% is used for public works projects, such as airports, sewage systems, and other municipal infrastructure. The remaining 40% is used in making roads. There are nearly 4 million miles of paved roads in the United States, and 94% of their asphalt is aggregate (the rest is the binding material, usually petroleum based). The asphalt and paving industry employs 330,000 people, while the broader transportation construction industry employs 2.5 million. Roads, clearly, are fundamental.

Near the Durbin Pit is the Hanson Spancrete complex, a construction yard and administrative headquarters for California's largest manufacturer of these prestressed precast concrete structural members. Spancrete was first used in the famous Arroyo Seco overpass next to downtown Los Angeles, called the first four level interchange in America. Spancrete is now an important premanufactured component expediting the assembly of ubiquitous functional structures like parking garages and freeway overpasses. Behind Hanson's yard is the "Touchstone" Business Center with the likes of "Gibraltar" Products, Inc., more evidence that this region is the rock products capital of Los Angeles.

The Santa Fe Dam

The Peck Road Quarry is across the engineered San Gabriel River, where large vertical concrete fins protrude from the spillway. This is the western edge of a pit complex nearly a mile long, which is being worked especially on the east side by the Hanson Materials Company, the nation's largest manufacturer of bricks, concrete pipes, and precast products (including Spancrete), as well as the third largest aggregates producer in the country.

Of the seventeen major pits in the Irwindale area only four are being mined at the moment. Many of the others are idle, having already been mined to their permitted depth of 200 feet, and having met their limitations in size by running up to the edges of adjacent properties and roadways. In many cases the material extends to a thousand feet deep and the quarries are trying to get permits to go deeper. Vulcan estimates that if they could go another 150 feet, their Irwindale pits would have another thirty years of life. The city, on the other hand, having literally lost so much of its taxable surface area, is interested in bringing the inactive pits back up to grade, so they can develop the land in a more economically productive way.

One of the filled-in pits has been capped with a giant slab of asphalt (itself, no doubt, made up mostly of Irwindale aggregate), and turned into the parking lots and tracks of Irwindale Speedway, one of a handful of large-scale car racing complexes in the Los Angeles area. Though it is normal for the track to host things like NASCAR racing, the Irwindale Speedway recently had been the host of the "D1 Grand Prix," the first major drifting event in the nation. Drifting is an emerging car racing sport in which cars move around in prolonged

controlled skids. These skids are made possible by using lightweight, rear wheel drive compact cars, mostly Nissans and Toyotas of late '80s and early '90s vintage.

Aggregate operation in the Reliance Pit

One way for these massive pits to be filled in, over time, is to turn them into dumps. While some pits have become household landfills, the city now discourages this sort of pit filling, as it is unsanitary, smelly, and potentially hazardous. And, as Los Angeles' disposal pressures mount, there was a serious concern that Irwindale might become the garbage dump for the city. Currently there are only three pits in Irwindale that are being commercially landfilled, and they generally accept construction debris but not domestic waste.

The Live Oak/Nu Way landfill, operated by Waste Management Incorporated, the nation's largest waste company, is one of these dumps. Between 1957-1973, this was an active quarry, and in the 1980s, much of the pit was filled with mining waste from another quarry. The eighty feet or so of pit that remains to be filled in is slowly approaching grade, being filled in by inert wastes, mostly construction debris including rock, drywall, concrete, bricks, and metal. Inside the pit are various recycling operations, where construction debris is broken down, divided into reusable and non-reusable metal, asphalt, and concrete piles.

Beyond the pits, one of the key landscape features in the region is the Santa Fe Dam, an arc of piled rock nearly five miles long. Built by the Army Corps, it has never really had to be used for its designed purpose—yet. It was made to defend the land downstream from catastrophic floods and debris flows. These are occasional storm events, which have been very destructive to some parts of the city, where unconsolidated rock from the mountains is mobilized by prolonged rain, and tumbles down the canyons and river valleys like a slow motion avalanche of coarse rock, gravel, and mud, destroying everything in its path. There are hundreds of check dams higher up in the mountains now, and these catch the majority of the flows before they reach the valley (the dam basins themselves are periodically emptied by the aggregate industry).

Structures like the Santa Fe Dam, the Sepulveda Dam, the Hansen Dam, and the Whittier Narrows Dam are the last line of defense, built downslope to hold back a major flow that makes it out of the mountains, like a geologic shock absorber. Behind these dams are undevelopable areas that need to stay empty to contain the material from this potential unscheduled aggregate delivery. The permitted uses of the land here is ephemeral: oddly disorganized wildlife areas and recreation zones.

The "Raider Crater" across from the Miller brewery

A paved, narrow recreational pathway runs along the top of the dam. The view from one side is of the margins of this sacrificial recreational zone within the dam together with the mountains looming above it. On the other side, the downstream industries and roads of Azusa and Irwindale are visible. At the center of the dam, above the gatehouse, are stairs set in the rock wall to the entrance of a tunnel which leads into the heart of the 24,100-foot-long, hundred-foot-tall rockpile.

The Santa Fe Dam is meant to keep the mountain's margins from merging with the city. Typically, in cities ringed by wilderness, things fray at the edges. At these margins, socialized behavior can give way to other, more marginalized activities. These edges contain dumping grounds, burned cars, and shooting ranges, places and activities nobody wants to see in the city's midst. At the San Gabriel Valley Gun Club, at the end of the road at the base of the mountains, small firearms are made available for anyone to shoot recreationally at the San Gabriel Mountains, adding to a new land layer of shells and bullets.

Debris travels down the mountains, from the mouth of the canyon that holds the San Gabriel River, down the wash, back down the alluvial fan, to the land of the pits. One pit is known to locals as "Raider Crater." Here, a decade or so ago, the Los Angeles Raider football team pledged to build a stadium inside a disused Irwindale pit. It was a plan that seemed to make sense: stands for 65,000 would be built on the sides of the pit, a playing field at the

bottom, and the Miller brewery was visible across the highway. The plan fell apart, and the team took $10 million of Irwindale's incentive money and eventually moved up to Oakland. The pit remains fenced and empty.

The nearby Reliance Pit is one of the most active in Irwindale. This is the site of Vulcan's main processing facility, an amazing maze of conveyors, hoppers, and sorters. Neat piles of crushed and sorted rock are mounded in elegant conical piles of uniform grain size and texture. All this takes place in a 200-foot-deep, massive rectangular hole, surrounded by office park buildings. An old concrete silo stands on a raised area in the middle of the pit. This massive structure once loomed high over Irwindale and prominently display a big CalMat logo on it (Vulcan bought CalMat in 1999). The silo is being torn down to permit excavation underneath it and to permit the reuse of the concrete it was made out of. The entire operation would then be nearly invisible, contained in the pit below the horizon line.

Outside the main gate of the Reliance Pit is Irwindale Boulevard, the main drag through the city, lined with fast food restaurants, particularly McDonald's. Irwindale is said to have the highest per capita consumption of Big Macs in the country. This is due, probably, to the fact that the population is less than 1,500, while nearly 40,000 people work here, many of them quite likely statistically to be hamburger eaters. The largest single employer in town is a frozen food company, Ready Pak Produce, followed by the cable TV company, followed by the Miller brewery.

Irwindale's 9.5 square miles are a hodgepodge of margins, non-places, and land not wanted by the neighboring cities of Duarte, Azusa, Baldwin Park, and El Monte. Its boundaries were made up by the existing limits of the surrounding cities, where their lines stopped in the unincorporated county white zone, in the wide gravel wash of the river, and along the Santa Fe sacrifice basin. But in 1957, during a building boom, the city finally incorporated, and its founders saw that revenue could be made by exporting its marginal real estate.

But not all the city got dug up and shipped out. The surface level land has typical office parks and bungalow rows. Irwindale Boulevard has muffler shops and storefronts. Like many L. A. basin cities, aerospace was an important employer here, and just off the main drag, over the line in Azusa, Aerojet, the defense contractor, developed a complex for manufacturing and developing satellite-based surveillance systems that allow for, among other things, monitoring other nation's rocket launches. Though Aerojet is mostly gone from the cavernous buildings down Optical Drive, the complex is now home to Northrop Grumman's Electronic Systems, and a division of Perkin Elmer, the company that built the camera system for the SR-71 spy plane.

Across Irwindale Boulevard stands the landmark Miller brewery. Like the sand and gravel of Irwindale, the city's water is mined, processed, and shipped across the country, in the form of beer products. Through its efforts to preserve the perceived purity of its water supply, the aquifer under the adjacent San Gabriel River, the plant has a direct effect on the landscape of Irwindale, using its leverage as one of the region's major employers. When a trash-burning power plant was proposed for a pit next to the highly visible brewery, Miller successfully stopped the project. When the county proposed building wastewater percolation ponds along the San Gabriel River, the company sued to have the project reduced. When the plant needed room for expansion, Irwindale bought 242 acres of adjacent property for $10 million and sold it to Miller for $1.

This plant uses over a million gallons of water a day to make nearly 200 million gallons of beer per year under dozens of labels, many of them for other brands, such as Old Milwaukee, Schlitz, and Colt 45. Raw material including grains and corn slurry, comes by rail, while the packaging material comes by truck. After a few weeks of fermentation, the finished product is shipped by truck to markets all over the west coast, but more than half of what is produced here goes to Los Angeles. This is one of six Miller breweries in the country, and the only Miller brewery in the west. Miller, now owned by a South African beer company, is the second largest beer company in the country, with around 20% of the market nationwide. Anheuser-Busch, with around 50% of the market, is indeed the king of beers.

Miller is fortunate that its plant and water source are relatively close to the undeveloped mountains. Just downstream, the San Gabriel River aquifer under Irwindale has been designated a Superfund site, with a subsurface plume of contamination a mile wide that extends 8 miles south to West Covina—from the 210 to south of the 10, on the east side of 605.

Contaminants include perchlorates from rocket fuel at the Aerojet plant as well as solvents and degreasers from the now closed Huffy bicycle factory.

The Azusa Land Reclamation Company was one of eight businesses cited in the Superfund lawsuit, and responsible for assisting with the $200-million clean up of the contaminated ground. The Azusa Land Reclamation Company site is a former quarry pit that became an unlined hazardous material landfill. It was shut down by the state in 1991, due to the groundwater contamination concerns. In 1994, it reopened as a landfill, with new engineering and lining, and is now operated by Waste Management Incorporated. One of the four mandated water treatment facilities for pumping out and treating the contaminated aquifer is located at the site, and vents can be seen poking out of the mounded earth at the hazardous end of the dump.

The old sanitarium is across from the Irwindale Chamber of Commerce, on the way to the new Irwindale Business Center, a showpiece for the kind of development the city would like to see at other pit sites. It is a fancy new office park that looks like other fancy office parks, except for the fact that it is about 30 feet below grade. Access roads climb down a slope, into the faint remains of a (mostly) filled-in gravel pit.

A 192-acre empty pit nearby, surrounded by homes, was purchased a few years ago by the Catholic Archdiocese for $3 million. The church has plans to develop the site by building a church, a school, a retreat center, and a cemetery there, one of the more unusual reuse proposals for the pits of Irwindale. The city manager is on the record as opposing it, however, and the city is trying to buy it back from the tax-exempt church.

California is the leading consumer—as well as producer—of aggregate in the nation. These holes may be owned by Vulcan, Hanson, United Rock, or the Catholic church, but they are holes that we all dug, together. For every pile there is a pit, for every pit there is a pile.

Preceding pages: Plate 1. The confluence of Bell Creek and Calabasas Wash in the San Fernando Valley marks the start of the Los Angeles River.

Lane Barden

THE RIVER

THE LOS ANGELES RIVER PICTURING LOS ANGELES: CONDUITS, CORRIDORS, AND THE LINEAR CITY, PART 1

Seeing Los Angeles from the air elicits a feeling of shock, matched by an equally intense feeling of fascination. It is the uneasy and extraordinary sense that this is more than proof of where we have gone wrong; it is an inscription across the earth's surface that describes who we are, what we have done, and where we are headed. It is also proof that our impact on the earth has become so vast and so intricately woven with causal relationships that it is becoming increasingly difficult to maintain an intellectual distinction between nature, culture, and the built environment.

From the air, the logic of the Los Angeles River and its status as infrastructure reveal themselves more clearly than from the ground, especially where the river turns, is joined by another channel, or undergoes structural changes. The conjoining of two channels in the west San Fernando Valley, for example, forms the river's official beginning (see plate 1). From the air, this convergence of two tributaries into one channel performs an impressive symmetrical flourish of engineering and infrastructure design. As it moves further downstream, the river channel demonstrates a remarkable spatial efficiency that is the extreme opposite of its natural state. In its authentic form prior to channelization, the river wandered and wove through a myriad of sandbars and willow stands in a vaguely defined, unpredictable wash that could stretch to hundreds of yards or even miles across.[1] Now, from the air,

[1] For a complete, detailed and fascinating description of the undeveloped Los Angeles River, see Blake Gumprecht. *The Los Angeles River: Its Life, Death, and Possible Rebirth* (Baltimore: Johns Hopkins University Press, 1999), 9-40.

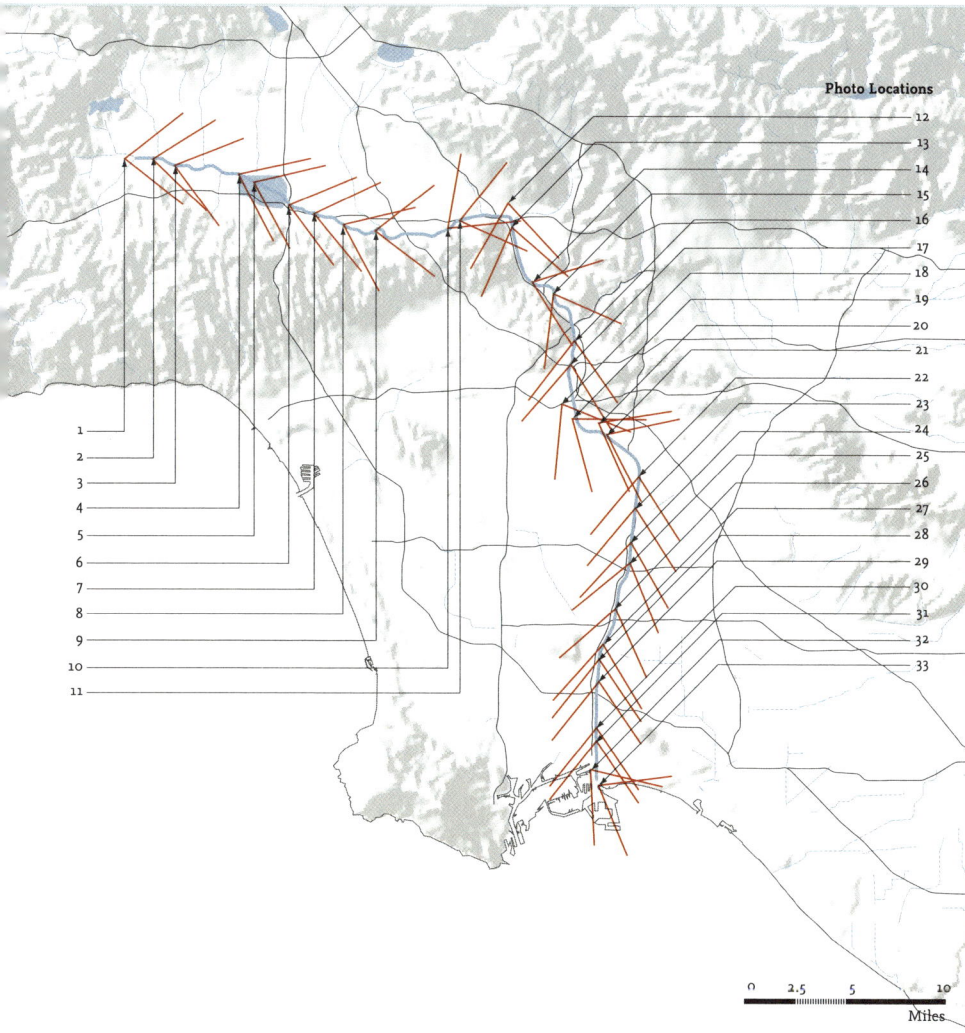

12
13
14
15
16
17
18
19
20
21
22
23
24
25
26
27
28
29
30
31
32
33

1
2
3
4
5
6
7
8
9
10
11

*Numbers correspond
to plate numbers of
photographs in this
chapter*

0   2.5   5   10
                    Miles

Photograph Viewshed
Los Angeles River
Interstate Highways

79

looking at the river across the sweep of the landscape and city surface, its form is narrow, smooth, and precisely executed. Its plotted curves and precise straightaways move smoothly and rhythmically across the landscape in a controlled trajectory, minimally affected by the lay of the land, slowly growing wider as it is joined intermittently by feeder channels in elegant, mathematically correct confluences. (See plates 2, 3, 9, 11, and 25).

Observers frequently describe it as an inadequate "trickle," undeserving of its status as a river. This trickle is hidden in a box-like ditch called the low-flow channel, and carved deep into the floor of the larger channel. The low-flow channel carries about 58,000 gallons of water per minute—sufficient to support a full riparian habitat (see plates 4 and 5).[2] Surges during heavy rains rise within a few feet from the top of the channel and are treated as a dangerous threat that must disappear as quickly as possible. They do. Within about sixteen hours after the end of a rainstorm the channel is nearly empty and back to normal base flow. The river is embedded in a super-efficient infrastructure that dispenses with the natural water in the watershed as though it were a nuisance.

This efficiency of the channel for flood control is mirrored in its efficiency for organizing easements, rights-of-way, and the placement of utility properties. Developers can build right up to the edge of the channel, with essentially no more threat from flooding than if they built half a mile away. Construction of the channel, therefore, created new real estate as well as a relatively uncontested path for the location of freeways and other forms of infrastructure. The Ventura Freeway, Interstate 5, and the Long Beach Freeway all run parallel to the river and crisscross it (see plates 11, 13, and 22). Railroads are hemmed in along the river on both sides through downtown

[2] Mark McKowski, *Upper Los Angeles River Watermaster Report* (Los Angeles: Los Angeles Watermaster's Office, 2006), 2.4.

where trains move smoothly up and down the channel's edge with no threat from flooding and no interference from automobile traffic. In the San Fernando Valley, a long string of movie studios is installed on huge tracts of land nestled right up against the river's edge (see plate 8) while in South L. A. vast warehouses line the channel on both sides (see plates 18-19). Literally thousands of outlets for storm water run-off dot the sides of the channel. Massive bridges, viaducts, and rail crossings occur at regular intervals. Enormous high-tension wires are draped along geometrically structured galvanized steel towers rising eighty feet into the air next to the river in a long necklace-like chain, stretching and fading into the distant haze. As far as urban infrastructure is concerned, the Los Angeles River is a full house.

The river is more than a river and more than a drainage channel. It is a corridor of public land that serves as a conduit for the movement of water, trains, cars, electricity, trucks, and freight for much of its fifty miles. In the moment of confronting this level of complexity, the kind of recovery destined for this landscape becomes evident. Historically, the river has an inextricable relation to infrastructure, and to undo this relationship with the aim of separating the natural environment from the man-made is at best, a shaky proposition.

Imagining the Landscape The Los Angeles River is hidden from view—literally (it runs on the bottom of a channel 30 feet below street level) and figuratively (the actual river in its natural form has been hidden behind the engineering of a flood control system). Los Angeles's landscape does not afford views of the river from a distance. To grasp the river, you need to be next to it, or on top of it, or in it. At that point its vast, empty, graffiti-laden concrete surfaces are alienating and overwhelming in their closeness. The channel, for obvious reasons, is usually described as ugly, an eyesore, or an embarrassment. Images made from the ground tend to become documentation of the undesirability of this condition, or obvious plays upon the strangeness of industrial landscapes. But from the air, the river's form becomes more singular, coherent, and self-explanatory.

While high aerial photography from an airplane, with the camera on an axis perpendicular to the surface, has its strengths in mapping the diagrammatic aspects of the landscape, it produces pictures in a thoroughly flattened perspective. There is no horizon, no vanishing point, no depth, and no modeling—all long-established codes in the history of landscape representation, particularly in painting, and in nineteenth- and twentieth-century landscape photography. In low altitude photographs, with the camera at an oblique angle to the river, a helicopter can be used like a very tall tripod, placing the object in pictorial space, with a more naturalistic, subjective point of view, detailing the river within a larger context of the surrounding environment.

5

Without the pictorial history of perspective drawing and easel painting, there would be few references for our perception of landscape. Painting was particularly influential in the construction of our concept of landscape and landscape photography in the American West, but this was hardly the beginning. Bird's eye view perspective drawings of palace gardens date back to the fifteenth century, pre-dating aerial photography by several hundred years. But the intent and the effect are the same. As Charles Waldheim observes, "Picturing the landscape is to infer its renovation."[3] Waldheim points out that the picturing of landscape is not simply a recording of an image as a document, it is a tool for the construction of space in a world that is created for its potential to be seen. It is as though our concept of landscape exists exclusively in its imaging.[4]

The series of photographs of the Los Angeles River consists of fifty images (33 of which are reproduced in this publication) taken in a single flight, with the helicopter held at an altitude between 400 and 500 feet. The camera is always pointed downstream. The horizon line is held relatively constant in the frame, and the light remains consistent from one image to the next. This repeated articulation of the landscape within pictorial references and frames became a kind of composite representation of the river in its engineered form—revealing its path through the city and its relation to other infrastructure in the conduit.

[3] Charles Waldheim, "Aerial Representation and the Recovery of Landscape," in James Corner, ed. *Recovering Contemporary Landscape: Essays in Contemporary Landscape Architecture* (New York: Princeton Architectural Press, 1999), 133.

[4] Waldheim in Corner, *Recovering Landscape*, 127.

The images remain within pictorial conventions, but include all the realities of what the landscape has actually become. The photographs represent the landscape *tel quel*, unembellished, and as is. What we learn from these pictures is the degree to which the river has become reformulated by engineering, and the intricate relationship it now has to larger systems of urban infrastructure. The question is what kind of recovery do these images suggest, and what kind of imagination do we need in order to visualize it?

What kind of river is this? There are two conventional answers to this question and a third, unconventional one—and all are accompanied by mental images. The first answer really answers a different question; "What kind of river *was* this?" as though recovery of the river amounts to a mandate to restore all original conditions and native habitat to something like it was prior to development. The simplified image is a broadly sketched wash, devoid of concrete and instead supporting native plants and an annual run of steelhead trout: a park combined with a flood plain. It is generally accepted, even within the most pure sectors of the environmental movement in Los Angeles, that putting everything back like it was is not an option, yet this image lingers on and frequently confuses the dialogue and debate about the river's future.

The second answer is the obvious one; the river is not a river, it is a drainage ditch. Its image is the present concrete channel as it is, a kind of anti-icon, a version of the river that nobody wants or visualizes a river to be. This image is flawed simply because it does not recognize the magnetic, theatrical dimension of the channel and the way it has drawn

the community into it to question the reasons for its existence. The third answer is that this is a river whose dry season base flow—the water that is in the river when it is not raining—consists almost entirely of treated sewage water. Ironically, this is the most interesting and the most honest answer to the question.

There is no single image attached to this answer by the public, because the public is not yet fully aware that the movement to restore the Los Angeles River is a movement to restore a river that will consist primarily of recycled sewage. Without this tertiary treated water, there is not enough water remaining to form a river. In the river's natural state prior to channelization, dry season flow did not come from springs in the surrounding mountains but from a surging, overflowing, gigantic abundance of ground water in the valleys—one trillion gallons in the San Fernando Valley alone. Now, only traces of that ground water ever find their way into the River.

Today, the San Fernando aquifer and adjoining aquifers in the Southern California region, are depleted sub-surface reservoirs controlled and administered by the city. Because excessive storm water run-off from Los Angeles hardscape is swiftly funneled into the river, even heavy rains do little to recharge the aquifers, so ground water reserves are below capacity. This groundwater is monetized and can only be pumped out with a license and a fee. Pumping ground water into the river for restoration purposes is not an option and will not become an option. The authentic conditions of an endless supply of groundwater feeding the Los Angeles River are lost and will not be reclaimed.

Prior to 1913, the Los Angeles River and its massive ground water supply was the sole source of water for the city. After tapping the Owens Valley and the Colorado River with aqueducts hundreds of miles in length, Los Angeles was freed from its dependence on local aquifers. Water from the aqueducts that once flowed in the Colorado and Owens Rivers now flows into our sinks and toilets, then into the sewers, and onto three treatment plants located next to the L. A. River. There it gets scrubbed three times and is discharged into the river channel only to be polluted again with street runoff that includes various chemicals, oil products, hundreds of thousands of plastic bags, and coliform bacteria coming from kennels, stables, and the street.

That's the contemporary Los Angeles River, a river that has been siphoned from outlying areas, has flowed though kitchens and bathrooms, treated before it goes into the riverbed as tertiary water, then polluted before going to the ocean. Robust community movements are now underway to clean up runoff and storm water before it enters the river to protect the tertiary base flow. Remarkably, this tertiary water, if it could remain unpolluted, is probably cleaner than the water in every urban river in the world.

Ideally, many years from now, the rain that falls in Los Angeles would be cleaned and diverted into the city's aquifers for storage. Then, tertiary water could become the primary source for the river year round. With this in mind, a third, more adaptable image becomes possible, enabled by a constant, steady supply of clean tertiary water that could feed a linear public garden fifty miles long. It would provide as yet unimagined cultural interpretations, natural habitat, recreation, and green infrastructure for a city that has become so dispersed, park-starved, and focused on short-term problem solving that its inhabitants are hard-pressed to imagine anything beyond what the river once was and what it has become.

9

The reputation of the Los Angeles River as a river has been restored by community efforts. It now stands at the beginning of a massive restoration effort that will go on for decades into the future. Regardless of the status of its waters, the Los Angeles River is the backbone in the structural map of the watershed. The Los Angeles River will always be a river no matter what form it takes. Reclaimed, tertiary water is currently approved for recreational and selected agricultural uses in California, but not for drinking water or ground water recharge. In Singapore, recycled sewage is bottled and re-sold as drinking water, but in this country there is a discomfort about tertiary water that may or may not persist into the oncoming water crisis. Either way, it is reasonable to assume that recycled water will be available to maintain the Los Angeles River or a greenbelt, as the concrete channel is gradually removed in the coming years. Los Angeles is a severely park-starved city, and the river is the only significant remaining real estate to address this problem effectively.

These photographs may be seen as a record of the river as it is but I cannot say I was motivated by the potential of documenting the facts for the public record. These photographs were produced with the intent to satisfy a near-voyeuristic need to visualize the river and the landscape around the river and to know it. After years of studying photography, I remain astonished at the capacity of a photograph to gather up the details in the visual world and render them in pictorial space with such concentration and clarity that the photograph seems more complete than the event in real space and time. No other technological or natural phenomenon can quite compare with it. Photography constitutes another way of knowing about the world.

11

13

14

16

15

17

19

21

24

23

25

27

29

31

33

FABRIC

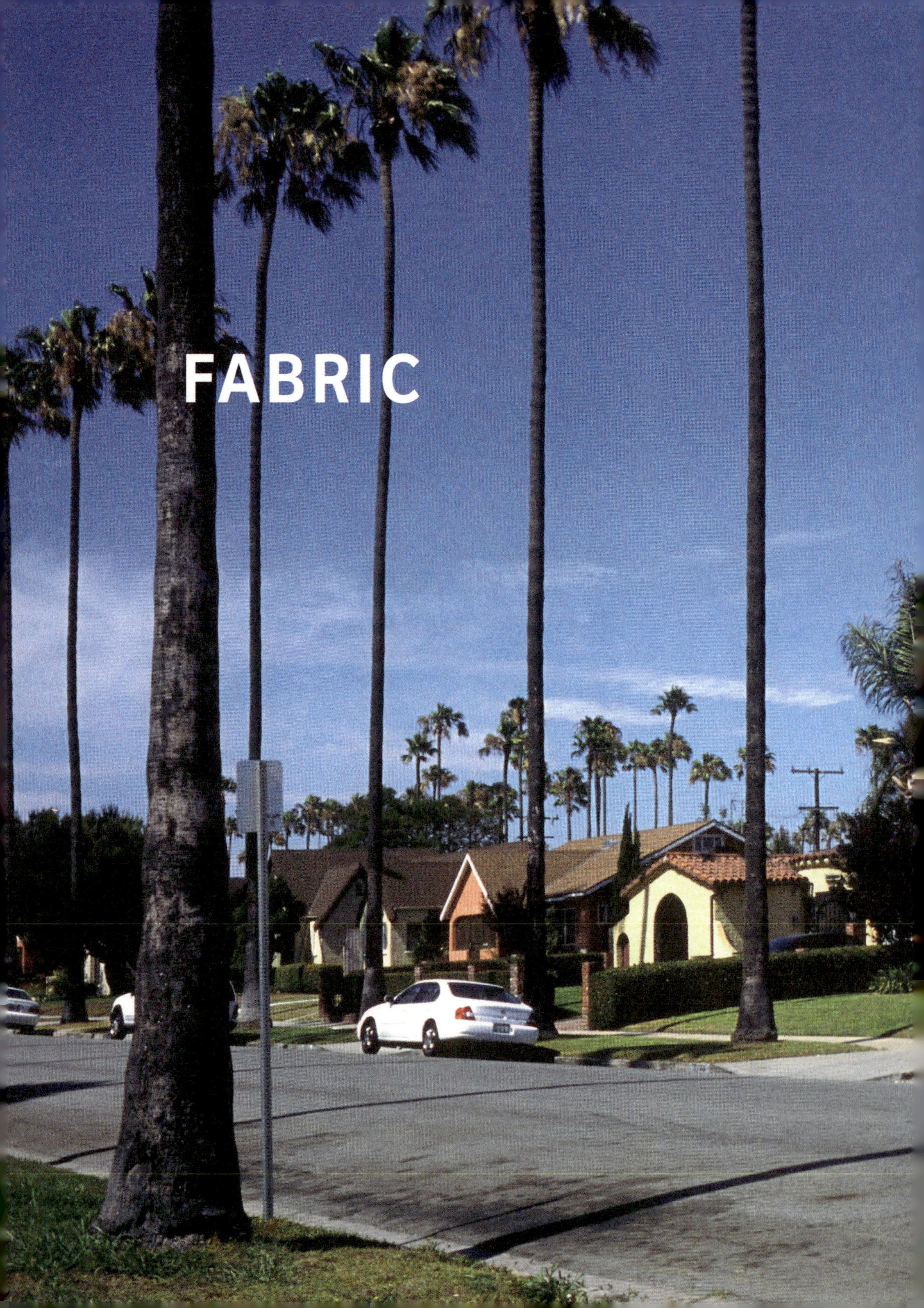

Sean Dockray, Fiona Whitton, and Steve Rowell

BLOCKING ALL LANES

TRAFFIC

If Los Angeles evokes sunshine, flashy cars, and movie stars, it also instantly brings to mind traffic. But the word "traffic" is always a little slippery, one of those words that escapes us when we try to pin it down. For engineers and the dictionary alike, "traffic" refers to the movement of vehicles along a roadway. For the rest of us, however, traffic has come to mean the exact opposite: that phenomenon of vehicles crowding a roadway until everything slows down to a frustrating crawl.

Ten years and 400,000 automobiles into the twentieth century—slowdowns were given a name, dubbed "traffic jams" by the *Saturday Evening Post*. Today the notion of a jam, which suggests something that can be unplugged, seems hopelessly optimistic for drivers accustomed to four-hour-long rush hours. Engineers continue to categorize the phenomenon as "traffic congestion" even without any consensus of what that means. Is it slowness at a point over time—or over an area at a point in time? If so, what defines "slow"? Is congestion just a feeling? In cities all over the world, congestion is becoming the rule, which is to say that it is simply becoming synonymous with traffic.

Tracing the history of the word, traffic originally referred to the movement of commodities. Only in the last two centuries did it explicitly take on vehicles and people. In terms of the modern definition, we are traffic (which reminds us that it was once quite acceptable for one to be a "computer" or a "typewriter").[1] Of course, we don't talk that way: we say that we are "in traffic," but we never admit to being traffic. Although this point was made into a

---

[1] Katherine Hayles, *My Mother Was a Computer: Digital Subjects and Literary Texts* (Chicago: University of Chicago Press, 2005), 1.

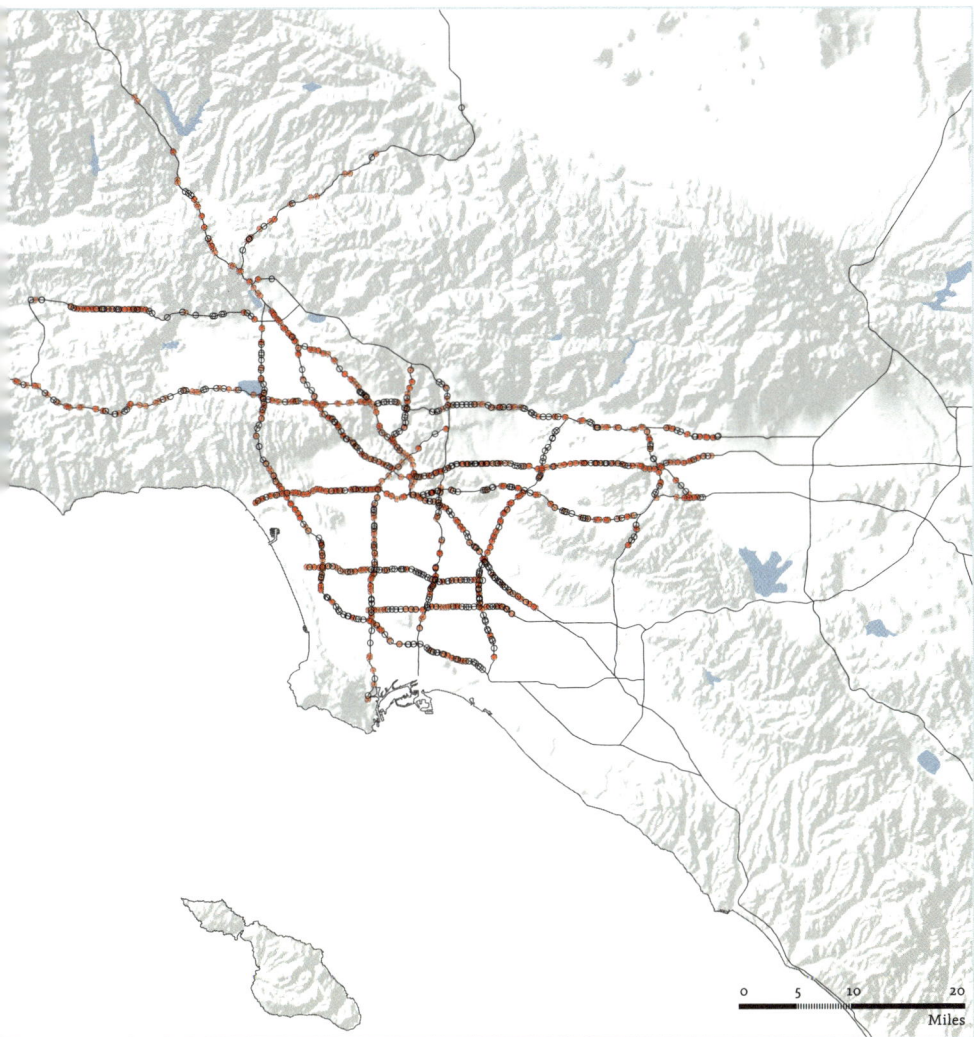

Mainline Freeway Loops,
CalTrans District 7

Source: "Freeway Per-
formance Measurement
System," CalTrans and
University of California,
Berkeley

Functioning Loops ○
Broken Loops •
Major Water Bodies ▬
Interstate Highways —

German roadside ad campaign—"You're not stuck in a traffic jam. You are the traffic jam," it hasn't found traction in our speech.[2]

But our need to remove our own culpability from congestion, our need to speak of being "stuck in a jam," is an expression of our profound ambivalence to driving. The automobile, the capitalist vehicle par excellence, promises freedom while the often-frustrating experience of driving leaves us feeling quite out of control. We hold on to the idea that although we might be stuck now, there is a way out. But what if our agency were underpinned by an organizing, computational mechanism? We stop. We go. We turn. We yield. What if these were not simply rules to follow (code as law), but instructions to follow (code as program), an instruction that gives a green light?

Control It's impossible to say where the first traffic jam was, but the origin of modern traffic control was probably in 1722 in response to "the great inconvenience and mischiefs which happen by the disorderly leading and driving of cars, carts, coaches, and other carriages over the London Bridge, whereby the common passage there is much obstructed."[3] To fix matters, the Lord Mayor of London ordered that three able-bodied men be appointed as public servants to keep traffic to the left, and keep it moving.

Beginning in 1860, New York City's police department was given the task of regulating the increasingly competitive and reckless horse-drawn bus drivers. Not long before, City Council had given permission for the livery corporations to franchise, and many pedestrians were killed in the aftermath as drivers raced each other to their destinations. The police officers that brought order to the streets were not ordinary men: they were some of the tallest on the force ("Broadway's Finest" were all over six feet in height) so they could be seen above the confusion of carriages and pedestrians, and they would point and wave, moving traffic with their hands, barking orders above the din to eliminate uncertainty.

The integration of the police into traffic flow marks the origin of modern traffic control. The policeman represents a system of rules and enforces them, apprehending violators. But he does more than this—he also directs the traffic and his professional presence keeps traffic from degenerating into a stall. As transportation engineer Burton Marsh wrote in 1927, "The officer can take advantage of variations in the volume of traffic on the two streets and give to each street that proportion of time best suited to it at that minute."[4] Each officer was a responsive, real-time traffic control system.

Problems with this system arose immediately. It was difficult enough for any single officer to coordinate his activities with another officer, one block away, but it was practically impossible for that officer to synchronize his signals with officers at the four adjoining intersections, each of whom might be coordinating with three more intersections, and so on, throughout the urban grid. Over time, the traffic cop was slowly transformed: his hands took on white gloves for visibility; his voice was replaced by a whistle; and, eventually, he was elevated in a tower and communicated with the traffic via signs or colored lights. The police officer slowly vanished, his body evolving into mechanical and electrical devices. His hands were replaced by standardized, colored signals. His eyes were replaced by sensing actuators, such as microphones, pressure sensors, electromagnets, or video cameras. All that was left was to replace his brain.

[2] Jane Kay Holtz, *Asphalt Nation* (Berkeley: University of California Press, 1998), 3.

[3] R. A. Paxton, "Traffic Engineering and Control Before the Motor Vehicle," *Traffic Engineering & Control* (August 1969), 7.

[4] Burton W. Marsh, "Traffic Control," *Annals of the American Academy of Political and Social Science* 133 (1927): 91.

A very early experiment with non-human control occurred in London in 1868. There, the first ever traffic signal using colored lights was installed at a busy intersection near the Houses of Parliament. These gas-powered semaphores attracted throngs of Londoners and merchants, selling food and drinks, rounding off the spectacle. Part of the intrigue of this sort of innovation was the premise that a machine could do some aspect of the policeman's job. These sorts of innovations proliferated in the 1920s, during which time most regulated intersections were equipped with discrete signals. Still, there was resistance to such automation. William Phelps Eno, "the Father of Traffic Safety," and author of New York's first printed traffic regulations in 1903, wrote a quarter-century later that "students of traffic are beginning to realize the false economy of mechanically controlled traffic, and hand work by trained officers will again prevail."[5] This nostalgic error was by no means unusual—it was said that the police officer could handle traffic "in a way which no mechanical device could do... often being able to 'weave' it through the traffic from the opposite direction without entirely stopping either line."[6]

Access ports for traffic signalization equipment, intersection of East Fourth Place and East Fourth Street

In spite of these reservations, the technological developments in automated traffic control accelerated. The explosion of automobile use in the first two decades of the twentieth century put an unusually large strain on police departments in major metropolitan areas. Until the early 1920s, traffic control, even in its most advanced forms, had been a series of independent installations—coordinated traffic signal systems had not yet been born. In New York and Detroit, officers positioned in a series of traffic towers synchronized with one another to allow automobiles to flow freely in one direction. Houston built this logic into a string of electronically interconnected signals in 1922. The police officer was practically unnecessary in such an automatic, "simultaneous system."

Systems Not all urban plans were conducive to this design however, and new methods were introduced in the following years: the alternate system created staggered movement through cross-traffic while the flexible-progressive system allowed for the tuning of timing gears within each individual signal. By 1926, Chicago had a room in the basement of City Hall full of such timers, from which a single employee could control dozens of important intersections. Perhaps in recognition that these mechanical turks were best kept hidden, the space of traffic control migrated from elevated towers to subterranean bunkers. In 1930, Philadelphia put the "master controller" (both a device and a person) of its flexible-progressive signal system in the basement of its City Hall.

Induction loop, intersection of Canfield Avenue and Culver Boulevard

Today, the groundbreaking Automated Traffic Surveillance and Control (ATSAC) center, created for the 1984 Olympics, operates four floors below City Hall in Los Angeles. The Traffic Management Center (TMC) for the Los Angeles district of the California Department of Transportation (CALTRANS) sits in an equally fortified building a few blocks away. ATSAC and CALTRANS combine with the Los Angeles County Public Works TMC to handle traffic flow in Los Angeles.

In this city of traffic, traffic management practices have created a feedback loop between the environment and the system. The environment can be described as the collective movement of vehicles across the urban grid. The system is the infrastructure designed to measure, monitor, and control the environment. The system, in Los Angeles, has two primary realms: the physical and the virtual.

---

[5] *Nation's Traffic*, December (1927).

[6] Marsh, "Traffic Control," 91.

In the physical realm, over 50,000 buried loop detectors—the insulated wire loops that passively detect subtle magnetic field changes from vehicles—combine with over 700 weatherproofed video cameras, some of which are remotely controlled to pan and zoom, to monitor and control traffic flow. Loops automatically trigger software in switching boxes linked to intersection signals but also send data to TMCs that allow traffic engineers to monitor flow patters and adjust timings remotely. A simple click of a mouse button can start or stop the flow of movement on the grid.

Transponder unit for bidirectional lane control of Fourth Street Bridge

The surveillance power of 700 cameras may seem oppressive, but neither CALTRANS, which controls 250 freeway cameras, nor ATSAC, which controls 350 street cameras, is allowed to archive footage or to feed even a single frame of video to the Los Angeles Police Department or other law enforcement agencies. Apparently, privacy concerns outweigh the value of traffic surveillance on this scale. The identity of the individual is meaningless compared to the importance of the flow. Aside from monitoring, an increasing number of these cameras actually control traffic flow through sophisticated software interfaces. As vehicles pass in designated zones of the frame, they are counted and measured for speed and direction. The policeman and the loop detector are replaced.

Data Taken together, actuators, control centers, and signals largely comprise the physical infrastructure of traffic control in Los Angeles, as they do in many other populated regions. Cameras and inductive loop detectors transmit data to a centralized location, from which computers can adjust signal timing and freeway metering—a process resembling the "sense-think-act" cycle of classical Artificial Intelligence. In 1935, twenty years before the birth of experimental AI, Bernard Schad wrote that "the control mechanism is the most important part of this so-called 'robot' system. Its function is to receive the impulses from the detectors and assign the right-of-way 'intelligently' by means of the signals, in exact accordance with the indications received."[7]

When the controller "receives" and "assigns," it does so from a distance: through buried phone lines, fiber optic networks, microwave signals, or whichever communication technologies are available at the time. Data circulates incessantly through these connections, animating the devices. It is as much a part of the story of traffic control as the hardware, but it is ephemeral and dynamic, useful only in the present. As new data supplants old data, the old fades into obsolescence, inscribed solely in the strange memory of traffic patterns.

Some of this data is disseminated through the Internet to the public, so that motorists can make adjustments based on current traffic conditions. By intercepting this feedback of information, we have been able to collect the data before it is deleted and lost forever. In this data, one experiences the elastic city through abbreviated narratives of minor mishaps, inexplicable slowdowns, and tragedy.

The eight diagrams that accompany this essay represent Los Angeles on Friday, June 11, 2004, the day of Ronald Reagan's funeral. After beginning the day in a ceremonial horse-drawn caisson in Washington DC, Reagan was flown from Andrews Air Force Base to Point Mugu Naval Air Station in California, and then taken by motorcade to his namesake library for burial. As the motorcade headed east on the 101 freeway at the tail end of rush hour, crowds along the route waved flags, and traffic going west came to a halt to pay its respects to the president.

[7] Bernard T. Schad, "Traffic Control at Signalized Street Intersections." (PhD dissertation, University of Michigan, 1935), 101. According to the Oxford English Dictionary, the word robot was used for automatic traffic signals in South Africa.

There is one diagram for each direction of four Los Angeles freeways. The center corresponds to one end of the freeway and the outer edge, the other—the distance between them corresponds to the amount of time required to drive from one to the other. Tracing the shape clockwise, from top to bottom, you pass from midnight to noon. Continuing from the bottom, up along the left edge, and back to the top, you pass from noon to the following midnight. A perfect day would be a set of concentric circles; as traffic builds, however, the circles deform outwards. Beneath each diagram are the "incidents" that occurred over the course of the day.[8]

Although traffic is generally grouped with the weather and the stock market on the radio, television, and Internet news, unlike those two complex systems it has no popular visual representation that would allow it to be remembered and internally differentiated. What is the analogy to the swirling radar image of a hurricane cloud or the plunging graph of a market crash? How can one day's traffic be distinguished from another's? The traditional topographical map of Los Angeles is radically divorced from each motorist's perception of it, expanding and contracting over time. These diagrams provide an alternative way of imagining the city, centered at an individual point—a person at an origin—and outwardly directed to any number of destinations.[9]

---

[8] The incident stream inexplicably went down at the time of Reagan's funeral.

[9] The diagrams were initially developed with guidance from Rebeca Mendez, and during a project with Ewan Branda and Heather Fraser at UCLA.

5 NORTH

A   *On Roxford Street offramp; 5:58am*
     Offramp closed for unknown duration due to police activity

B   *At Florence Avenue; 11:35am*
     2 vehicles on the right shoulder

C   *Just south of Broadway; 11:46am*
     Nissan Maxima versus Ford Taurus now on right shoulder

D   *Just south of CHP road; 2:22pm*
     An Amtrak bus blocking the right lane

E   *Just north of Alondra Boulevard; 2:49pm*
     Vehicles on right shoulder at callbox

F   *At Los Feliz Boulevard; 3:21pm*
     A large amount of smoke on the west side of the freeway

5 SOUTH

A   *Just north of Lakewood Boulevard; 7:05am*
     Overturned vehicle

B   *Just south of Slauson Avenue; 7:06am*
     Solo overturned vehicle blocking unknown lanes

C   *Just north of Burbank Boulevard; 8:35am*
     Vehicle on right shoulder

D   *To southbound 110 connector; 10:19am*
     Unknown type vehicle blocking the transition road

E   *Just north of Colorado Boulevard; 11:04am*
     2 vehicle traffic collision in center divider

F   *Just south of Pico Canyon Road; 1:18pm*
     4 vehicles in center divider

G   *At Balboa Boulevard; 1:33pm*
     Vehicle on right shoulder

H   *Just north of Norwalk Boulevard; 1:47pm*
     Visual of 2 vehicles on the right shoulder

I   *Just north of Garfield Avenue; 2:30pm*
     Victim in '96 black Nissan pickup truck on right shoulder

J   *Just north of the 14; 2:45pm*
     Red gas can in the car pool lane

110 NORTH

A   *At westbound I-10 connector; 9:15am*
     Multi-vehicle traffic collision

B   *Just south of Vernon Avenue; 10:14am*
     Roadway clear

C   *Just north of Slauson Avenue; 10:54am*
     Large red dog walking in car pool lane

D   *Just south of Florence Avenue; 1:34pm*
     Metal in #2 and #3 lanes

E   *Just south of Pacific Coast Highway; 1:39pm*
     Debris in lanes
     1:39pm. Appears to be a dog house

110 SOUTH

A   *Just south of Manchester Avenue; 9:51am*
     Mostly in car pool lane then across lanes

B   *Just south of 39th Street; 10:41am*
     Reporting party said dog was closer to Adams

101 NORTH

A   *At Vermont Avenue offramp; 8:53am*
     Vehicle on right shoulder

B   *At Vignes Street; 9:39am*
     2 pickup trucks involved in traffic collision

C   *Just east of Kanan Road; 11:02am*
     Large piece of metal caused flats on 2 separate vehicles.

D   *Just east of Shoup Avenue; 1:04pm*
     Trash can in traffic lanes

E   *Just south of Edgeware Road; 3:23pm*
     Big rig on right shoulder

101 SOUTH

A   *Just north of Mission Road; 1:10am*
     Black Honda hit center divider and is now overturned in slow lanes.

B   *On Van Nuys Boulevard offramp; 8:23am*
     2 vehicles involved

101 North   101 South   405 North   405 South

C   *At Beaudry Avenue; 8:45am*
     Roadway clear

D   *On Vermont Avenue offramp; 8:53am*
     Vehicle on right shoulder

E   *Just south of Glendale Boulevard; 10:05am*
     Off-duty freeway service patrol has visual of 5-vehicle
     traffic collision.

F   *Just west of De Soto Avenue; 11:15am*
     Vehicle versus Mercedes

G   *At Woodman Avenue; 12:03pm*
     3 vehicles

H   *Just east of Balboa Boulevard; 3:30pm*
     Roadway clear. We have it over to the right shoulder.

I   *Just east of White Oak Avenue; 3:31pm*
     Black Nissan Maxima versus tan Toyota Camry

J   *Just south of Whittier Boulevard; 3:35pm*
     Vehicles are blocking delivery truck that rolled back
     and hit his car.

405 NORTH

A   *Just south of Devonshire Street; 6:21am*
     Clothes in all lanes

B   *Just north of Palms Boulevard; 10:02am*
     3 vehicles blocking the transition road

C   *Just north of National Boulevard; 11:10am*
     Vehicles on right shoulder
     11:13am. '97 Black Dodge Dakota partly in slow lane

D   *Just south of Montana Avenue; 1:15pm*
     Mercedes on right shoulder

E   *On Montana Avenue offramp; 3:18pm*
     Green Dodge Caravan on right shoulder of offramp

F   *Just south of Jefferson Boulevard; 3:46pm*
     2-vehicle traffic collision in slow lane, several cars
     still going

405 SOUTH

A   *Just north of Century Boulevard; 2:08am*
     Pickup truck involved versus right shoulder
     2:08am. Vehicle facing wrong way

B   *Just south of Manchester Boulevard; 2:48am*
     Is the light pole knocked down?
     2:50am. Light pole is down completely off of its base.

C   *At Lennox Boulevard; 3:06am*
     White vehicle with damage on right shoulder

D   *Just north of Waterford Street;*
     7:54am. Pickup truck hit center divider and overturned.
     7:56am. Red pickup truck rolled over.

E   *Just north of Burbank Boulevard; 8:48am*
     Big rig versus vehicle on right shoulder
     9:05am. Silver Ford with front end damage

F   *Just north of Sunset Boulevard;*
     9:24am Carpool lane 2 vehicles
     9:29am. Suspicious black Toyota pickup truck hit
     several cars, still going, approaching Getty Center.
     9:30am. Suspicious vehicle has hit 3 vehicles.

G   *Just north of Getty Center Drive; 9:30am*
     3 lanes blocked

H   *Just north of Avalon Boulevard;*
     2:13pm Silver vehicle and blue vehicle on right shoulder
     Just south of Getty Center Drive
     2:23pm. Suspect vehicle originally hit reporting party
     from behind.

J   *Just north of Wilshire Boulevard; 2:28pm*
     Toyota Tacoma versus Ford F150 pickup truck

K   *Just south of Washington; 3:20pm*
     Green Nissan Maxima partially blocking slow lane on
     right shoulder

L   *Just north of Getty Center Drive; 3:38pm*
     Silver BMW 325i and a green Buick completely burned
     on right shoulder

Also unlike the weather and the stock market, traffic exists at the human, bodily scale. We built the roads, we created its rules, we drive the vehicles, and yet it remains an inaccessible mystery. As the possibilities for adding new highways—or even lanes—dwindle in many cities, most new progress is made at the level of code (both legislative and software). To put off the inevitable stall of a truly monumental traffic jam, we incrementally transfer agency to optimizing algorithms. But still, in the heart of the rational system, there is the incessant irrationality of human behavior, the imprecision of reflex, and a perpetual reappearance of chance.

Incidents Despite the success of the Los Angeles traffic management system and its contributions to the evolution of systems in other cities, states, and nations, the environment it manages is organic and ultimately impossible to fully control. When the system breaks down, an "incident" occurs: drivers lose control of their vehicles, vehicles malfunction and dump cargo; animals stray onto roadways; wind-blown fires engulf mountain passes and mudslides bury highways.

When traffic incidents occur, the system acknowledges and responds in various ways depending on the technological level of the area's infrastructure. In the case of most freeways or major intersections in the city itself, cameras are the first observers, recording the collision or obstruction and the immediate effect on the surrounding flow. In California, an extreme incident is called a "Sig Alert," defined by the California Highway Patrol as "any unplanned event that causes the closing of one lane of traffic for 30 minutes or more, as opposed to a planned event like road construction, which is planned separately." Sig Alerts are named after radio broadcaster Loyd C. "Sig" Sigmon, who died in June 2004. Sigmon developed a customized radio receiver and tape recorder that would detect a particular tone and record the bulletin, providing radio announcers with an analog database of recent traffic incidents.[10] This relieved dispatch from answering phone calls from the press. Ironically, Sigmon passed away only days before President Reagan and his Sig Alert-causing postmortem journey.

What follows is an example of a Sig Alert on the 405:

Incident on 405 South

10:56 AM / 405 South Before Getty Center Dr / Possible Fatality
10:56 AM 4 Vhs and Motorcycle Blocking #1, 2, and 3 Lanes
11:02 AM Car Pool, #1, 2 Lane is Blocked—Please Issue Sig Alert
11:02 AM Rider Hit Possible By a Taxi That is Still On Scene
11:03 AM Transportation Management Center Copies Message/
Item Delivered Media and Chiefs
11:08 AM Per 64 Says the #1, 2 Lanes Blocked on the North Lanes
of the 405--Please Update the Sig Alert
11:12 AM Per S3 the Body is Blocking the North Lanes of the 405
Freeway[11]

---

[10] Roy Rivenberg, "Loyd C. Sigmon 1909-2004; Radio Broadcaster Put the 'Sig' in Traffic Alerts," *The Los Angeles Times*, June 4, 2004, A1.

[11] E-mail message from: Msg@Sig Alert.com, "Possible Fatality—405 South Before Getty Center Dr," April 06 2004 16:26:29 PDT.

On neighborhood streets or on remote stretches of highway outside of the reach of the system's network, visual reporting by a passerby with a cell phone is the only immediate link.

Incident: 0298

Type: Traffic Collision—No Details Location: EB I40 JWO ESSEX RD Map Page: Info as of: 7/31/2004 8:07:33 AM

ADDITIONAL DETAILS: 8:03 AM -1039 ACTIVE TOW / 8:02 AM -ROLL 1185—2 FLTS ON LFT SIDE OF TOYT / 7:17AM -PER RP THEY RAN TO CBX THEY ARE AT MM 872 / 7:08 AM -SIL NISS 4D SPUN OUT TO R/S INTO DESERT —

Engineers at control centers take note of the calls, examine camera feeds and speed graphs, and notify the appropriate dispatch offices of the police, highway patrol, fire, public works, or the animal response team as necessary. In extreme incidents, they might call on the bureau of Alcohol, Tobacco, and Firearms or the National Guard. Incidents involving spills and animals call for less drastic action, but are still a constant problem and become an element in the feedback loop.

Incident: 0218

Type: Traffic Hazard Location: SR145 AT COTTONWOOD CIR Map Page: 7 8H Info as of: 7/31/2004 8:11:49 AM

ADDITIONAL DETAILS: 8:03 AM—NEED SAND FOR 200 YARDS OF SPILL / 8:03 AM—NOTIFY CALTRANS, GRAPES AND GRAPE JUICE, IN BOTH LANES / 7:40 AM—1039 TO 10, AT DOC / 7:37AM—GREEN TOMATOS, OR GRAPES, SPILLED ACROSS THE ROAD

8:05AM Incident: 0350

Type: Traffic Hazard—Animal Location: 3604 N FERNDALE AV Zoom Map: 547 7B Info as of: 7/31/2004 8:13:20 AM

ADDITIONAL DETAILS: 8:05 AM—KIDS ARE IN THE ROAD TO LOOK AT THE CAT / 8:05 AM—1144 CAT IN THE ROAD—

Most incidents are accidents, meaning that they are unplanned events occurring without the design of the parties involved. Other incidents are intentional, planned events that still interfere with traffic flow, much to drivers' dismay. Hollywood production companies close entire blocks in downtown Los Angeles, affecting not only immediate parking and routing, but also entire flow patterns if crucial one-way streets are blocked. Detours can send drivers into unknown and unwelcome areas. Construction crews and LAPD officers interact with confused conventioneers, who are pitted against jaywalking pedestrians in Skid Row between the business district and Little Tokyo; commuters exiting the freeway to avoid a fuel spill are routed to avoid rigging trucks and make-up trailers through throngs of Lakers' fans in front of the Staples Center, causing further confusion and compounding delays.

During the course of incident response, field units and control continue working until the blockage is removed, the disruption relieved, and steady flow reinstated. Dispatch, or control, relays information via data, text, voice, and instant messaging to units in the field. The same infrastructure used to monitor traffic patterns is put into use here, but with the involvement of humans. People still talk to each other to report incidents and route response crews, but increasingly data is streamed, automatically routed, and detected by units in the field, computers autonomously interacting before relaying information to their masters.

Lines of Flight As bodies in vehicles are captured by cameras, averaged into speed data, and described in the machine-prose of incident reports, the informational essence of the body is amplified. Data streams to and from the central computer. The motorist's foot presses and releases to the rhythm of red lights. One gets the feeling that the optimizing algorithm connects everything—that a car going a little too slow at Point A will produce a shorter green light, on the other side of the city, at Point B.

Still, commuters find openings in the traffic system. Engineers at ATSAC—experts in the ebb and flow of traffic—move to outlying cities and customize their work schedule around unusual commute times, others have stopped driving and rely on under-funded public transportation systems, while still others drive motorcycles between lanes in a refusal to participate. But the population of the Los Angeles area grows, the openings become fewer, and motorists can only dream of escape in 350 horsepower sports cars that rarely exceed 35 miles per hour. For frustrated Angelenos, only the Mojave Desert to the north and east can provide a blank canvas for traffic-weary drivers. If they can navigate the steep, jammed, and narrow passes out of the city, maybe, they hope, they can attain escape velocity under skies once plied by the X-15 and SpaceShipOne. Like sub-atomic particles hurtling away from a densely packed nucleus, energy scatters as each vehicle spins from the city in limitless directions into this void. Where there is no grid, the dream continues, there should be no gridlock.

Kazys Varnelis

INVISIBLE CITY
TELECOMMUNICATION

The patch of asphalt at the east end of Wilshire Boulevard, where it dead-ends into Grand Street, is covered in what appears, at first glance, to be random graffiti. A closer look, however, reveals it to be a secret code. Known as "Underground Service Alerts" to technicians, engineers, excavators, drillers, trenchers, and pavement saw operators, these colored arrows, abbreviations, and marks delineate the presence of utilities hidden under the pavement. A party intending to dig issues an Underground Service Alert or "USA," marking its proposed route on the pavement in white and sending a notice to a "call before you dig" or utility location service. In turn, the agency notifies any utilities that might have buried lines in the area, the utilities check their records, and, if necessary, send out workmen to delineate the extent of their stakes using special spray cans of fluorescent paint that can operate upside-down.

Utility location services are key to the smooth operation of the city, ensuring that unwitting backhoe operators don't break through gas mains and launch themselves into the stratosphere or that hapless landscapers don't sever fiber optic cables connecting Los Angeles and Tokyo. The American Public Works Association has standardized the hidden code of the streets: red denotes electric power; orange signifies communication; yellow refers to natural gas, oil, steam, petroleum, or other gaseous or flammable matter; green marks sewers and drains; blue represents drinking water; violet identifies reclaimed water or irrigation lines; pink indicates unknown or unidentified facilities and is used for temporary survey markings; and white outlines the proposed excavation.

PROPRIETARY
DATA
NO INFORMATION AVAILABLE

Fiber optic networks,
Los Angeles

Source: author

Since the nineteenth century, boosters have claimed title to the busiest corners on earth for their cities: State and Madison in Chicago (perhaps in the nineteenth century but very unlikely today), the intersection outside of Shibuya station in Tokyo (if nothing else, the busiest corner for pedestrians texting each other while in motion), and Wilshire and Westwood in West Los Angeles (for vehicular traffic) to name a few. If, however, that title could be awarded on the basis of underground communications or the density of florescent paint markings, then this patch of pavement at the intersection of Grand Street and Wilshire Boulevard would win. The markings on the world's most spray-painted asphalt are predominantly orange, referring to the wealth of fiber optic lines running in and out of One Wilshire.

Subsurface infrastructure map, Grand Street and Wilshire Boulevard

Located off-axis at the end of Wilshire Boulevard, this nondescript thirty-nine-story skyscraper functions as the prime communications hub between Asia and the Western world (there is no good overland telecommunications route between Europe and Asia yet) and hosts installations for over 260 telecom-related companies. Here pavement is ripped up with such regularity that the rules of USAs are modified; instead of adding paint when a service alert is issued, companies preemptively mark asphalt as soon as an excavation is patched over.

Subsurface diagrams of the area, filed with the Los Angeles City Building Department, reveal the tangle below. This frenzy of spray-paint and the subterranean labyrinth of fiber under the streets are a key part of Los Angeles's role in the global economy. After what seemed like an inexorable decline after the city's loss of its aerospace industry following the end of the Cold War, it reemerged at the end of the 1990s as a key gateway in Pacific Rim trade and finance. To facilitate cross-border trade and financial transactions and to support its other critical role in the global economy—serving as the world's center of media production—the city has a highly developed fiber optic telecommunications network, both a large Metropolitan Area Network to serve intracity communications (in particular, the high-bandwidth needs of Hollywood) as well as long-distance and submarine connections to the United States and the rest of the world. All this comes together here, in the city's telecom district, centered around One Wilshire.

Beyond the Bonaventure The convergence of an unmappable hyperspace at a single structure in downtown Los Angeles echoes the seminal observations Fredric Jameson made about the Bonaventure Hotel, the city, and the state of society in postmodern culture in his essay "Postmodernism, or the Logic of Late Capitalism," first published in 1983.[1] Here, Jameson focuses on a single structure, John Portman's 1977 Bonaventure Hotel, a building constructed as part of that era's attempt to revitalize Los Angeles's decaying downtown. Jameson describes the city through negation, as a reflection in the mirrored curtain wall of the hotel's towers. Los Angeles, in his view, becomes nothing more than the end-product of multinational capital, void of any political capacity, Utopian aspiration, or reality, glimpsed only as a distorted glimmer on the surface of one-way mirror glass.

Unlike Mies van der Rohe's Friedrichstrasse skyscraper or Le Corbusier's Unité d'Habitation, which shatter the existing city with their modernist promises of a new order, Portman's Bonaventure lacks aspirations to a better world, reflecting the city, as given, back upon itself. Jameson writes, "The Bonaventure ... is content to 'let the fallen city fabric continue to be in its being' (to parody Heidegger); no further effects, no larger protopolitical Utopian transformation, is either expected or desired."[2]

[1] Fredric Jameson, "Postmodernism, or the Cultural Logic of Late Capitalism," *New Left Review* 146 (July/August 1984): 53-92.

[2] Jameson, "Postmodernism, or the Cultural Logic of Late Capitalism," 81.

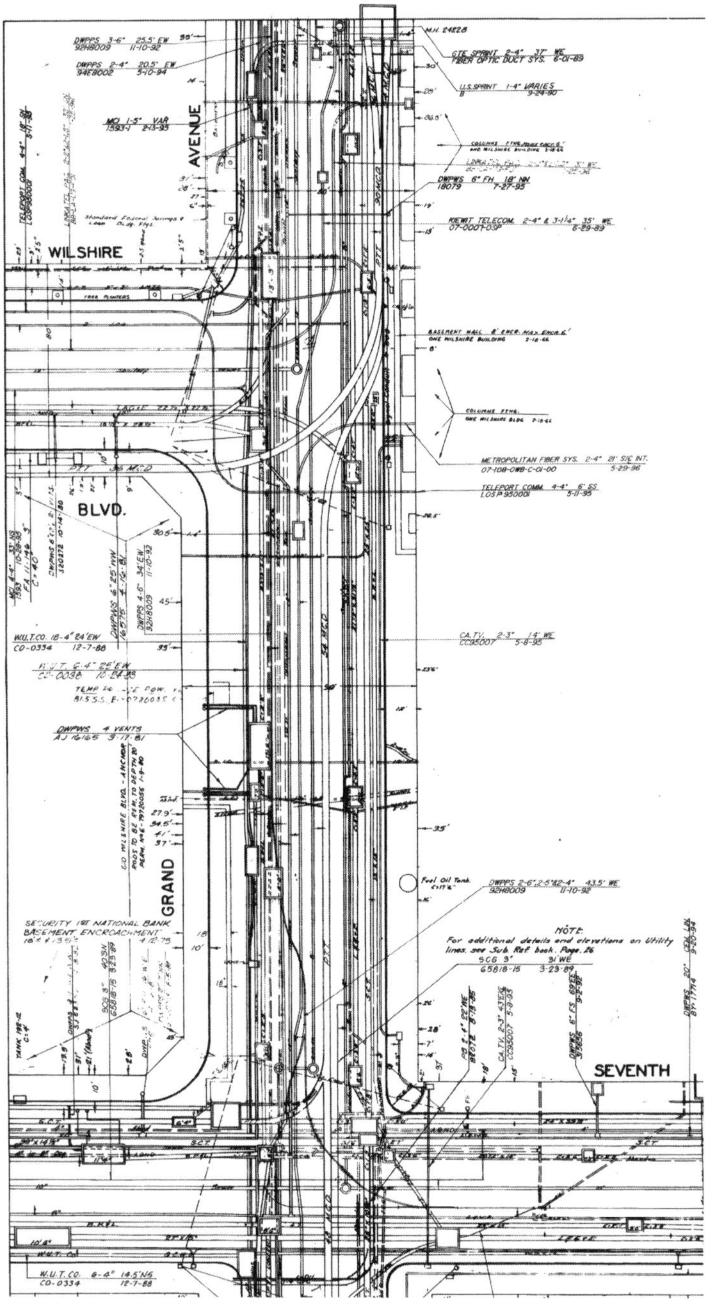
ADJOINING MAP NO. 1-96-15
WILSHIRE
AVENUE
BLVD.
GRAND
SEVENTH
DWPPS 3-6" 25.5' EW 92H8009 11-10-92
DWPPS 2-4" 20.5' EW 94E8002 3-10-94
MCI 1-5" VAR 1593-1 2-15-93
M.H. 24228
GTE SPRINT 2-4" 37' WE FIBER OPTIC DUCT SYS. 6-01-89
U.S. SPRINT 1-4" VARIES B 9-24-90
DWPWS 6" FH 18' NN 18079 7-27-95
KIEWIT TELECOM. 2-4" & 3-1/4" 35' WE 07-0001-0SP 6-29-89
METROPOLITAN FIBER SYS. 2-4" 21' S/C INT. 07-108-OWB-C-01-00 5-29-96
TELEPORT COMM. 4-4" 6' SS LOSP 950001 5-11-95
CA.TV. 2-3" 14' WE CC95007 5-8-95
W.U.T.CO. 18-4" 24' EW CO-0334 12-7-88
DWPWS 4 VENTS AJ 16165 9-17-81
DWPPS 2-6", 2-5" & 2-4" 43.5' WE 92H8009 11-10-92
SECURITY 1ST NATIONAL BANK BASEMENT ENCROACHMENT
NOTE:
For additional details and elevations on Utility lines, see Sub. Ref. book, Page. 26
SCG 3" 31' WE 65818-15 3-23-89
W.U.T.CO. 6-4" 14.5' NS CO-0334 12-7-88
Fuel Oil Tank

Disjunct from its surroundings, its street-level pedestrian entrance invisible, the Bonaventure Hotel hooks up to the networks of multinational capital through ramps to neighboring skyscrapers and via adjacent boulevards and freeways. A world onto itself, the hotel is inwardly focused, allowing visitors to avoid ever going into the city outside it.

John Portman, Bonaventure Hotel, mall interior

Giving no sense of the city beyond its walls, the hotel's notoriously confusing layout defies the visitor's capacity to map it. Instead, the Bonaventure, Jameson writes, "stands as something like an imperative to grow new organs, to expand our sensorium and our body to some new, as yet unimaginable, perhaps ultimately impossible dimensions." But this is not a question of bad planning; perversely, the floor plan of the hotel is deceptively clear, a late modern take on Beaux-Arts bilateral symmetry. Instead, for Jameson the hotel's complexity is an analogue for our inability to understand our position in the multinational, decentered network of finance and communications that comprises late capitalism.[3]

The Bonaventure, in Jameson's reading, represents culture under late capitalism. In this phase of economic development, capital has colonized all spheres of human activity including those, such as culture, that had remained autonomous from—and resistant to—its hegemonizing forces.[4] Unable to find a place outside the capitalist system, the postmodern subject loses any possibility of fulfilling the Enlightenment ambition of drawing a map that could claim to mirror reality. Master narratives such as *Marx's Capital* or the plans kept by Haussmann for his incisions into the body of Paris are impossible today.

In response, Jameson proposes "an aesthetic of cognitive mapping," a term he borrows from urban theorist Kevin Lynch "to endow the individual subject with some new heightened sense of its place in the global system." Rather than calling for complete understanding, cognitive mapping is incomplete, beginning from a position of inadequacy and acknowledging any map's built-in futility. Thus, we might understand postmodern Los Angeles through filmic allegories such as the incestuous, all-pervasive networks of Roman Polanski's *Chinatown*, the doomed journey of D-Fens in *Falling Down*, or the allegorical total vision of the city in Ridley Scott's *Blade Runner*.[5] Jameson's reading of the Bonaventure itself acts as a cognitive map suggesting that through this one structure the entire state of the city outside and indeed, of contemporary society, can be discerned. To this end, Jameson leads the reader in circles around the concept of the postmodern, replicating for us the experience of meandering through the Bonaventure's internal hyperspace or trying to navigate the global flows of capital.

Frank Gehry, Disney Concert Hall

But the Bonaventure is over twenty-five years old now, and during the late 1990s the damaged body of Los Angeles proved capable of a remarkable turnaround. The City of Quartz has been replaced by a downtown that more or less works. The city core, in which the Bonaventure was just one of countless failed attempts to resurrect the neighborhood, has finally recovered, at least in part.

Frank Gehry's Disney Concert Hall, a block away from the Bonaventure would seem its likely successor. A manifestation of the "Bilbao-Effect," the concert hall is a product of the further penetration of culture by capital, embodying the contemporary city's role as a site of culture through visual display. The structure's unprecedented formal gestures embody the placeless, hyperkinetic international flows of late capital, affirming that the joyous equation of culture, high technology, and capital produces an irresistible destination point.

---

[3] Jameson, "Postmodernism, or the Cultural Logic of Late Capitalism," 80-83.

[4] See Ernest Mandel, *Late Capitalism* (London: NLB Atlantic Highlands Humanities Press, 1975).

[5] Jameson, "Postmodernism, or the Cultural Logic of Late Capitalism," 89-92.

But in its relentless need to appear, the Concert Hall is a red herring. The visible is no longer a prime determinant of the urban. Instead, our networked society is increasingly dominated by what Lewis Mumford called the "invisible city," the unseen world of cables, wires, connections, codes, agreements, and capital.[6] Today more than ever, the role of this invisible city in determining the structure of urban areas is vast. Visible form is merely an irruption of other forces, a graphic user interface for a more powerful command line below.[7]

Invisible City Instead of Disney Concert Hall, it is One Wilshire, together with the patch of marked-up pavement in front of it, that is the more appropriate successor to the Bonaventure. A banal skyscraper completed by Skidmore, Owings and Merrill in 1966, this structure is not just devoid of the qualities that make the Disney Concert Hall, it is its inverse—retrofitted rather than new, anonymous rather than distinctive. Yet, it supplants the Bonaventure by being not just an index but a key switching point in the networked economy.

One Wilshire is a byproduct of the officially sanctioned monopoly on telecommunications in the United States once held by AT&T. In the nineteenth century, telephone service was a local product. A central office, inevitably located in the downtown business district, would handle interconnections between calls. When long-distance was introduced, it terminated there. In Los Angeles, the central office is the "Madison Complex," one of the largest such facilities in the country, located at 400 South Grand, roughly between the Bonaventure and One Wilshire. Long-distance calls would connect here to be distributed to local exchanges, at first with coaxial cable and later via microwaves beamed from nearby hills to the microwave tower, designed by Parkinson Field Associates and completed in 1961, an addition that made the Madison Complex the tallest building in the city for many years.[8]

With deregulation in the 1980s, competing carriers were allowed to make connections to this crucial local interface. Pacific Telesis (acquired in 1998 by SBC and now renamed AT&T), the regional telephone company spun off from AT&T to handle local calls in California and Nevada, refused to let carriers mount antennas on top of the Madison Complex, allowing them to install only the minimum equipment required by law. This was strategic: the company knew that one day it would be allowed to compete in the long-distance market in exchange for letting other carriers use its wiring from the central office to the handset.

To circumvent this restriction, MCI mounted microwave antennas on One Wilshire, one of the tallest buildings downtown, just down the street from the Madison Complex. Seeing a competitor-friendly environment close to the central switching station, long-distance carriers, Internet service providers, and other networking companies began to lay fiber to One Wilshire. As fiber technology has improved, the microwave towers on top have dwindled in importance—Verizon now uses them to connect to its cell phone network. With more and more companies based in One Wilshire, the building managers set up a "Meet-Me Room" on the fourth floor. In that space, carriers could interconnect without a fee by running a cable between their equipment. Now if a Guatemalan phone card company needs to connect to Sprint, they can simply run a fiber optic interconnect between their routers. Likewise, data networks use the Meet-Me Room to make peer-to-peer interconnections without costly fees. One Wilshire's function as a major hub in the global network makes it the most expensive real estate in the country: in 2003, it rented out at $250 per square foot per month.

[6] Lewis Mumford, *The City in History* (New York: Harcourt Brace, 1961), 563-567.

[7] For more on the regime of the invisible, see my article "Breve Historia de la Horizontalidad: 1968/9-2001/2," *Pasajes de Arquitectura y Crítica* (Marzo 2003), 38-41.

[8] Los Angeles Madison Complex, thecentraloffice.com, http://www.thecentraloffice.com/Calif/LA/Madison/LAMadison.htm.

If the Bonaventure remained disjunct from its surroundings, barring the ramps connecting it to the nearby skyscrapers, One Wilshire has reshaped its surroundings. As corporations eager to take advantage of high data bandwidth move into or near the tower, over a dozen nearby buildings have been converted to house telecom installations, reviving the real estate market in southwest downtown. This centralization of information defies earlier predictions that the Internet and new technologies will undo cities. Instead, the reliance of contemporary communications on fiber creates a new concentration at command points in the organization of the world economy.[9]

If the Concert Hall represents late capitalism's obsession with the visual, One Wilshire represents the rise of invisible networks and unmappable forces in our lives. The invisible city that grows from telecommunications is, by and large, a privatized infrastructure, its possession by private forces making it impossible to map. Although the postmodern hyperspace of the Bonaventure is unmappable by the body, a legible floor plan can still be found. No such plan exists for networked capital. Diagrams of the Internet and of fiber optic lines are hard to find: the data is proprietary, a matter too important for corporations to allow free access. Moreover, the complexity emerging along with the massive proliferation of connections increasingly makes it hard for even corporations owning the networks to understand their dimensions. A floor plan of One Wilshire tells you little about what happens there. Even for the corporate hive mind, the map is exceeded by a hypercomplex reality. The space

Conduit for carrying fiber optic cable is ready to be deployed on Highland Avenue.

[9] Manuel Castells, *The Rise of the Network Society*, 2nd ed. (Malden, MA: Blackwell Publishing, 2000), 409.

of global technological flows does not desire to become visual or apparent: perhaps only some spray-paint or a flag in the ground marks the presence of fiber below, and sometimes even that is elusive.

Late capitalism has entered a new phase—data and capital are now inextricably intertwined, creating a new spatial regime. The shimmering, ghostly computer-generated shapes of recent architecture only detract us from the invisible city, the less visible, but more real, work of programming and organizational processes. One Wilshire's form doesn't matter: what matters is how it's been re-programmed. Ultimately this can be said of the Guggenheim-Bilbao or the Disney Concert Hall as well: it is not the architecture that is crucial here but rather the union of governmental, institutional, and capitalist forces producing it.

What was allegorical in the Bonaventure has become real at One Wilshire. In our own era, the task of cognitive mapping lies at the point in which media and cities, network and economy, substructure and superstructure become inextricable. The real operating system, not the graphic user interface are our concern. Only by engaging the code below can we remain relevant to future cities.[10]

---

[10] For more on One Wilshire, see "Ether" by Robert Sumrell and Kazys Varnelis [AUDC] *Blue Monday. Stories of Absurd Realities and Natural Philosophies* (Barcelona: ACTAR, 2007), 48-89.

Warren Techentin

TREE HUGGERS
LANDSCAPE

Ask anyone—native Angeleno, recent transplant, or casual visitor—for their image of Los Angeles and you will hear the usual list: surf, sand, and palm tree-lined boulevards marked by the rise and fall of celebrities, shaped and clogged by the automobile, wreaked by repeated racial strife, menaced by impending natural disaster. Through more than a century of exposure through literature, cinema, and media these images insinuated themselves in the imagination. Of all of these clichés, however, the palm tree is the most easily distilled into a single frame, deployable whenever necessary to establish that the action takes place in Los Angeles. And if the city lacks an architectural skyline—not a single downtown skyscraper has managed to burn itself into the collective unconscious—its rows of palm trees substitute.

Virtually every aspect of life in Los Angeles is modulated with plants: its streets and parks, front yards, parking lots, fast-food drive-thru islands, even indoor corridors of malls and stacked office landscapes. Instead of acting as a civilizing measure, however, Los Angeles's plants suggest wildness; just as Paris is known for its arborescent *grands boulevards* lined with columns of identical trees, regimented like the Napoleonic army, Los Angeles is known for its formless, polyglot landscaping. So long as it can somehow acquire access to water, it seems, any plant can thrive in the California sun. Deliberately planted or accidentally imported, around a thousand different species of trees can be found in the area, making it perhaps the most bio-diverse region on the planet. This essay will analyze landscape as a foundational infrastructure in Los Angeles.

Los Angeles National Forest

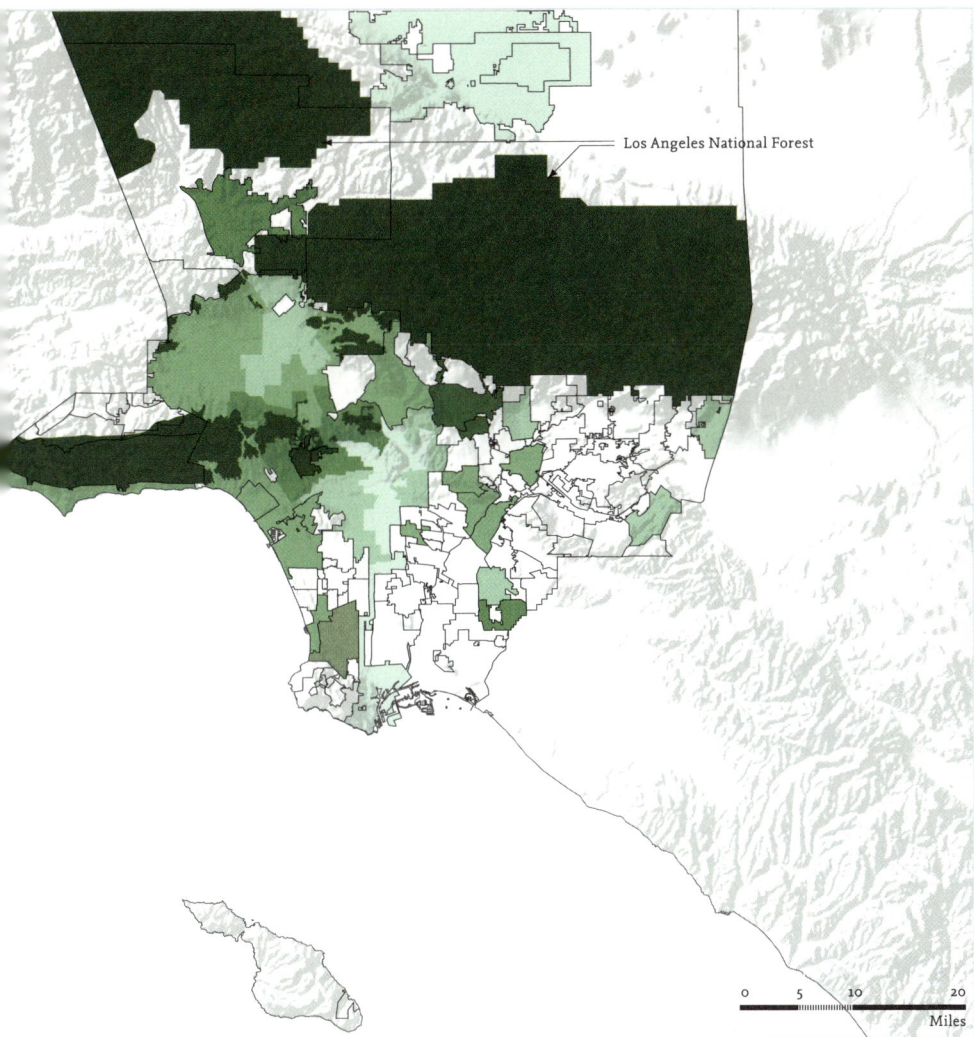

Percentage of canopy
cover in Los Angeles
County, by city

Source: author

Los Angeles County Cities   —

Tree Canopy Cover

< 10%
10 - 15%
15 - 25%
25 - 35%
35 - 45%
> 45%
No Data

Ed Ruscha, A Few
Palm Trees, 1971

According to the Bureau of Street Services, 10 million trees over 465 square miles
comprise Los Angeles's urban forest. And yet, when compared to other cities, Los Angeles
isn't particularly "well-treed." More well-paved than well-treed, it boasts a city canopy
(a measure of what percentage of the city has tree coverage) of only 18% compared to the
national average of 27%.[1] Not surprisingly, greater effort has been expended on the roads:
reputedly over two-thirds of the city's surface is paved.[2]

Starting in 2006, Los Angeles began augmenting its organic infrastructure by planting
one million trees.[3] The palm is not on the list of new trees the city will plant. Officially the
city is omitting the palm "because of its lack of shade."[4] But there are other factors as well.
Demand for palms from desert cities—most notably Las Vegas—has driven up the cost of
new specimens, doubling the price over the last decade. Nor does the higher cost end with
planting: palms are nearly twice as expensive as other trees to maintain, and the cumulative
mass of the fallen fronds and their impact on storm drains and landfills is substantial.

[1] Laura Mecoy, "L. A. sets goal to plant 1 million saplings: Race is on, and Sacramento may lose standing
     among world's great tree cities," *Sacramento Bee*, September 5, 2006. According to Mecoy's article the top 10
     tree cities defined by the number of trees per capita) are as follows: 1. Moorestown, NJ, 2. Morgantown, WV,
     3. Atlanta, GA 4. Calgary, Alberta, 5. Woodbridge, NJ, 6. Syracuse, NY 7. Freehold, NJ 8. Sacramento,
     CA 9. Baltimore, MD 10. Oakland, CA.

[2] Tree people. excerpts from Harry Wiland and Dale Bell, *Edens Lost and Found. How Ordinary Citizens are
     Restoring Our Great American Cities* (White River Junction, VT: Chelsea Green, 2006), Tree People Web Site,
     http://www.edenslostandfound.org/home/preview.php?id=32.

[3] Million Trees Los Angeles, "Frequently Asked Questions," Million Trees Los Angeles, Los Angeles http://
     www.milliontreesla.org/mtabout8.htm. "We will be encouraging the planting of California friendly trees;
     that is, trees that are adapted to our semi-arid climate and will not use too much water. There have been a
     lot of questions about Palm Trees. We have no intention of eliminating or replacing Palm Trees. If people
     choose to plant them, they will count as part of the Million Trees LA program. Palm Trees have cultural and
     historic value in this city, and they add to its aesthetic and visual texture. We are not targeting replacement
     of any trees; rather, we want to plant new trees where there are none currently. We want to bring shade
     to areas that don't have any. While there is no current plan to put Palm Trees in those targeted areas, our
     program is not planning to replace or eliminate them where they are now. Further, we will work with the
     communities of Los Angeles to determine what trees they would like in their neighborhoods."

[4] For more information about approved street trees, see the Web site of the Los Angeles Department of Water
     and Power (LADWP), "Tree Planting Frequently Asked Questions," Los Angeles Department of Water and
     Power, http://www.ladwp.com/ladwp/cms/ladwp000747.jsp. The LADWP will provide free trees from a
     selected list to all customers who take a short, on-line course to help reduce cumulative energy consump-
     tion through the shading of their homes.

Considering that the average lifespan of a palm tree is seventy to a hundred years and that most of the palms visible now were planted to beautify the city for the 1932 Olympics, the bulk of Los Angeles's palm trees will disappear within a decade or two. But regardless of its link to the city's popular image, the palm has never been the city's official tree. Instead, that honor goes to the flower-bearing Coral Tree (*Erythrina caffra*), another non-native species requiring large amounts of water to maintain. In a city that, Norman Klein reminds us, has always depended on the creative destruction of forgetting, the palm tree's impending doom has generated widespread debate and anguish.[5] Perhaps in anticipation of the need to commemorate the loss of the palm as city icon, Robert Irwin, the artist in charge of designing the new gardens at the Los Angeles County Museum of Art is proposing a palm oasis, an idealized fragment of landscape that would serve as a memorial for the palm, fittingly located nearby the fossils of the La Brea Tar Pits.

At LACMA, Irwin pays homage to the crucial role that palm trees play in the city and its cultural landscape, but he is not the first artist to do so. In the 1960s and 1970s, Los Angeles artist Ed Ruscha produced a series of small books cataloging various elements of Los Angeles. Along with his other books on key forms of Los Angeles infrastructure such as gas stations, swimming pools, and parking lots, *A Few Palm Trees* reveals that palms are not merely a decorative accident of urbanism, but rather a constituent element in the urban landscape. The book reads as both a catalog and a collection of family portraits. Selecting a tree (or small clump of trees) as the subject of each page, Ruscha exposes their twofold existence in the city. On the one hand, each photo serves as a guide to identifying and potentially selecting a palm for use in the city, as if from a catalog. On the other hand, each photograph personalizes each tree, showing the reader the unique features of each as if they were old friends from the neighborhood. Together, Ruscha's books point to the repetitive nature of the city and the banality of the objects of which it is composed. *A Few Palm Trees* builds an image of the city out of a series of barely noticed, minor elements, an index of Los Angeles's dispersed and decentralized urbanism.

---

[5] Norman Klein, *History of Forgetting* (New York: Verso, 1997).

Landscape as agriculture As a symbol, the palm tree suggests that Los Angeles—once a desert—is now an oasis. In truth, this isn't far off the mark. Historically, the landscape of the Los Angeles basin—with the exception of a few riparian episodes—was largely featureless, a semi-arid mix of swamp and scrub virtually devoid of trees.

Carl Jung suggested that all things spring from the archetypical World Tree. Los Angeles is no exception. The Gabrielino Indians formed their central village, Yangna, near what is present-day downtown Los Angeles by the "Council Tree" (a giant sycamore or Aliso tree) around which elders would meet to discuss tribal affairs. The Spanish settlement took roots near this tree as well—ignoring the Laws of the Indies' demand that new towns be settled away from indigenous settlements. Historians suggest that the missionaries chose the area because the sycamore was one of the few trees of any significance in the vicinity that provided substantial outdoor shade from which to retreat from the heat. From the start, then, trees and the very real need for urban shade and shadow have been part of the city.

Nearly a hundred years later, the Aliso tree would fall to make way for the vineyards of Jean Louis Vignes, generally considered the man who brought grape vines and serious wine-making to California. In conjunction with many others, Vignes contributed to the wholesale planting over of the region with agricultural trees and other crops. The most prominent of these was the orange tree. Thousands of acres of orange and other citrus trees were planted, contributing not only to the early wealth of the region but also to the exotic, bountiful image of the fledgling city. Soon, the refrigerated railcar would allow the city's produce to reach across the entire country within a week.[6] But like Eve's apple, the orange was a fruit that set in motion an unstoppable process, a fall from grace. The need to water the economic base of the orange groves required radical interventions to bring water to the Los Angeles basin. In turn, the tax revenue agriculture brought in helped fund those projects. With the construction of the Owens Valley aqueduct, the area would be utterly transformed, satisfying the needs of agriculture, but also allowing for an ever-increasing population that eventually supplanted the agricultural order, bringing with it a diverse, immigrant, ornamental plant life. Thus, in contrast to a medieval village that carved out civilization from the wild nature of the forest, the urban forest of Los Angeles was entirely planted—a confluence of the desire to transform an empty landscape and to take advantage of the city's imported water. It is also during this period that Los Angeles realized the painful fact of its existence: the city would forever be destined to live beyond its means, irrigated by water from far away lands.

Landscape as image Planted for its looks, not for its produce, the palm tree replaced the orange tree in the city's landscape and its collective image. During this period, the ranchos created by the original Spanish land grants gave way to agricultural plots which, in turn, gave way to subdivisions. Large tracts of houses were laid out in grids not unlike the orchards of trees that they obliterated. Developed autonomously, incrementally, and with little master planning, these tracts generated the multiplicity of grids that now blanket the region's terrain.

In today's Los Angeles, both the original landscape and its agricultural successor have been virtually supplanted by alien, ornamental trees. In fact, nearly all the trees that we now identify with the area were imported. Of the twenty-three palms commonly found in the city today, only the California Fan Palm (*Washingtonia filifera*) is native. Palms from the world over were imported to emulate the exotic environments of Mediterranean cities, thematizing the city with historic allusions and supporting the city's original role as a resort town desti-

---

[6] Kevin Starr, *California* (New York: The Modern Library, 2005), 151.

nation for over-heated, asthmatic Midwesterners. Palms evoked the space of salvation associated with an oasis: a thirst-quenching landscape, discovered after a long and harrowing journey and blessed with opulent palaces tucked in amongst lush, exuberant foliage. Trees in Los Angeles were used as props of seduction, fueling an image of the city as an exotic place. During the era of Valentino's Sheik, allusions to European traditions in Orientalism supported by a motif of neo-Egyptian civic architecture were enlisted in the palm-tree-fueled dreamscapes of travel brochures promoting the city as a mysterious but welcoming, sensual land. Films set on the streets of the city, such as Mack Sennett's *Keystone Cops* comedies made evident the temperate, verdant luxuriousness of the Los Angeles landscape and served as vivid propaganda for the city.[7] Events such as the annual Tournament of Roses Parade in Pasadena demonstrated the perpetual spring of Southern California at a time of year when the rest of the country was under snow. The palm, however, was not the only protagonist: many other alien species, particularly those from regions with sympathetic climates, invaded the southland and took root.[8] According to Sunset Magazine's *Western Garden Book* the most widely planted non-native tree was the eucalyptus tree, promoted by Abbott Kinney, the developer of Venice Beach. Seeking to beautify the state while simultaneously providing windbreaks, firewood, and shade, he led the "Eucalyptus Crusade" in which thousands of acres of the trees were cultured from Australia and obsessively planted throughout the state.[9]

Kinney understood that trees provided a foil against the relentless sameness of the Los Angeles grid. Lacking other "natural" features, developers actively deployed—and continue to deploy—trees to give presence, history, and a sense of luxury. The repetitive, geometric layout of palms along the newly formed streets helped give value to the platting and parceling of otherwise abstract, featureless land. Many streets today still memorialize the efforts of early developers who planted palm trees to attract potential buyers. Visible from a distance, the palm-lined streets symbolized the arrival of a new, upscale neighborhood, allowing visual navigation to the latest home sites. Many communities planted-over their streets with monocultures: Elm Street, Oak Street, Magnolia Avenue, Palm Street announce clearly what grows on them.

After people moved in, so did businesses, and trees and plants were again used to raise the value of commercial properties. The front doors of many businesses in Los Angeles are accessed through parking lots so the effective use of landscaping to provide relief from the acres of asphalt is important for business.[10] In a city built around cars, new forms of landscaping comprised of edging, hedging, containment, concealment, signage, embankment, topiary, and décor emerged simultaneously with the developing car culture. When the pedestrian space of the sidewalk disappeared amidst the spaces of strip malls and parking lots emerged between the street and the building, landscape again helped to soften the deleterious effects of the quickly erected, often bland commercial architecture. Particularly at fast food restaurants, new concepts of landscape were deployed exuberantly, often monstrously,

---

[7] Starr, *California*, 275.

[8] E. Gregory McPherson, George Gonzalez, Greg Monfette, Ron Lorenzen, "Expanding Street Tree Canopy Cover and Repairing Sidewalks in the City of Los Angeles" *Western Arborist* (Fall 2003): 22. According to the article, "The most abundant species are Crape myrtle (*Lagerstroemia indica*, 8%), Mexican Fan Palm (*Washingtonia robusta*, 7%), American Sweetgum (*Liquidambar styraciflua*, 7%), Southern Magnolia (*Magnolia grandiflora*, 6%), Indian laurel fig (*Ficus microcarpa* 'Nitida,' 5%), camphor (*Cinnamomum camphora*, 3%), and London plane (*Platanus acerifolia*, 3%)."

[9] Kathleen Norris Brenzel, ed., *Sunset Western Garden Book* (Menlo Park, CA: Sunset Publishing Corporation, 2001), 337.

[10] Million Trees Los Angeles, "Frequently Asked Questions." Studies show that commercial landscaping can increase sales as much as 12%.

to enhance the meal. Images of the pastoral suburban landscape of the Garden City, the exotic landscape of Eden, and the topiary gardens of France and Japan were marshaled to screen the growing proliferation of urban artifacts: trash cans, electrical transformers, water meters, building edges, air conditioning condensers, and the sidewalk or roadway itself. All of these objects disappear through carefully selected plantings, thus allowing patrons to enjoy an authentic indoor-outdoor eating experience a few feet away from their automobiles. At any drive-through of a fast food restaurant, a country road is evoked as drivers circle their way between the speaker and pick-up window amidst plants that beautify the wait for food with a pleasing, planted environment that has grown over the stains, graffiti, garbage, insects, and dust of the city.

Palm trees line a street in Beverly Hills

Landscape as machine While the city may be in the process of abandoning the palm as its foremost icon, trees continue to be enlisted as supplements to urban life. Trees have been intricately intertwined with humanity for centuries as providers of shade, fruit, building materials, and firewood. But the relationship of humans and trees has hardly been equal: we have unceremoniously cut down our arboreal brethren to fuel a vast urban expansion. Recently, however, this relationship has become more symbiotic as we have come to an understanding of the importance of trees in the urban ecosystem. Taken in conjunction with plant life everywhere, trees collectively function like a giant machine—an enormous oxygen-producing and pollutant-filtering infrastructure for the city. Urban forests generate oxygen, absorb airborne and ground toxins, beautify, shade, create privacy, reduce water run-off into storm systems, stabilize soil to prevent erosion, mitigate reflected heat off roads and sidewalks, produce "curb appeal" thereby increasing real estate values, provide wind control, animal habitat, and a source of food and flowers.[11] A single mature tree can absorb carbon dioxide at a rate of 48 pounds/year and release enough oxygen back into the atmosphere to support two human beings.[12] In one year an acre of trees can absorb as much carbon as is produced by a car driven 8,700 miles, roughly the same number of miles that an average driver in California drives every year (according to this rough measure, 8,125 square miles, or an area twice the size of Los Angeles county—most of which is desert or mountains—would have to be forested to make up for the amount of carbon produced by the county's 5.2 million motor vehicles).

Trees play an important psychosocial role in the city. Trees are stand-ins for nature. Simultaneously evocative of the raw, dark power of forests and the generous perfection of the Garden of Eden, trees symbolize man's uncomfortable relationship to the natural world. But this is an inversion of the natural order. Wild nature, or what may be left of it, seems all but removed from collective experience. Instead our cities become dioramas, providing us with the safe experience of, and carefully pruned effects of, nature in episodic demonstrations and specimens.

Trees also mirror the life of an individual—we mimic their branch and root structures with our branching systems of knowledge. In myth, trees and forests typically serve as powerful foils. Bruno Bettelheim, in his analysis of the fairy tales of the Brothers Grimm, uses forests as a site of individual reckoning: "The forest, where [the Two Brothers] go to decide that they want to have a life of their own, symbolizes the place in which inner darkness is confronted and worked through; where uncertainty is resolved about who one is;

[11] Tree People, http://www.treepeople.org/.

[12] Mike McAliney, *Arguments for Land Conservation: Documentation and Information Sources for Land Resources Protection* (Sacramento, CA: Trust for Public Land, 1993)

and where one begins to understand who one wants to be."[13] Individuals standing erect with their arms outstretched, more like humans than like our quadruped cousins (who in turn resemble bushes), trees remind us of ourselves. It is amongst the trees, analogues to individuals, that the sense of the wisdom of the ages and human continuity is gleaned. Even in the city, a typical street tree will outlive the inhabitants that come and go around it.

These are familiar uses of urban trees. If, however, trees in the city have traditionally been appreciated because they were useless—removed from their non-urban cousins, which exist to provide us with lumber and fuel—they are increasingly becoming machines, bits of living infrastructure. The fall of the palm—that vapid, high-maintenance Hollywood starlet— is tied to this idea of trees moving from being merely ornamental to more performative organic machines—walling us in, generating the air we breath, shading our cities. The rise of the performative tree can also be seen in the emergence of synthetic, mimetic trees—cell phone towers often known as "Frankenpines." Sprouting in our urban forest, these imposters produce new hybrid mechanic-organic systems, grafting onto natural systems and performing better than the original, all the while packaged in familiar, friendly shapes. Cell phone trees suggest that technology is itself natural.

[13] Bruno Bettelheim, *The Uses of Enchantment* (New York: Random House, 1975), 93.

With the Frankenpine thriving, it is possible to speculate on an urban future in which thousands of artificial trees might be deployed throughout the city: on streets, in malls, and in our office landscapes. In the next generation of office or mall equipment, we may see new tree-machines proliferating amongst this landscape—providing wireless communication, video monitoring, air filtration, security, and space for storage, digital or otherwise. One can imagine a whole forest of imitative, performative, and embedded artificial "trees" deployed amongst real trees or, for that matter, prosthetic systems that would augment living trees, providing necessary features that we otherwise would find disagreeable to look at, some of which may provide a solution for some of today's urban ills such as the reintroduction of animal habitats, methane gas venting, hazmat and security monitoring systems, and so on.

The new importance of trees in Los Angeles can be seen in how they are increasingly codified in local and regional laws. Against its rapid decline due to population expansion, significant steps have been taken to protect the native oak tree.[14] Fines of $10,000 have been assessed for cutting down specimens with trunks larger than eight inches in diameter. The law has generated a reversal of sorts from early modern paradigms and dictums for the making of architecture: "The PLAN fits the trees, not the trees fit the plan."[15] Communities such as Pasadena and districts such as the Mulholland corridor have protected their mature native trees through legislation. Increasingly, each year sees more lawsuits filed relating to trees and property rights. In all new housing developments the city requires one tree planted for every four units built. In commercial parking lots, there is a similar code that requires one tree for every four cars, in hopes of shading the pavement as "the net cooling effect of a young, healthy tree is equivalent to ten room-size air conditioners operating 20 hours a day."[16] Because trees are, on the one hand, often entangled with the city's power lines and,

---

[14] 24. Los Angeles County Zoning Regulations. 22.56.2050 – Established Purpose: "The oak tree permit is established (a) to recognize oak trees as significant historical, aesthetic and ecological resources, and as one of the most picturesque trees in Los Angeles County, lending beauty and charm to the natural and man-made landscape, enhancing the value of property, and the character of the communities in which they exist; and (b) to create favorable conditions for the preservation and propagation of this unique, threatened plant heritage, particularly those trees which may be classified as heritage oak trees, for the benefit of current and future residents of Los Angeles County. It is the intent of the oak tree permit to maintain and enhance the general health, safety and welfare by assisting in counteracting air pollution and in minimizing soil erosion and other related environmental damage. The oak tree permit is also intended to preserve and enhance property values by conserving and adding to the distinctive and unique aesthetic character of many areas of Los Angeles County in which oak trees are indigenous. The stated objective of the oak tree permit is to preserve and maintain healthy oak trees in the development process. (Ord. 88-0157 § 1, 1988: Ord. 82-0168 § 2 (part), 1982.)" 22.56.2060 Damaging or removing oak trees prohibited—Permit requirements "A. Except as otherwise provided in Section 22.56.2070, a person shall not cut, destroy, remove, relocate, inflict damage or encroach into a protected zone of any tree of the oak genus which is (a) 25 inches or more in circumference (eight inches in diameter) as measured four and one-half feet above mean natural grade; in the case of an oak with more than one trunk, whose combined circumference of any two trunks is at least 38 inches (12 inches in diameter) as measured four and one half feet above mean natural grade, on any lot or parcel of land within the unincorporated area of Los Angeles County, or (b) any tree that has been provided as a replacement tree, pursuant to Section 22.56.2180, on any lot or parcel of land within the unincorporated area of Los Angeles County, unless an oak tree permit is first obtained as provided by this Part 16. B. 'Damage,' as used in this Part 16, includes any act causing or tending to cause injury to the root system or other parts of a tree, including, but not limited to, burning, application of toxic substances, operation of equipment or machinery, or by paving, changing the natural grade, trenching or excavating within the protected zone of an oak tree. C. 'Protected zone,' as used in this Part 16, shall mean that area within the dripline of an oak tree and extending therefrom to a point at least five feet outside the dripline, or 15 feet from the trunks of a tree, whichever distance is greater. (Ord. 88-0157 § 2, 1988: Ord. 82-0168 § 2 (part), 1982.)"

[15] Los Angeles City Bureau of Street Services, Urban Forestry Division, "Oak Trees in Southern California, Can Urban Foresters and Arborists Stop the Bleeding?" http://www.lacity.org/boss/StreetTree/oaktrees.ppt.

[16] U. S. Department of Agriculture Natural Resource Conservation Service. "Conservation Plant Identification —Trees and Shrubs" http://plant-materials.nrcs.usda.gov/technical/plantid/woodies/.

on the other, provide energy-saving benefits, the Department of Water and Power is responsible for maintaining the urban forest and has created a program whereby it will give people up to seven free shade trees to help raise the cooling effect over the city.[17]

The codification of trees and landscaping into legislation is a response to the contested nature of the landscape in Los Angeles, a "second nature" of legislation and conflict between individuals. Subjective views on landscape's functionality and aesthetics together with concerns about the landscape's impact on property values create arguments in communities. Neighbors sue each other to save a tree from being cut down. In 2004, citing concern that high hedges impede driver's views of pedestrians, the City of Santa Monica began enforcing a nearly forgotten sixty-year-old statute prohibiting hedges higher than forty-two inches. When the city announced it would fine violators at a rate of up to $25,000 a day, outrage ensued, provoking a great deal of discussion. Playwright and Santa Monica resident, David Mamet contributed an Op-Ed piece to the *Los Angeles Times* on the topic.[18] The issue came to a boil in an animated debate at a meeting of the city's council on May 10, 2005, in which the two sides battled it out, one side citing rats, the need for safety, and the "right to public viewing" of a resident's property, the other side proclaiming the "traditional, beautiful, historical, healthful" properties of these hedges and the need for privacy. Both sides cited the presence of drug use and thirteen registered sex offenders in Santa Monica in arguments for or against the offending hedges. The council largely backed away from stringent enforcement.

As space in Los Angeles becomes tighter and more segmented, trees and landscape have become more contentious. While Los Angeles begins its project for a million trees to beautify, shade, and help purify the city, and Santa Monica residents fight for the right to shroud themselves in landscape for their own privacy and sense of luxury, instances of violence toward trees have been documented. Because of the laws passed to keep individuals from cutting down trees, parallel ordinances have been enacted requiring the maintenance of trees to protect views. In towns such as Palos Verdes, neighbors can appeal to a ten-member, neighborhood "View Restoration Committee" to force the maintenance and thinning of another neighbor's trees if they block views of the ocean. In fits of vigilantism, view-deprived neighbors use escrow periods during home sales to prune, trim, or even cut down offending trees. In one instance, entertainment leader David Geffen was paid $700,000 in damages for the unauthorized cutting of eight pines and four eucalyptus trees on a property he was holding under escrow.[19] More dramatically, residents of a neighborhood in San Clemente, masquerading as CALTRANS workers, cut down or poisoned fifty eucalyptus trees that had grown into their views.[20] Trees have gained an enormous hold on the local, public imagination in California, generating more complaints than any other element in Los Angeles with the exception of traffic.[21]

[17] Los Angeles Department of Water and Power "Tree Planting Frequently Asked Questions."

[18] David Mamet, "Community Theatre: The High Drama of Tall Shrubbery," *Los Angeles Times*, May 08, 2005.

[19] Bob Pool, "Los Angeles; Covert Tree Trimming Prompts Suit," *Los Angeles Times*, November, 30, 2002, Home Edition, B3.

[20] Richard Marousi and Jack Leonard, "A Killer View? Tree Cutting Sprouts Suit," *Los Angeles Times*, March 24, 1999, Orange County Edition,1.

[21] Julie Tamaki, "Many Tree Debates are routed in old age; Passionte battles grow from sidewalk-ripping. view blocking maturity of urban plantings" *Los Angeles Times*, April 29, 2003, Home Edition, B1.

Los Angeles continues to be a laboratory for urban forestry and gardening, embracing efforts toward sustainability, energy production, and organic gardening as well as continued efforts to increase the public recreational character of the landscape with the creation of bike paths and horse neighborhoods. Experiments toward this end include Lauren Bon's 2005 "Not a Cornfield" project in which the artist planted and harvested corn on the site of a nine-acre brownfield that was once a railyard, making it temporarily the largest, if not the only, urban cornfield in the world.[22] In a nod to earth art, the project surreally juxtaposed large-scale monoculture agriculture with the towers of Downtown. Bon's work parallels efforts all over California to bring agriculture back to the cities as a viable alternative to earlier, unsustainable private pleasure gardens.

In their "Fallen Fruit" project, Silver Lake artists Matias Viegener, David Burns, and Austin Young map all of the fruit trees in their neighborhood. Based on the premise that according to Los Angeles law, fruit overhanging public property is available to all, the project sees the fruit as forming an urban Garden of Eden, capable of year-round sustenance and urging residents to seek out the free fruit.[23] Simultaneously a way to subvert the waste of agribusiness and the divisiveness of trespassing laws with simple strategies for community building, the maps provide a template for a new form of neighborhood ethics and generosity, asking those who download their maps to "take only what you need—say 'hi' to strangers—share your food—take a friend—go by foot."[24]

Los Angeles is the result of a unique interaction and engagement of city form and space with the organic landscape, intimately intertwined since the city's inception. As we hit the limit of available land parcels in Los Angeles, the city finds itself in a quandary. Developers continue to demolish the landscape of single-family houses to build apartment buildings. While the city may yet become hyper-vertical like Manhattan, can the transformation of Los Angeles occur on its own terms and in consideration of the tradition of the many experiments with the landscape, indoor-outdoor living, density itself, athleticism and play, and a new understanding of the productive capacity of landscape? The symbol of Los Angeles has indeed become its landscape—the organic infrastructure—and the city has flourished as has the art and architecture that has used it as an ingredient for exploration.

With the palm tree following the orange tree into the city's history of forgetting, it is again possible for the city to reshape itself through landscape, to look again at the city's trees and its urban forest. The need for a more sustainable environment will demand that the tree and the landscape of the city, in general, offset the diminished global capacity of nature to counteract the effects of globalized urbanism. But the Los Angeles landscape has many other capacities as well. Given a climate so sympathetic to year-round inhabitation of the outdoors, can a new Los Angeles blossom whereby architecture and landscape, inside and outside, become increasingly indistinguishable; in which country and city become less estranged with more of today's functions typically relegated to each, inverted; and the proliferating equipment of the city become more bio-mimetic and responsive to the needs of the city? As infrastructure, landscape has much potential. The dying palms have only provoked us to explore what those are. Down with the Palm! Long live the Palm!

---

[22] Not a Cornfield, http://www.notacornfield.com/.

[23] David Burns, Matias Viegener and Austin Young, *Fallen Fruit Project*, http://www.fallenfruit.org.

[24] Burns, et. al. *Fallen Fruit Project*.

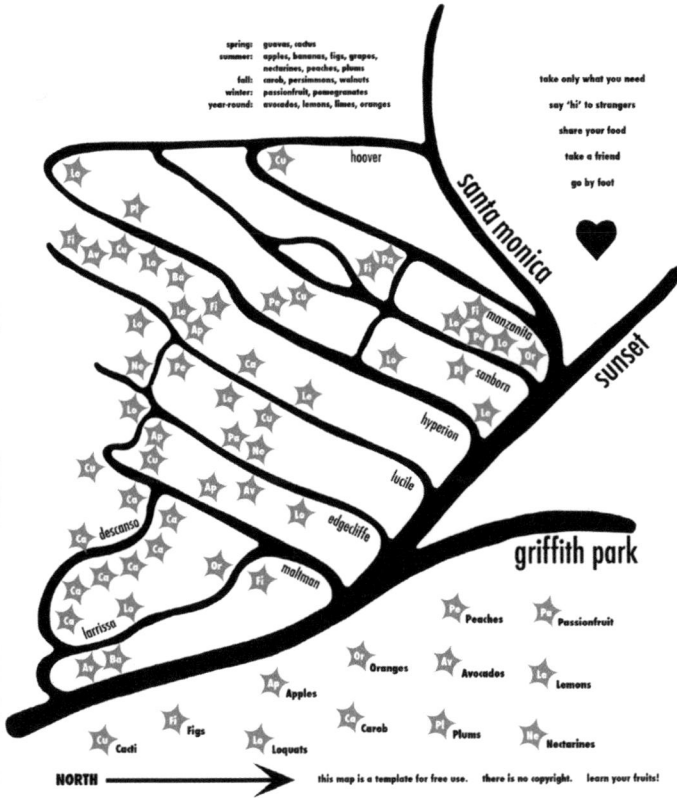

spring: guavas, cactus
summer: apples, bananas, figs, grapes, nectarines, peaches, plums
fall: carob, persimmons, walnuts
winter: passionfruit, pomegranates
year-round: avocados, lemons, limes, oranges

take only what you need

say 'hi' to strangers

share your food

take a friend

go by foot

hoover

santa monica

sunset

manzanita

sanborn

hyperion

lucile

edgecliffe

descanso

maltman

larrissa

griffith park

Peaches   Passionfruit

Oranges   Avocados   Lemons

Apples

Carob   Plums   Nectarines

Cacti   Figs   Loquats

NORTH ⟶   this map is a template for free use.   there is no copyright.   learn your fruits!

Ted Kane and Rick Miller

CELL STRUCTURE
MOBILE PHONES

A new stratum of infrastructure is settling over Los Angeles. Unlike previous developments, this new infrastructure isn't planned by publicly directed municipal entities but
rather is developed by competing, privately operated corporations. Lacking the heroic
visibility of past civil works (from Mulholland-era aqueducts to Eisenhower-era freeways),
these new systems are projected along the airwaves or through fiber optic cables, inhabiting
realms all but invisible to the average citizen. Even their sole outposts in the material world,
cellular phone towers, seek to disappear, camouflaged as palm trees or church steeples to
blend into their suburban surroundings. But the disguises need not be so clever, as the visual
background noise of the city already effectively hides towers in plain sight.[1] Belying their
invisibility, these new networks of communication have as much impact on the development
of the city as the freeways before them. Nor is this simply a question of technology; the rise
of privately funded infrastructure and the subsequent decline of public control represents a
new corporate model of urban planning, with implications for the future development of
the city.

---

[1] For example, throughout the city many WWII-era air-raid sirens still stand, typically beige in color, atop
steel posts. This earlier system of telecommunications is rarely ever noted, as it too has faded into the visual
clutter.

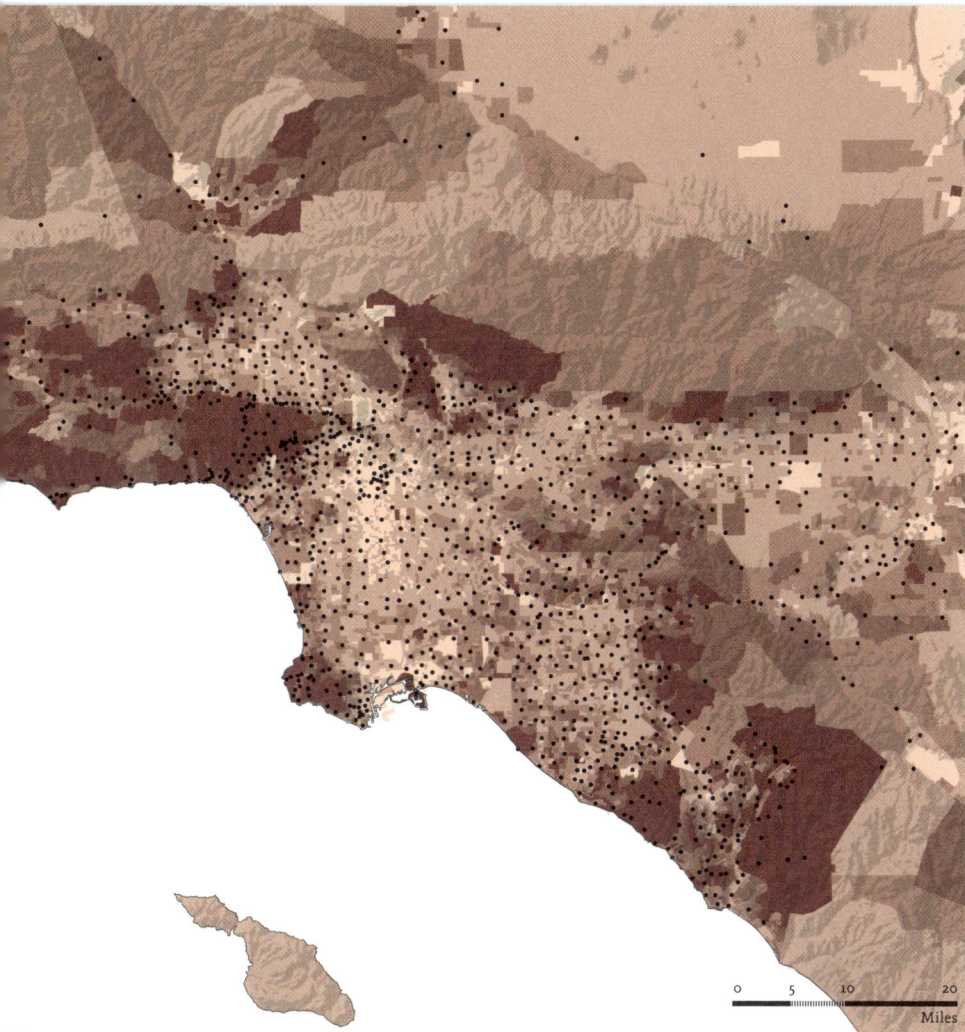

Cell phone coverage
vs. median house-
hold income, Los
Angeles.

Source: Sprint PCS &
U.S. Census Bureau

Sprint Nextel Cell Towers ●

**Median Household
Income (1999)**

< $25,000
$25,001 - 50,000
$50,001 - 75,000
$75,001 - 100,000
> $100,001

Regional Patterns Los Angeles has relied on infrastructure for much of its history. Free-ways, aqueducts, and dams were essential to the area's growth into a city of over 12 million inhabitants.[2] More than anyone else, the city's greatest hero remains William Mulholland, and, punctuating the city's history more than any other positive accomplishments, these enormous undertakings have become emblematic of the collective urban psyche. Histori-cally, infrastructural developments reacted to the urban needs of both private and public constituencies, addressed localized real estate interests, responded to the need for commer-cial links between disparate communities, and implemented Cold War defense logistics.[3]

Cell phone tree in Santa Clarita

Federal, state, and regional interests acted together to build the freeway system, elevating transportation to a public network of regional proportions, thereby permitting new trajectories of movement removed from the ubiquitous homogeneity of the urban grid.[4] Los Angeles's residents quickly adopted the car and celebrated the freeway for its ability to connect the larger political entity of the city while maintaining the autonomy of the indi-vidual. The freeway imposed a different sense of place, one in which each driver is the center of his or her own universe. As Reyner Banham observed,

> A domestic or sociable journey in Los Angeles does not end so much at the door of one's destination as at the off-ramp of the freeway...in part this is a comment on the sheer vastness of the movement pattern of Los Angeles, but more than that it is an acknowledgement that the freeway system in its totality is now a single compre-hensible place, a coherent state of mind, a complete way of life.[5]

But if the freeway is a place, it is a place separate from the rest of the city. As the freeway connected the dispersed city, it undid any possibility of a cohesive regional plan, fueling a further dispersal of the region into a patchwork of entities each seeking greater autonomy. The region became a city of multiple overlapping jurisdictions—a legal quagmire. Gerald Frug describes the resulting state as one in which "residents of metropolitan areas live in a multitude of legally defined jurisdictions with different borders: the areas defined by school districts, transportation districts, redevelopment authorities, park districts and the like often differ not only from city borders but from each other."[6] If the freeway provided connections to the area, it ensured that a greater sense of wholeness would not emerge as the region's inhabitants were condemned to shuttling from off-ramp to off-ramp in tiny metal pods.

Private infrastructure flourishes in this vacuum of myopic jurisdictions, taking advantage of gaps in oversight to create new, private realms unburdened by the equal access that has historically been the obligation of utilities operating in the public realm.

[2] As William Fulton explains in *The Reluctant Metropolis* (Point Arena, CA: Solano Press, 2001), the growth machine that characterized Los Angeles for much of the last century was largely driven by real estate development, which in turn was dependent on a strong infrastructure of water and electricity to subsidize the continuous expansion of the city through developments on the periphery.

[3] As Fulton has explored, many of the civic and government officials of Los Angeles have been inextricably linked to land development for much of the past century.

[4] See Albert Pope, *Ladders* (New York: Princeton Architectural Press, 1997) for an extensive look at American cities and their transformation from places formed on the equal access of the gird to a closed system of the cul-de-sac or ladder.

[5] Reyner Banham, *Los Angeles, The Architecture of Four Ecologies* (1971; Berkeley: University of California Press, 1995), 195.

[6] Gerald Frug, *City Making: Building Communities Without Building Walls* (Princeton, NJ: Princeton University Press, 2001) traces the powerlessness of today's cities and the subsequent rise in Public Corporate powers, to our legal system and its favoring of individual rights over state rights. This historical power shift from public corporations to private corporations is a product of our current legal systems propensity to ensure that Private Corporations are protected from state domination, while Public Corporations are subject to such domination.

Like the freeways before them, wireless networks hold out the promise to spatially liberate the citizen by connecting the city without undermining the autonomy of the individual citizen. The wireless network spans the extensive geographic breadth of the city, creating new connections where the freeway left off. However, this new infrastructure is no longer a part of a regional plan; rather it is carved out by private corporations competing for market share. These are commercial enterprises, which by their very nature are competitive yet redundant. Today in Los Angeles four telecommunications corporations—Verizon, Sprint/NEXTEL, T-Mobile, and AT&T—operate simultaneously, stitching together independent wireless phone networks based on their own strategic models.

Though these companies are publicly held entities in legal terms (their stocks being traded on Wall Street and open to anyone to own), their day-to-day operations and the extent of their networks are shielded from public view, making it difficult for municipal authorities to influence their formation and trajectory. Opening further fissures, the Telecommunications Act of 1996 further curtailed local jurisdictional oversight by preventing states and local governments from "regulating the placement, construction, and modification of personal wireless service facilities on the basis of the environmental effects of radio frequency emissions to the extent that such facilities comply with the Commission's [FCC's] regulations concerning such emissions."[7] As interpreted by the cell phone companies and defended by the Federal Communications Commission, this law has effectively eliminated the ability of local governments to oppose the construction of wireless towers in their communities. Instead local governments are limited to regulation based on community planning standards, largely imposing some form of visual control.

Camouflage The result is the camouflaged cell phone tower, the by-product of the only position available to communities who oppose cell phone towers, that is, to demand their invisibility. Hiding its presence from public view, the ubiquitous cell tower camouflaged as a palm tree becomes an appropriate icon for the private infrastructural network of our day.

Stealthy networks of towers and transmission stations span the city in a hexagonal matrix, honeycombing a sprawling metropolis already shaped by generations of commercial development.[8] Wireless phone networks have been built in stages. Because of the piecemeal construction of cellular systems and relative low cost per transmission location, the cellular industry has lent itself to a type of financing much different than the heavy construction of power lines, freeways, or aqueducts.[9] These earlier projects necessitated a large, up-front investment and long-term construction schedules, making them virtual monopolies by their nature. In contrast, the first layer of wireless networks provided thin coverage zones— generally in high-traffic, high-income areas—that produced revenue to finance perpetual growth over successive phases.

Such insubstantial and nimble systems that can be built out in stages and paid for by their own growth have transformed the rules of urban development. This new paradigm has an impact beyond wireless systems, spurring other forms of public infrastructure to seek out privatization and future development based on urban buying habits rather than public discourse. Today the private sector has assumed a leading role in energy production, education, prisons, and road systems, all of which seek to move toward a new concept of adaptability and efficiency modeled on the open market using new forms of communication and technology to monitor peak demands and cost models. The move from government-backed infrastructure to private networks has shifted power to such a degree that city governments are forced to behave like corporations in the market, competing with each other to attract the latest technological developments that corporations offer, giving tax incentives and public lands to private entities in exchange for access to the latest gadgetry.

---

[7] Telecommunications Act of 1996, S. 562, 104th Congress, 2nd Session, Section 332 (c) (7), http://www.fcc.gov/Reports/tcom1996.pdf, 117.

[8] The hexagonal grid is often referred to in the technical writing surrounding radio-based technology because it represents an ideal efficiency. The hexagon's symmetry means the distance between a given cell and its immediate neighbors is the same along any of the six main directions, thus it contains twelve-fold symmetry as opposed to the rectangle's eight-fold symmetry.

[9] Industry estimates suggest that the cost for a transmission tower is around $150,000.

In principle, privatization appears to be an efficient and sound strategy for extending the reach and depth of the new urban infrastructure without taxing citizenry further. Nevertheless, when we examine the implications of technology meeting the landscape, we begin to understand the real impact of this model.

Wireless coverage maps of Los Angeles expose a definable hierarchy following the dense corridors through a city where the consumer roams, while neglecting neighborhoods with less viable demographics. Wireless companies tap consumer polling, interest group research, and statistical usage data to understand the needs of the cellular citizens at the expense of the collective needs of the community. As inevitable byproducts of this hierarchical development, dead zones—areas not economical to build out as part of the network—emerge. That parts of the city remain victims of "Swiss cheese" coverage concerns the networks only when the density of lost calls and complaints in a particular area exceeds a predetermined threshold. Although the operations of a smooth corporate hierarchy are unquestionably efficient, universal access is too expensive to be an immediate goal and the corporation is accountable to citizens only through many filters: stockholders, marketing demands, cost-benefit ratios, and the bottom line.

Wireless nodes represent a dispersed network that typifies the contemporary city at both the macro and the microlevels. The integration of the wireless network into the daily workings of the city is particularly evident in the creative industries where film and television crews come together for short durations. In this model, teams of experts form to work on a creative production with a limited duration—from a single day for a commercial, up to several months for a film—before dispersing again. Within this culture a wireless connection is a necessity for instant communication with other workers about job leads and changing opportunities. This "Network Economy," as Manuel Castells has explained, "represents a new form of entrepreneurship in which the individual worker markets his or her human capital portfolio among various 'buyers.'"[10] The culture of the network permeates the everyday life of the city, often times blurring the boundaries between work and leisure. Today business is transacted in spaces like libraries, cafés, and coffee shops, and not just among heavy brokers, but at all levels of network culture.

That wireless use has grown from being a luxury a decade ago to a necessity today demonstrates the importance now placed on instant communications. In the Los Angeles wireless region alone (Los Angeles, Orange and Riverside counties), network users have doubled over the last 5 years; today there are over 14.6 million subscribers to the network, in a population of 18 million.[11] We are seeing the influence of this shift beyond the middle class, into the growing economy of freelance and gray market jobs. Wireless technology is now a common tool for day laborers, landscapers, maintenance workers, mobile food vendors, and other "migratory" workers who must keep in constant touch with clients and colleagues to negotiate for and locate work. With communication freed from the confines of land-based systems and adapted to the peripatetic body through mobile phones, smartphones, and laptops), such individuals are able to leap beyond previous spatial barriers to create their own connections.

Hidden in the fabric of the city are the informal networks that sustain the contemporary economy of global Los Angeles. As Paul Virilio has observed, "we may have reached a point in the development of the city where the individual has supplanted physical territory as the dominant form of urban identity."[12] The wireless infrastructure heightens our mobility, transforming our notion of the city; it is no longer easy to decipher where Los Angeles begins or

[10] See Manuel Castells, *The Rise of the Network Society* (New York: Blackwell, 1996).

[11] According to the FCC Southern California district potential customer base.

[12] Paul Virilio, *Pure War* (New York: Semiotext(e), 1998).

ends (something made vaguer by telephone number portability, which attaches area codes to individuals rather than to localities). The boundaries of the city blur, as the interactions that used to happen in face-to-face transactions have now been transplanted by distance-shrinking telephone conversations, e-mail, and network connections.

Caller Identification With the personal freedom afforded by a mobile system, individuals must give up and become completely transparent to the system. With an increasing number of users opting out of land-based phones, the 911 emergency phone system and its capacity for address tracking became obsolete. In response, a 2005 directive from the Federal Communication Commission mandated that all cell phone carriers provide the ability to trace cell phone calls to a location within one hundred meters or less. To comply, the wireless industry integrated "assisted GPS" into phones, using triangulation between cell phone towers to ensure that carriers can track its customers to within approximately five meters. Perversely, although the mobile phone user is always connected and always locatable, this system is rarely made available to handset owners.

When a cell phone call begins, a signal is sent to the nearest tower, which verifies the user's name, billing information, and authorization to use the network. Once the caller is approved, the tower connects the call, but as the caller begins to move out of range of the first tower a signal is sent out, allowing the call to be handed off to the next tower. What appears to be one phone call is actually composed of many relays over different towers, as the network constantly tracks the caller in space. The information is then cataloged in digital form, open not only to data mining to expose possible new markets or for identifying areas of call density, but also to surveillance in the name of "security." The fundamental subservience inherent to a communication system was expressed by Jean Baudrillard: "The essential thing is to maintain a relational décor, where all the terms must continually communicate among themselves and stay in contact, informed of the respective condition of others and of the system as a whole, where opacity, resistance or the secrecy of a single term can lead to catastrophe."[13] To be mobile, the individual becomes transparent.

Niche Markets In such an open market, the individual is increasingly vulnerable to demographic mining and subject to new forms of carefully targeted advertising. NEXTEL distinguished itself early, finding its niche with building contractors and the predominantly Mexican-immigrant construction labor force. Developed to take advantage of the two-way radio communication that had already been established in practice on construction jobs, push-to-talk technology—which acts like a two-way radio or walkie-talkie—appealed to both management and construction workers on site. But NEXTEL's advantage had deeper implications. Though the company could only sell a limited number of phones to workers in the building trades, when accounting for other members of a construction worker's family and social group, the target group grows exponentially. As the primary wage-earner, a laborer might be the first in his family or social group to purchase a phone, and would do so as a necessary expense of his employment. But when subsequent members move into a social or economic position to also subscribe to phone service, even if push-to-talk may not be a required feature for their use, they would have become familiar with NEXTEL via second-hand exposure to the product and would want to be on the same network as their relatives to take advantage of free mobile-to-mobile service.

[13] Jean Baudrillard, *Ecstasy of Communications* (New York: Semiotext(e), 1998).

NEXTEL took an early lead in the Latino market, but more telling still are the corporation's attempts to maintain this lead. Although its marketing has relied on traditional schemes, such as underwriting concerts for Latino music, NEXTEL also undertook strategies more intricately tied to its customer base. While American companies are politically limited to the nation of their operation—agreements with a Mexican firm in which the company holds a partial stake do exist—the signal has the ability to cross boundaries unfettered. In the early 2000s, while not explicitly claiming an ability to use NEXTEL from the border regions of Baja California, billboards nevertheless made reference to the possibility that portions of northern Mexico were suddenly "in network." Even as federal policy solidified the boundary of the United States against illegal Mexican immigration, an American corporation dematerialized the very same border to increase its appeal to a particular population that lived on both sides of that line.

Freeways, telephones, satellites, Wi-Fi, radio and television each provide means by which the everyday city flows and composes itself. This new open-ended infrastructure doesn't dictate its form in concrete, but still has an immense impact on the life and consciousness of the city. While privately operated wireless infrastructure has had positive implications for individual freedom, allowing new opportunities for citizens to form their own connections to their surrounding community, it also exposes a troubling sovereignty now afforded corporations in the planning of American cities. Privatized infrastructure is becoming increasingly prevalent while civil institutions are declared obsolete. The privatization of governance through private police forces, prisons, school districts, and toll roads, all lead us toward a city further divided along economic lines and lacking a cohesive means of ensuring equal access. Under this private mantle urban development decisions more closely match the exchanges used in business: market share and price point find their relationship not with the public, but with other, competing infrastructures. Amortization of costs becomes part of the thought process, and those who do not fit a prescribed buying demographic are suddenly no longer part of the equation.

There is widespread faith today in the ability of the market to respond to our needs, making the activities of government seem almost irrelevant in comparison. However, as Gerald Frug has noted, there is a measurable difference between how a consumer acts individually (seeking the cheapest price for the largest return) versus how they will act when voting on government measures that can benefit the many.[14] The individual will often put the needs of society and the less fortunate ahead of his own when casting a vote for initiatives like school bonds or street maintenance. The citizen/shopper in a market system, by contrast, will only look out for his pocketbook interests, at the expense of a larger urban vision.

Fragmented and dispersed, the mega-city must come to grips with the new reality of mobile and malleable infrastructures. It has no choice but to compete with private networks. If we are to continue the development of a privatized infrastructure, we must find ways of reactivating the operative logic of the "the greater good" within the new, privatized economic regime. Like cellular networks themselves, today's cities must form connections beyond their distinct geographic boundaries, carving new systems of interaction and collective space on a regional scale. Only in a borderless, regionally scaled city plan organized by purpose rather than geographical boundaries, can the public realm hope to compete with the smooth surfaces of corporate control.

---

[14] See Frug's *City Making* for a look at this concept of personal gain vs. greater good and its loss in most discussion of privatization of public services.

1

Lane Barden

THE STREET
WILSHIRE BOULEVARD PICTURING LOS ANGELES: CONDUITS, CORRIDORS, AND THE LINEAR CITY, PART 2

Los Angeles evolved from a pueblo established by Spanish conquistadors on the Los Angeles River where the river emerges from the Santa Monica mountains onto a vast alluvial flood plain (see "The River," plate 16). This location, over twenty miles from the beach, was ideal for agriculture and access to drinking water. After the automobile became the primary means of transportation, Wilshire Boulevard became the first traffic corridor to the ocean, following the westward expansion of Los Angeles. Initially the street was residential, but the amount of traffic using Wilshire made it less attractive for living and more attractive for shopping and business. Stores and offices alike began to populate Wilshire and, because of their easy accessibility to automobiles, proved so successful that they pulled the city out along the strip.

This series of photographs proceeds in a reverse path along Wilshire, from the beach in Santa Monica toward downtown (see plates 2 and 3). As the helicopter leaves Santa Monica and passes over the Westwood financial district, the street disappears into a curving ribbon of inexplicably white office towers that gleam so brightly in the sun they exceed the dynamic range of the camera (see plates 10 and 11). After crossing the 405 freeway intersections like Santa Monica Boulevard (see plates 14 and 15) and San Vicente Boulevard (see plate 17) glance off at an angle and disappear into the Los Angeles haze. Then the street leaves Beverly Hills, entering the Miracle Mile, a cultural and historic corridor that continues past the Los Angeles County Museum of Art (see plates 1 and 18), where it enters another historic section that is now the vast ethnic community of Koreatown. At Hoover Street, the north-south alignment of the western Los Angeles grid comes to an end, and Wilshire enters a new grid

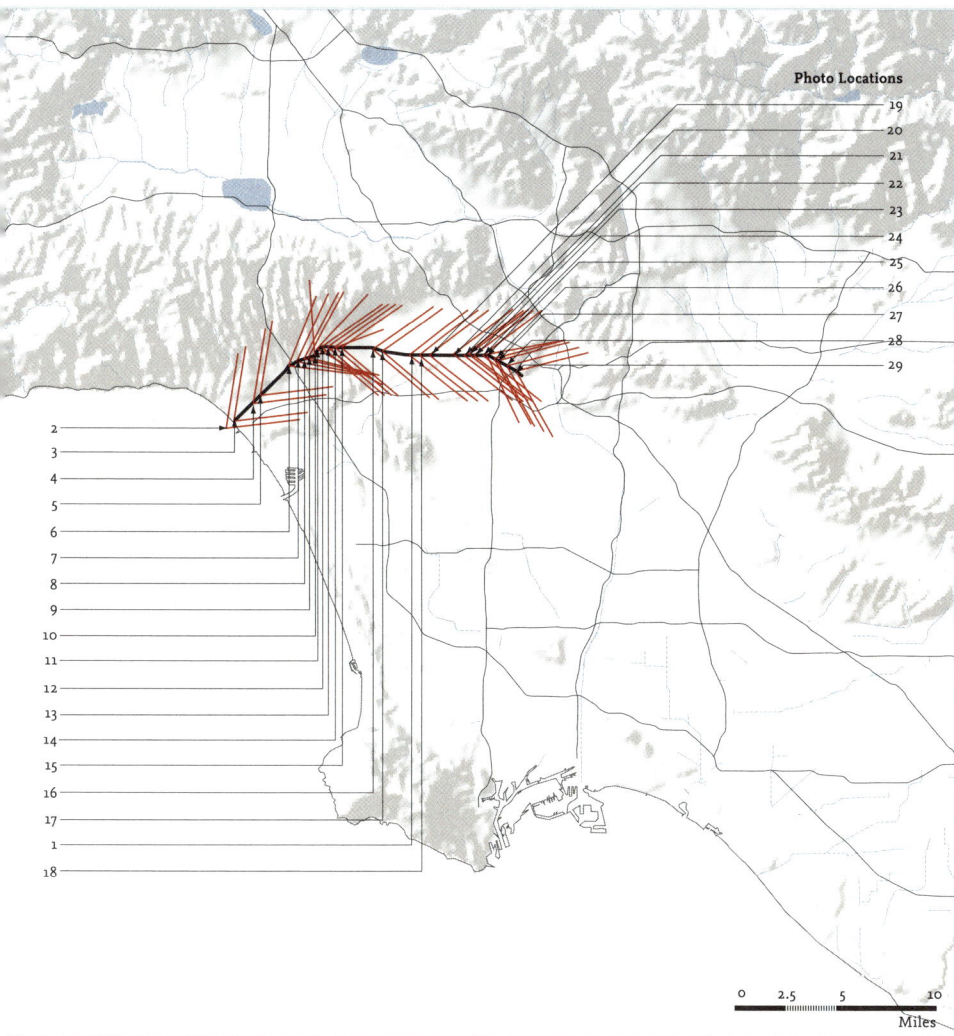

Photo Locations

19
20
21
22
23
24
25
26
27
28
29

2
3
4
5
6
7
8
9
10
11
12
13
14
15
16
17
1
18

0   2.5   5   10
Miles

Numbers correspond to
plate numbers
of photographs in
this chapter

Photograph Viewshed ⟨
Wilshire Boulevard ▬
Interstate Highways —

aligned with the river on a northeast–southwest axis. Here the street bends southeast, passing through MacArthur Park (see plate 27) and enters the downtown business center where it abruptly ends, or begins, depending on your point of view, at One Wilshire, actually located on Grand Avenue and placed strangely off-axis to the street it is named after.

It is often observed that Los Angeles does not have a center like other cities. Yet, extra-ordinary and painful efforts have been made to create a city center in the Bunker Hill area of downtown Los Angeles. The result is that downtown Los Angeles will have a more active cultural life, but it will probably function in the greater city just as Hollywood, Santa Monica, or for that matter— Glendale and Encino do. It will be one place among many in Los Angeles, but a place that happens to be located in the middle—a center but not a center, an edge city located in the city core.

Le Corbusier's Linear City[1] would come as no surprise to anyone living in this city. Avenues like Vermont and Normandie, or boulevards like Sepulveda, Sunset, and Wilshire, stretch out into the Southern California landscape for more than twenty miles. Their trajectories, like the Los Angeles River, form lines that disappear into the haze of the city long before they reach their vanishing point. From a distance, buildings and palm trees are the only landmarks in the flat, gridded land-scape, delineating the street below. As if to mimic Le Corbusier's ideas of the linear city, where buildings rise up in long, formal, Archimedian spaces, the towers of Wilshire Boulevard suggest a city within a city on a linear trajectory that slices across the landscape like a knife (see plates

[1] The linear city was a concept Le Corbusier explored in various idealized iterations that rendered city plans along viaducts, parallel open spaces, and straight boulevards or corridors. See for example the plan for Algiers and the plan for Sao Paolo in *The Radiant City* (New York: The Onion Press, 1967), 222, 232.

3

18-24). Le Corbusier's sketches are architectural corridors of grand proportions, with implications for an urban space where the "center" is the vanishing point—always just ahead of you as you move down a linear corridor constructed for efficiency and economy. To live in it requires believing that having a true geographical center to the city is not really that important. So it is with Wilshire, the ideal center to a city that dreams of itself in perpetual, vehicular motion.

In Los Angeles, the conventional model of the city with a center that serves business and cultural life surrounded by suburbs, and beyond that, open countryside—has been replaced by a polycentric matrix of aging suburbs embedded in a larger urban fabric. This is a regional metropolis where the same infrastructure serves multiple centers with overlapping networks of transportation, communication, and consumption.[2] This is not to excuse the sprawl or justify it, or to make our population appear to be contemporary and enlightened. In Los Angeles, we are, in fact, consumptive cretins with very little culture and soul—but in a good way, an adaptive way, and an exciting way, we like to think.

Expanding outward and adding to hardscape is unsustainable. The water crisis has not yet hit Los Angeles, but when it does, it will make the depletion of oil resources look pale by comparison. Sprawl prevents groundwater recharge and is bad for water conservation. Increasing the population density within the city is the only logical response to sprawl. Wilshire Boulevard—a direct link between the beach and downtown and possessing a history of its own as a cultural and commercial corridor—is already a dense linear city, making it the ideal location for more

[2] Alex Wall, "Programming the Surface," in James Corner, ed. *Recovering Contemporary Landscape: Essays in Contemporary Landscape Architecture* (New York: Princeton Architectural Press, 1999), 34.

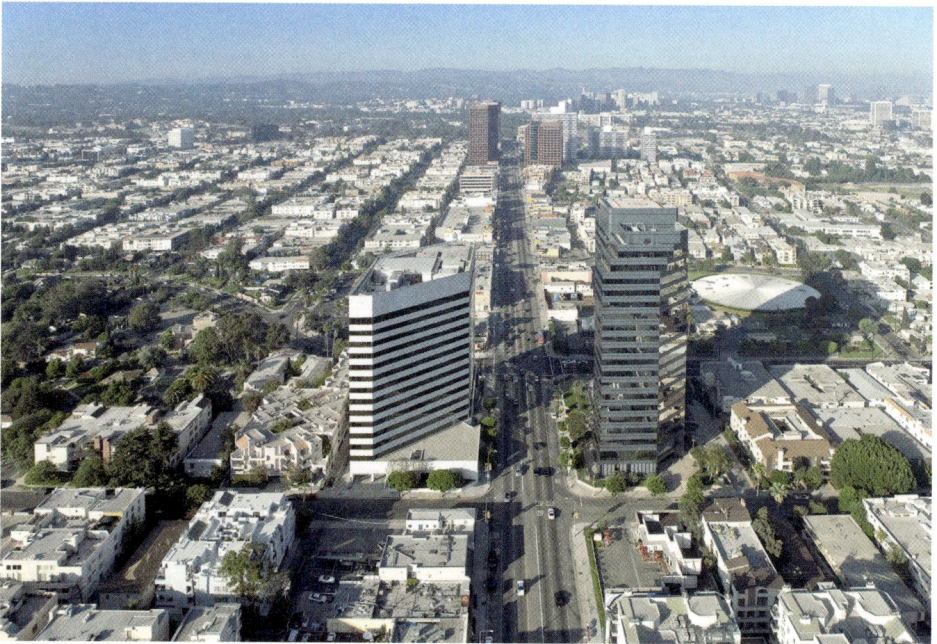

density and growth. Construction of the proposed subway running its entire length—
connecting the existing MTA Red Line from downtown's Union Station to the beach in Santa
Monica over twenty miles to the west—would make the street into a functional, linear center
for the greater metropolitan area. Anyone living on that line would have access to downtown's business and cultural center, Koreatown, the Miracle Mile's museums and galleries,
Beverly Hills's shopping, Westwood's museums and UCLA, as well as Santa Monica's beach
culture, and new amenities stimulated by development along the line. Living without a
car would become attractive in Los Angeles for the first time since the Red Car trolley was
dismantled. No relocation and little rezoning would be required. Wilshire, like the river, is
an established trajectory for linking and connecting the disparate points on the Los Angeles
grid and could create ideal conditions for high density.

   Maybe for Corbusier, this was radical, futuristic thinking. Not anymore. This is basic.
New subway lines in Los Angeles have been successful, with high-density development
growing around new stations. More public transportation and high-density development
along those lines is the only obvious alternative to the problems of a dispersed metropolis
and the arrival of another four million people by 2025.[3]

[3] Stephen P. Erie, *Beyond Chinatown* (Stanford: Stanford University Press, 2006), 5.

5

Time moves forward like a car accelerating into a faintly imaginable vanishing point. In plate 21, the LG cell phone photographed August 12, 2005, towering so proudly some 80 feet above Wilshire on the side of a building in Koreatown, is already beginning to look like an old Westinghouse refrigerator. In twenty years it will look like an artifact from a bygone era. Energy costs, and the fallout from environmental malaise will eventually trump the short-term thinking of a city heedlessly streamlined for the economy of real estate profit and the automobile. How that change will happen is yet to be seen; but surely Wilshire Boulevard, like the Los Angeles River, will remain.

7

9

11

13

15

17

19

21

23

25

27

29

OBJECTS

Roger Sherman

COUNTING (ON) CHANGE
PROPERTY

Cities today develop at a rate that outpaces architects' and planners' efforts to shape them. Political and economic circumstances change so rapidly that by the time a plan is realized, it is often already obsolete; a mere election or market downturn can radically alter the assumptions and objectives of a project or master plan. In this milieu, the path of least resistance for urban development calls for action rather than reaction—to develop not in comprehensive wholes, but in realizable chunks or increments, placing an emphasis more on augmentation than organization.[1] For architects, the time has come to recognize, finally, that contemporary urbanism is better rethought around conceptions of progress and potential—via design strategies for unfolding the future—rather than by another utopian horizon.

This lack of sufficient time to plan brings with it an atmosphere of higher risk. Yet for the most part, architects and designers today either blithely ignore the change of conditions to which their projects will imminently be subject, and focus their design effort on simply "expressing" the way that things currently work, or employ a one-size-fits-all approach purporting total flexibility, wherein so many contingencies are accommodated that it serves none of them well.[2] Like the panic room, these responses choose to play it safe. However if architecture is to recover its social, economic, and political value amidst the instability and

[1] Penelope Dean, "Deadline Urbanism," *Log* 5 (2005): 46-9.

[2] Here the Parametric and New Urbanist projects are strangely alike. While the Parametric project portrays itself as avant-garde, this is defined only narrowly with regard to technological development, not the social and political future, with respect to which it is ironically and surprisingly accepting of the status quo.

Hollymont Car Wash   1
Strawberry Field   2
Flower Tower   3
Curley's Cafe   4
Major Water Bodies ▬
Interstate Highways ┄┄┄

uncontrollability of the contemporary city, it needs to be rethought in a manner that assumes risk, not averts it. Instead of hedging its bets, design must provide sufficient looseness with respect to future scenarios, but actually help tilt the odds in favor of certain of them.

Rather than assuming stability and explaining change, this means that architects must learn to assume change and explain stability. Fortunately, for all their complexity, cities— like self-organized systems—are not entirely unpredictable. Their ability to adapt to change is related to simple behaviors, or rules-of-thumb. Not unlike an ecosystem, these rules constitute a kind of protocol which urban buildings, spaces, and communities must engage if they are to re-organize themselves at critical points of instability such as floods, acts of terrorism, real estate market collapses, and so on.[3] In order to do so, those environments must be strategized not just in terms of how they are intended to work today, but also how else they might work at another time or under different circumstances. More than any other city, Los Angeles has been an incubator for strategies of urban development which are thought out in exactly this way—marrying pure speculation with the built-in plasticity necessary to adapt to, and even preempt, future scenarios (Culver City, whose downtown was designed both as a decoy for home buyers and as a backlot for the two major movie studios adjacent to it, is just one example). The numerous models of urbanism that L. A. has produced, which can now be seen replicated around the globe, have succeeded in propagating largely due to their ability to take productive advantage of the economic and political risk that is associated with the rapid urban growth that is more the norm in many cities today.

Like well-designed software, these new plans possess not one, but a variety of alternative organization patterns and pathways. Instead of the inclusion of a "Plan B" only as a back up to a preferred plan, their design—which combines top-down and bottom-up thinking— builds in several plans of equal value (as in the Culver City model). Such versatility allows a design strategy to spread the risk—not unlike a diversified stock portfolio—thereby lessening its susceptibility to failure or obsolescence due to a change in conditions. But as importantly, by building in the capacity to host a range of future scenarios, it also carries the projective potential to attract a wider set of prospective audiences. Unlike the paradox of the "lowest common denominator" approach exemplified in the multi-purpose room, (the "dumbing down" of form to a universal generic), this speculative approach to design calls for a deceptively simple, if evocative formal conceit that is cleverly embedded with an infra-structural capacity to support a variety of possible futures. Specific shape or surface characteristics create a formal peculiarity that is both highly imageable and at the same time serves as an unlikely point of tangency between the possible constituencies it might attract.[4] Only as the future unfolds does its full formal complexity and political potential become evident.

The other key trait of change-based thinking—one that Landscape Urbanism has been more successful at addressing in landscape proposals than those concerning urban develop-ment—draws from what ecologists term successional dynamics, referring to the evolution of species and their habitat. In a man-made ecology, these "species" are the interest groups that, driven by the free market, negotiate (compete, cooperate) with one another for the fixed resources of a given property or lot. (This so-called "bundle of rights" includes air and mineral rights, easements, and privileges, to name just a few.) The ripple effect caused by the combined and complex interaction of these stakeholders' efforts to assert these rights is

---

[3] Protocol is here defined as a detailed plan for the course of a scientific experiment or medical treatment, the rules of which are sufficiently open as to be contingent upon the particular feedback/outcome of each stage of the experiment/treatment.

[4] Although clearly reminiscent of Venturi's double-functioning element, here multi-functionality does not refer to the distinction between its symbolic pragmatic roles, but rather that it possesses different diagrams of pragmatic operation, each which attracts a different audience.

1656 N. Vermont Ave. (Hollywood)
Multiple Exchange Diagram

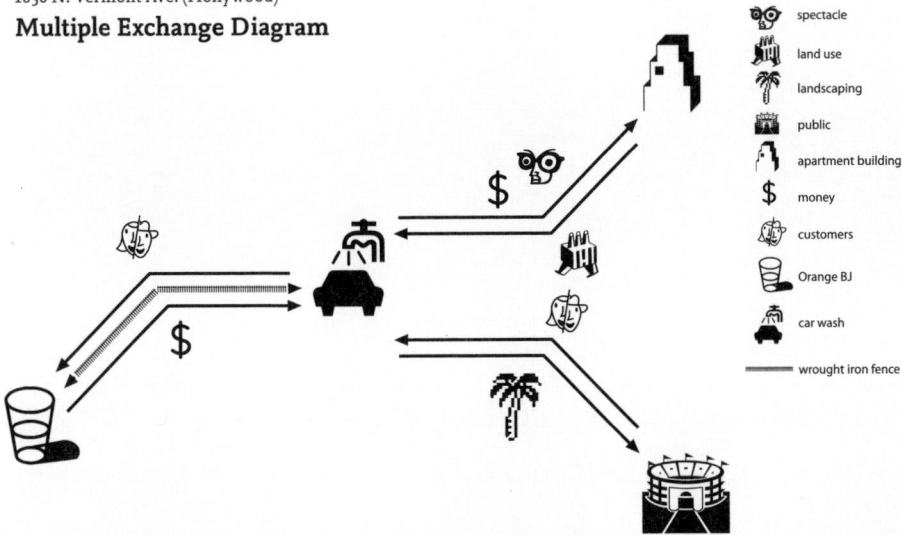

👀	spectacle
🏚	land use
🌴	landscaping
🏛	public
🏢	apartment building
$	money
😊	customers
🥤	Orange BJ
🚗	car wash
▬▬▬	wrought iron fence

1

the major force in shaping the way that capitalist cities change today. It is these behaviors, not zoning ordinances, which constitute the above-mentioned protocols, ones to which every urban plan is subject, however small, whether the architect wishes to engage them or not. These rules, such as the equality between the incentive for cooperation and that of competition, or that land will always seek its highest and best use, also make the dynamics of urban development somewhat less unpredictable, and therefore possible to work with.

There is no more transparent example of how these logics operate than in Los Angeles, whose rapid development was enabled by the fact that speculation (self-organization) always preceded infrastructure (planning). There, connectivity was, as it largely still is, neither a priori nor continuous, instead developing contingently through the opportunistic, piecemeal, lets-make-a-deal process that operated on an as-needed basis only, as necessitated by an ever-changing present.

In Robinson Crusoe-like fashion, the approach to infrastructure in L. A. is and always has been more software than hardware, a method or protocol that looks for ways to cleverly piggyback one thing upon another not originally conceived to harbor that use, but in which a latent value or potential (future) is "discovered." In the northeastern corner of Hollywood, for instance, a property has been assembled out of three lots to construct a virtual urban ecosystem. It is "habitat" to four entities: two by right (a car wash and juice bar), and two by adjacency (an apartment building and public right-of-way). Though each use attracts a different audience, the structures and territories they occupy connect to one another spatially in a way that at the same time articulates their socioeconomic interdependency (figure 1). These

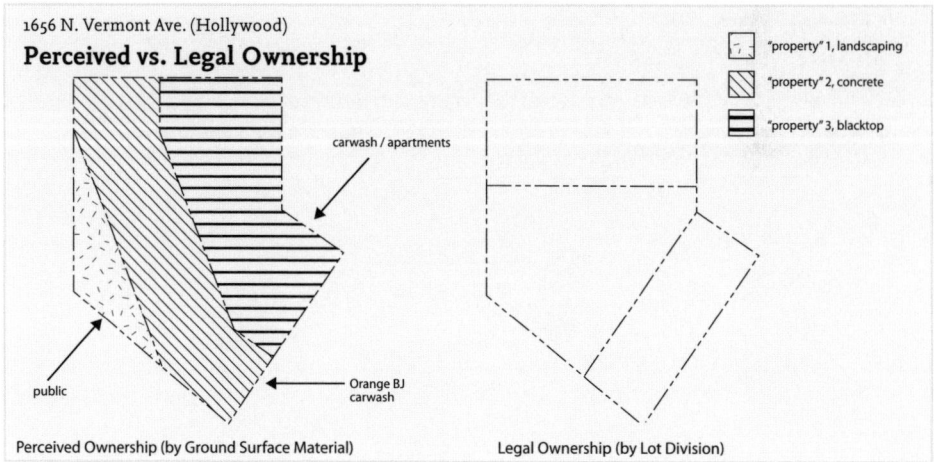

1656 N. Vermont Ave. (Hollywood)

Perceived vs. Legal Ownership

"property" 1, landscaping
"property" 2, concrete
"property" 3, blacktop

carwash / apartments

public

Orange BJ carwash

Perceived Ownership (by Ground Surface Material)

Legal Ownership (by Lot Division)

2

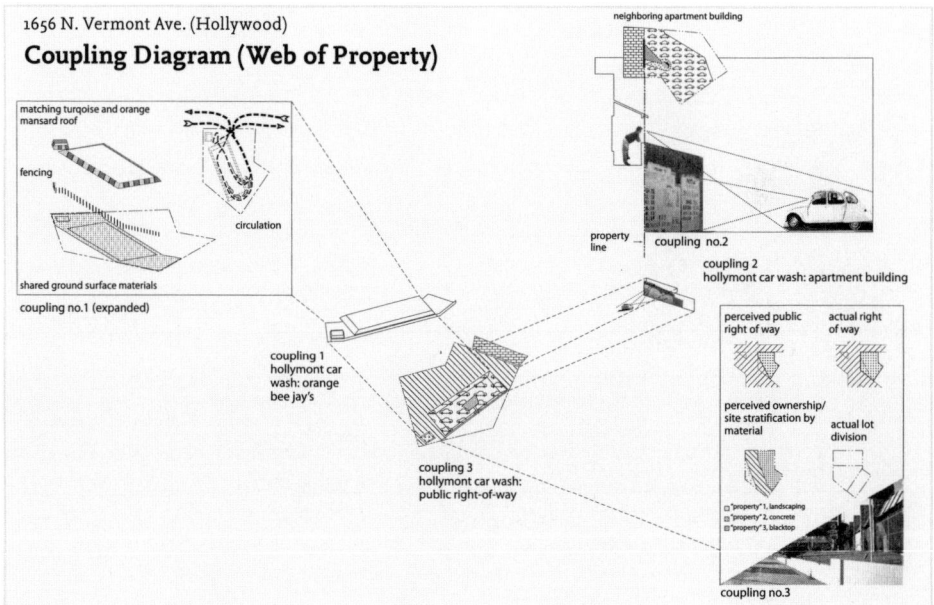

1656 N. Vermont Ave. (Hollywood)

Coupling Diagram (Web of Property)

neighboring apartment building

matching turqoise and orange mansard roof

fencing

circulation

shared ground surface materials

coupling no.1 (expanded)

coupling 1
hollymont car wash: orange bee jay's

coupling 3
hollymont car wash:
public right-of-way

property line

coupling no.2

coupling 2
hollymont car wash: apartment building

perceived public right of way

actual right of way

perceived ownership/ site stratification by material

actual lot division

"property" 1, landscaping
"property" 2, concrete
"property" 3, blacktop

coupling no.3

3

organize themselves into three socioeconomic couplings, of which the actual property owner, Hollymont Car Wash, is the lynchpin (figure 3). The wash building itself sits diagonally across the southeast corner of the site, in order to optimally accommodate the layout of its various (gas/vacuum/wash/dry) functions. The juice bar (Orange BeeJay) camps at the northeast corner of the property and depends, parasitically, upon the car wash, whose patrons are a captive audience while they wait for their cars. This first coupling—a kind of economy-in-miniature—extends to the exchange of practices and materials, as when the Orange BeeJay's

4

5

plates and glasses are rinsed in Hollymont's (rag) washing machines (figure 4). Their association is also branded in visual terms, through the orange-and-turquoise roof fascia and wrought iron fence that wraps both enterprises (figure 2).

The second of the couplings occurs between the car wash and an adjacent apartment building. This relationship consists of an agreement in which the car wash is entitled to the use of the party wall of the apartment building as a "menu" of services. Seemingly in exchange, tenants in the second floor apartments above the sign lounge on a patio above, taking in the spectacle of people washing their cars—a cultural practice widely-popular in L. A.—below (figure 5). The last coupling is perhaps the most subtle and interesting, however; it involves no monetary transaction, but instead trades in what might be termed "impression management." By positioning itself so as to cut across the lot's obliquely-angled street corner, the wash leaves a triangular-shaped residue of its own land (figure 6). Carpeted with lawn and populated by topiary, this area is rendered as an ornamental landscape, presenting itself as a virtual extension of the public right-of-way. The fact that it is actually private property is hinted at only by a billboard (technically a fifth, "uncoupled" rightsholder), and sign for the wash itself. Why would the owner of the wash willingly cede a portion of his own property? Simply put, the car wash, realizing that it could not use that odd sliver of land for its operation, recognized the value it possessed as a tool with which to construct a "clean" public image for itself. That the wash also uses its grey water to irrigate this landscape further underlines their awareness of the collateral benefits that could accrue to them through a seemingly unselfish gesture.

The field of Game Theory, which studies the dynamics of negotiation, lays out similar bargaining strategies players (in the case of the city, these include property owners, neighbors, merchants, city agencies, etc.) use as they cross their own political and economic objectives with a finite set of available options. Following scenarios like the Prisoner's Dilemma, Tit for Tat, Divide-and-Rule, and Even Up, each bargainer (including the owner and his/her architect) must learn how to "play" this dynamic logic according to a consistent and premeditated strategy that must be sufficiently elastic to permit tactical adjustments which take advantage of the knowledge of what the other player(s) hopes to accomplish himself. Even if never precisely predictable, the endgame is nearly always the same: to settle upon an equilibrium enforced by each player's self-interest. More than any other single logic, it is the nature of how this inevitable quid pro quo, or tradeoff is settled that offers the greatest potential as a productive instigator of change-by-design: where design is nothing less than a strategy of both staging and creatively working out the causal relationships that comprise the city-as-ecosystem, and in so doing not only makes evident but actually constitutes the tie that binds them.

An example of the way that the protocols effecting urban change work may be found on a cul-de-sac in a residential neighborhood in Encino, in the San Fernando Valley. Here, amidst an increasing trend toward enclavization, a privately developed public space has been cultivated through the entrepreneurial gerrymandering of neighboring property owners, by using the aforementioned protocols to "hack" the very zoning code that purports to regulate the operating system of suburbia. The owner of the property in question, in a manner consistent with his negotiating style as a talent agent, did not follow an intricately worked out plan in pursuit of his goal, but rather a protocol, or loose set of rules flexibly dependent upon the responses of his bargaining partners. Instead of being pre-determined, the form of the project emerged from this give-and-take process, enabled by the owner's adroitness at operating in the extra-legal area beyond the reach of his property's zoning stipulations regarding land use and setbacks.

In living there, the owner, Rick Messina became frustrated with the inefficiency of the pie-shaped configuration of his lot and the lack of utilizable yard space. It occurred to him that his neighbor had the same lack of utilizable side yard that he did and that together the two adjacent sideyards could be combined into one to form a larger wedge-shaped space that would make for a regulation-size Wiffle ball field (opening spread, figure 7).

For Messina, an inveterate bachelor, playing and watching sports was an opportunity to invite over his friends and clients on the weekends to socialize and network. Being entrepreneurially oriented, Messina sold his neighbor on the idea, with the understanding that

6

7

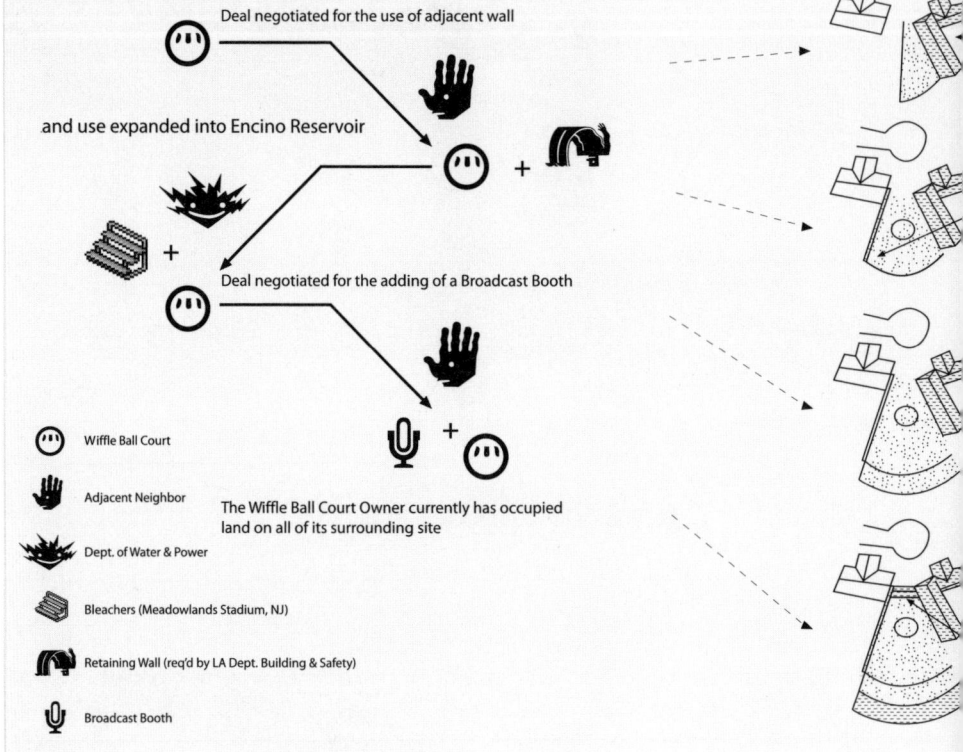

17169 Strawberry Drive (Encino)

Land Acquisition Diagram

Deal negotiated for the use of adjacent wall

and use expanded into Encino Reservoir

Deal negotiated for the adding of a Broadcast Booth

Wiffle Ball Court

Adjacent Neighbor

Dept. of Water & Power

Bleachers (Meadowlands Stadium, NJ)

Retaining Wall (req'd by LA Dept. Building & Safety)

Broadcast Booth

The Wiffle Ball Court Owner currently has occupied land on all of its surrounding site

the latter was entitled to equal use of the jointly owned field. The project began to acquire a momentum and spatial logic of its own, one that, like the bargaining process itself, propelled a sequence of further agreements (figure 8). Though the splay of the field was wide enough, the outfield was still rather shallow, due to the fact that the rear of both properties ran up a hillside. Messina proposed to excavate the lower portion of the hillside and install a fifteen foot-high retaining wall in order to extend the length of the playing surface (figure 9, 10). The land immediately behind the wall, however, belonged to the Department of Water and Power (DWP). Once approached by Messina however, the DWP agreed, because it turned out that the project would improve both hillside access and drainage—provided that Messina build a ramp and stairs to the flat area they required behind the wall. Quick to recognize this as an opportunity to add bleacher seating in the outfield, he immediately agreed. As coincidence would have it, his contractor had a cousin working at the very same time on the demolition of New Jersey's Meadowlands Stadium—within days, several rows of seating arrived in Encino. The most recent of Messina's deals was the erection of a second-story bridge over home plate, spanning between his own residence and that of his neighbor's, to serve as a public portal to the field from the street (figure 11)—also an improved easement for the

ORIGINAL

ACQUISITION 1
(Neighbor's Sideyard,
Rightfield Wall)

9

ACQUISITION 2
(DWP Property)

ACQUISITION 3
(Add Bleachers)

10

ACQUISITION 4
(Add Broadcast Booth)

11

17169 Strawberry Drive (Encino)

Series of Bilateral Exchanges

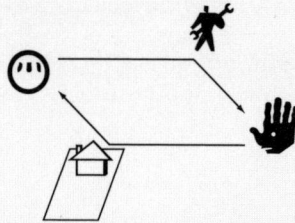

Wall given to Messina in exchange for usage of field

1 Deal negotiated for the use of adjacent neighbor's sideyard

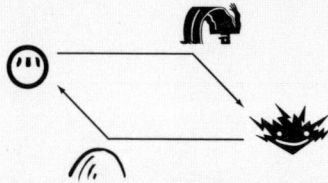

Hillside given to Messina in exchange for ramp access

2 Lend use expanded into DWP Property

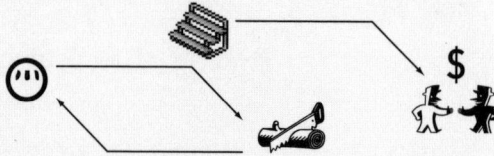

Stadium seats given to Messina in exchange for cash and favor

3 Deal negotiated for the Stadium Seats

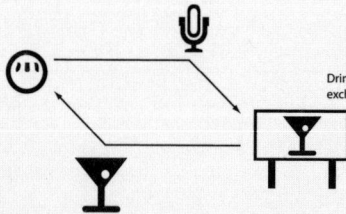

Drinks given to Messina in exchange for advertisment

4 Deal negotiated for the free drinks

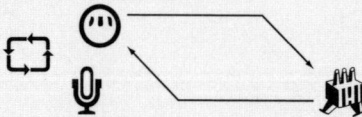

Space given to Messina in exchange for landuse

Hillside

land use

Favor

Dept. of Building & Safety

Beer + Liquor Distributors

Ramp Access

Work?

Wiffle Ball Court

Adjacent Neighbor

Dept. of Water & Power

Bleachers (Meadowlands Stadium, NJ

Broadcast Booth

12

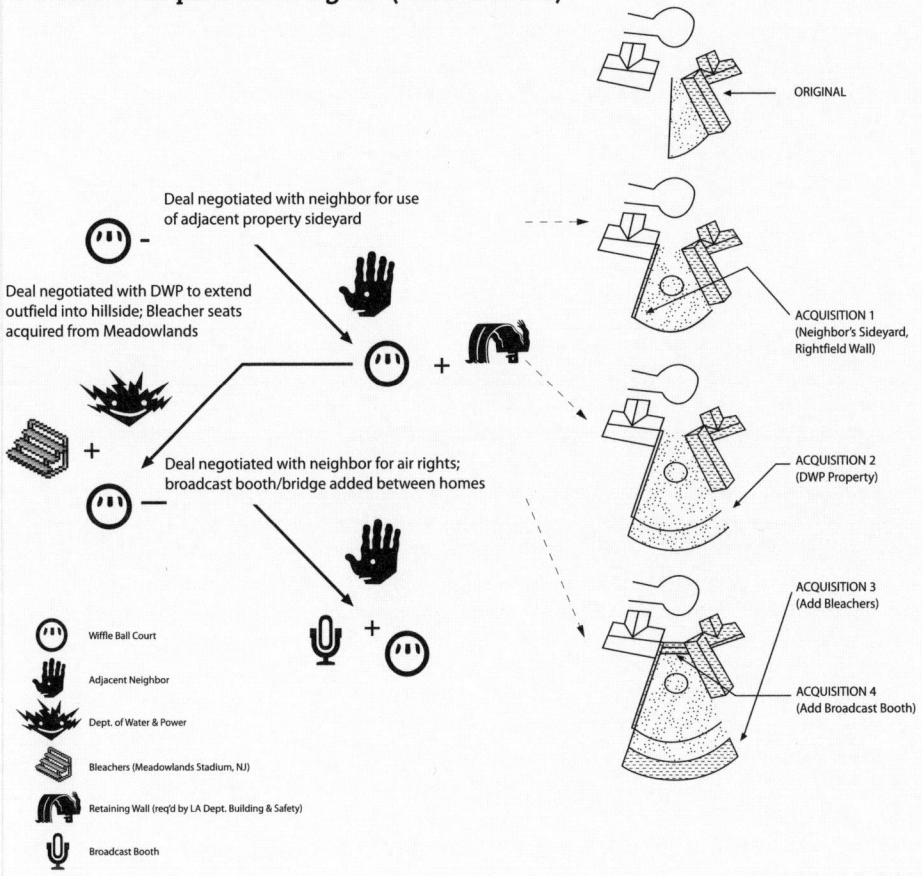

17169 Strawberry Drive (Encino)

Successive Acquisitions Diagram (Site Evolution)

ORIGINAL

Deal negotiated with neighbor for use of adjacent property sideyard

Deal negotiated with DWP to extend outfield into hillside; Bleacher seats acquired from Meadowlands

ACQUISITION 1
(Neighbor's Sideyard, Rightfield Wall)

Deal negotiated with neighbor for air rights; broadcast booth/bridge added between homes

ACQUISITION 2
(DWP Property)

ACQUISITION 3
(Add Bleachers)

ACQUISITION 4
(Add Broadcast Booth)

Wiffle Ball Court

Adjacent Neighbor

Dept. of Water & Power

Bleachers (Meadowlands Stadium, NJ)

Retaining Wall (req'd by LA Dept. Building & Safety)

Broadcast Booth

13

DWP to access its property. The bridge itself actually functions as a broadcast booth for his comedian-clients to entreat friends and neighbors to a humorous play-by-play of the games.

The public status of Strawberry Field (named after the street on which the owner lives) was not preordained. While he may not have had a fixed plan in mind, he was never without one altogether either—it was, like a protocol, simply plastic in its design, poised to take advantage of the opportunities that came his way (figure 12, 13), all of which could in the end be easily tied together visually with a coat of the same paint color. With each new deal Messina struck, another stakeholder was welcomed into the fold, and the web of interests arrayed around his property so widened—just as it will continue to in response to any future circumstances or opportunities that may present themselves.[5]

[5] Roger Sherman, *Under the Influence: Negotiating the Complex Logic of Urban Property* (St. Paul, MN: University of Minnesota Press, forthcoming 2008).

Another remarkable instance of the same phenomenon may be found on a tiny triangular patch of land located in Los Angeles at the border between the City of Beverly Hills and the commercial towers of Century City. On it stands an enigmatic tower-like structure clad in a multi-colored floral pattern graphic (figure 14).[6] Though a familiar landmark to thousands of Angelenos who commute past it daily on their way to and from work, few could identify what it is or to whom it belongs. In fact, this "accidental obelisk" is an oil derrick marking the drilling operations of Venoco Oil Company, which owns the mineral rights to a roughly 800-acre oil field. The rig has been at the site since 1908, preceding Century City by several decades, although it has been inactive since 1982. It remains on the site only in order to legally enforce the company's interest, reserving its right to drill in the future should they see fit. The derrick's more readily recognizable skeletal structure was exposed until the 1970s, when the development of Century City brought thousands of office workers nearby, and political pressure was exerted on Venoco to muffle the noise emitted by the drilling, which it did by covering the rig in gray acoustical cladding.

However, since the derrick became inactive and the cladding was no longer needed, the tower has undergone yet another transformation, thanks to a non-profit arts organization that recognized that the padding still had a value in being retained as a means of camouflaging what would otherwise be considered by its tony Beverly Hills neighbors to be a visual nuisance or eyesore. Additionally, Portraits of Hope, the non-profit, saw potential for the tower as a three dimensional billboard terminating a two-mile long axial view down a major thoroughfare, waiting to be given a message. They bargained with both Venoco and the City of Beverly Hills to transform the inadvertent landmark (which they refer to as Project 9865) to memorialize and call attention to the plight of terminally-ill children by having such children paint the subsequent floral pattern that now appears on the cladding.

Over the history of the site's development, the "Flower Tower", as it has come to be called, has proved to be more than resilient in response to the change in circumstances both on-site (from drilling to no more drilling) and off (neighboring development and cancer awareness). With the intensification of land use came a singular imageability, born of the history of and party to the negotiation itself (figures 15, 16, 17, 18). Significantly, this is largely the result of a certain formal potential that was, however unintentionally, built in from the start, giving the derrick the decoy-like ability to attract unforeseen audiences that later proved to be agents of (its) formal transformation. Though privately operated, it operates as a form of, what could be called, speculative infrastructure, in its ability to be retroactive and pro-active at the same time. Instead of expressing or indexing change, as seems to be the preoccupation of much contemporary architecture, it precipitates future change, for which it is also "designed" to adapt in real time. By being catalytic rather than merely conciliatory, it represents a paradigm that is both more truly adaptive—and speculative—than the indexical model which claims those emergence-related traits as its moniker.

---

[6] Sherman, *Under the Influence.* Special thanks and credit to Alexandra Loew, who was responsible for the site analysis, including the drawings appearing here.

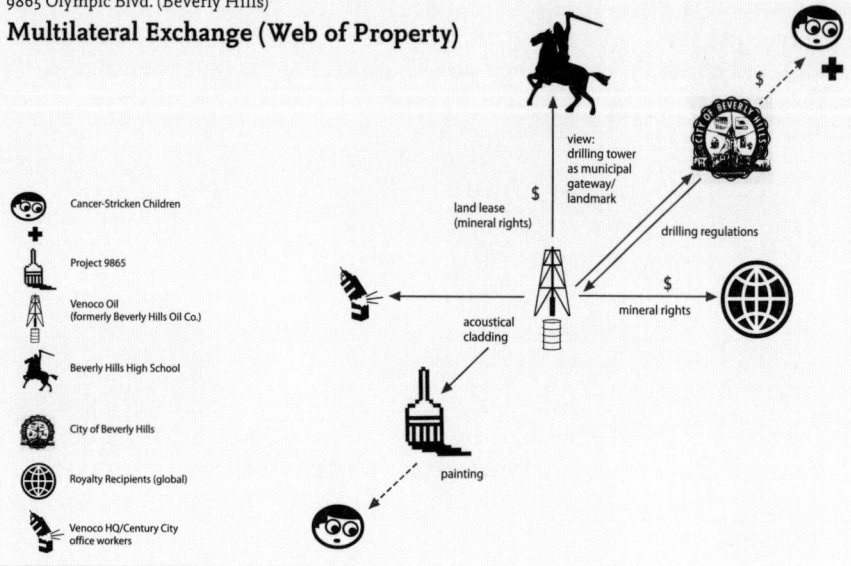

9865 Olympic Blvd. (Beverly Hills)

Multilateral Exchange (Web of Property)

Cancer-Stricken Children

Project 9865

Venoco Oil
(formerly Beverly Hills Oil Co.)

Beverly Hills High School

City of Beverly Hills

Royalty Recipients (global)

Venoco HQ/Century City
office workers

view:
drilling tower
as municipal
gateway/
landmark

land lease
(mineral rights)

drilling regulations

acoustical
cladding

mineral rights

painting

15

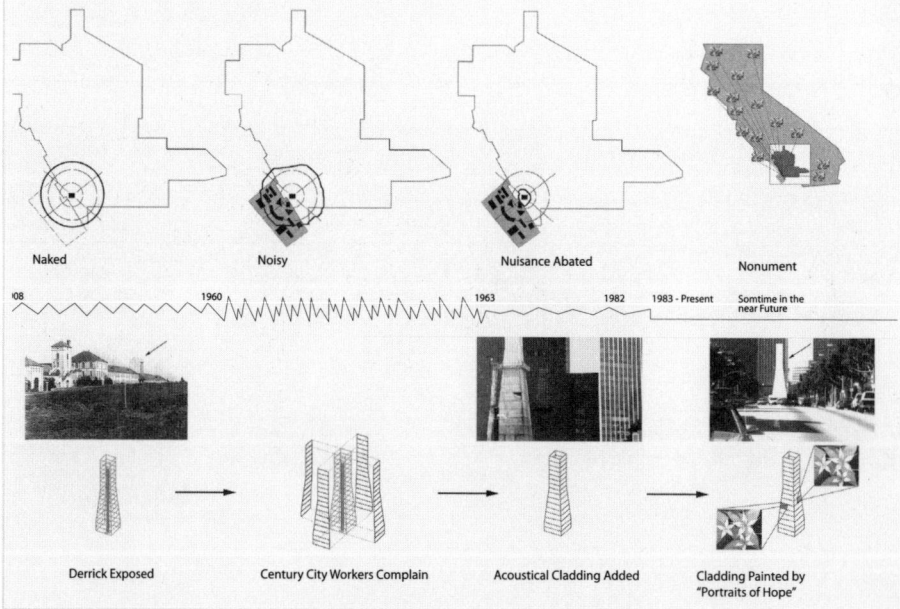

9865 Olympic Blvd. (Beverly Hills)

Petroleum Palimpsest (Site Evolution)

Naked

Noisy

Nuisance Abated

Nonument

'08   1960   1963   1982   1983 - Present   Somtime in the
                                                                            near Future

Derrick Exposed

Century City Workers Complain

Acoustical Cladding Added

Cladding Painted by
"Portraits of Hope"

16

194

9865 Olympic Blvd. (Beverly Hills)
Interruption Diagram

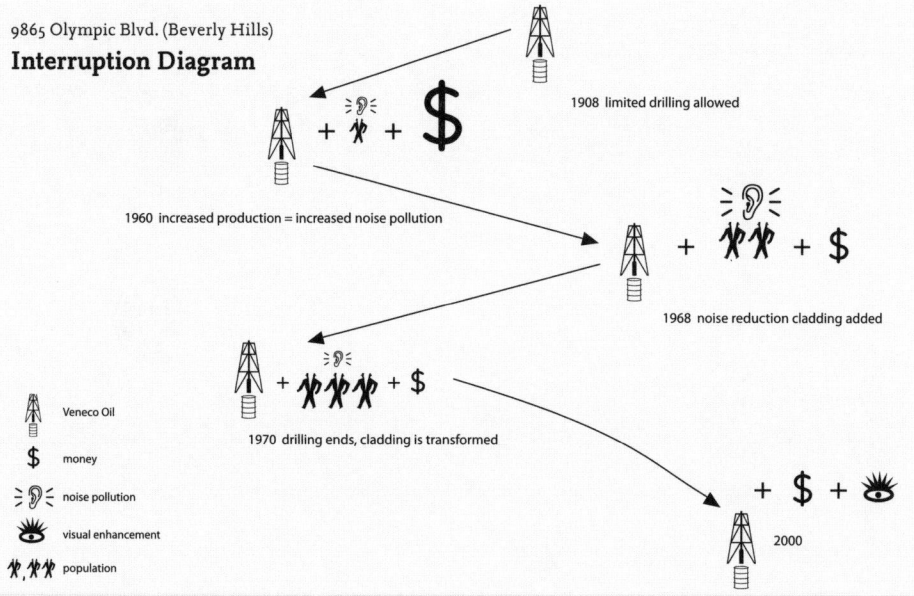

1908 limited drilling allowed

1960 increased production = increased noise pollution

1968 noise reduction cladding added

Veneco Oil

money

noise pollution

visual enhancement

population

1970 drilling ends, cladding is transformed

2000

17

9865 Olympic Blvd. (Beverly Hills)
Accidental Obelisk (Coupling Diagram/Web of Property)

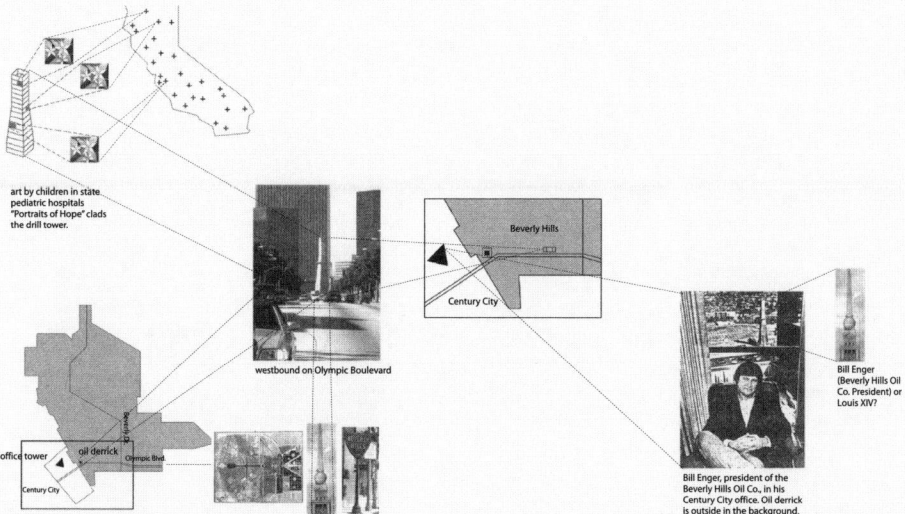

art by children in state pediatric hospitals "Portraits of Hope" clads the drill tower.

Beverly Hills

Century City

westbound on Olympic Boulevard

office tower   oil derrick
Century City

Bill Enger
(Beverly Hills Oil
Co. President) or
Louis XIV?

Bill Enger, president of the
Beverly Hills Oil Co., in his
Century City office. Oil derrick
is outside in the background.

18

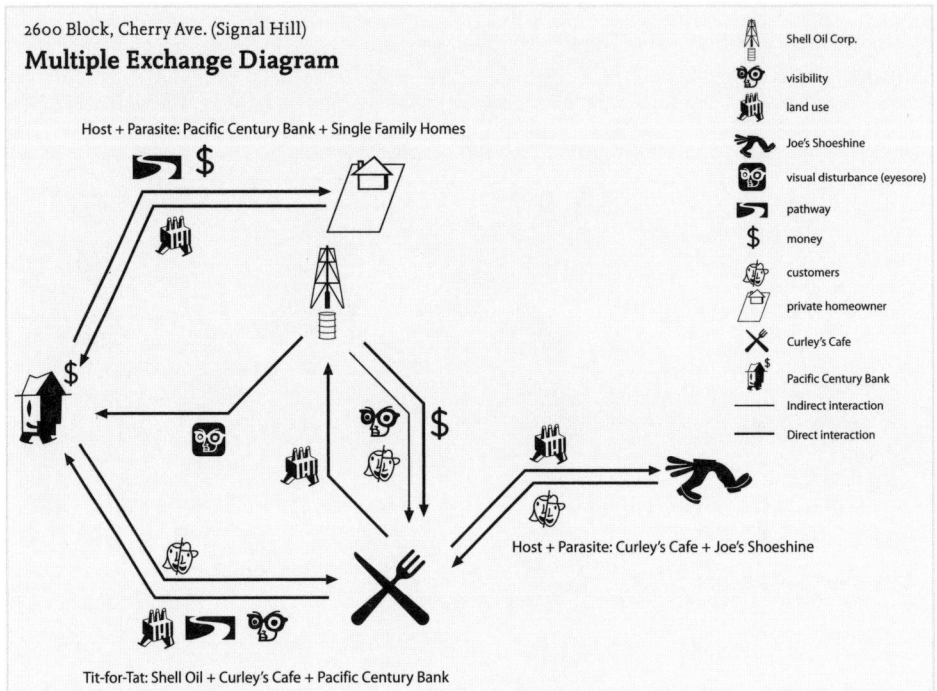

2600 Block, Cherry Ave. (Signal Hill)
Multiple Exchange Diagram

Host + Parasite: Pacific Century Bank + Single Family Homes

Host + Parasite: Curley's Cafe + Joe's Shoeshine

Tit-for-Tat: Shell Oil + Curley's Cafe + Pacific Century Bank

Shell Oil Corp.
visibility
land use
Joe's Shoeshine
visual disturbance (eyesore)
pathway
money
customers
private homeowner
Curley's Cafe
Pacific Century Bank
——— Indirect interaction
——— Direct interaction

A fourth site, on Cherry Avenue in Signal Hill (figure 20), presents perhaps the most robust demonstration of the earlier discussed protocols of adaptation. The extraordinary interdependence between the parties—which range in scale from homeowner to global conglomerate—together constitute a veritable urban economy-in-microcosm (figure 19). The players include: Curley's Cafe; Joe the Shoeshine Man (figure 21); three derricks owned and operated by Shell Oil (figure 20); to the north, Home Bank, with its surrounding parking lots; and to the west, across the alley, two Craftsman Style residences that date back to the earliest days of Signal Hill, currently belonging to the Denny and Hockenbrocht households. Though each land user sits on and controls the development and use of its own individual parcel(s)—with the exception of Shell, the Shoeshine and Curley's, which share a single property—these parties interact with one another in a way which lends the block a curious cohesiveness without any of the buildings looking the least alike. In tracing its development, one finds that a remarkable cause-and-effect pattern in the (trans)actions of the landowners has resulted in the complex land use arrangements which exist there today. This is exemplified in the subset of relations forged between the cafe, the shoeshine, and the oil company (figure 22). The shoeshine is physically and economically dependent on Curley's, sharing its sidewall, parking area and clientele. Shell's rigs also share the lot, having been the first rightsholders there.

The positioning and re-positioning of the two rigs traces the evolving relationship between the two parties and how they "learned" to accommodate one another. The original orientation of the pumps was, like all those of Shell, to cardinal north. With the arrival of Curley's, a second organizational "template" was overlaid upon the same parcel, primarily

20

21

2600 Block, Cherry Ave. (Signal Hill)

Negotiated Access (Shell Oil Rigs: Curley's Cafe Parking)

Shell Oil Corp.

Joe's Shoeshine

private homeowner

Curley's Cafe

Pacific Century Bank

future
site of
Curley'

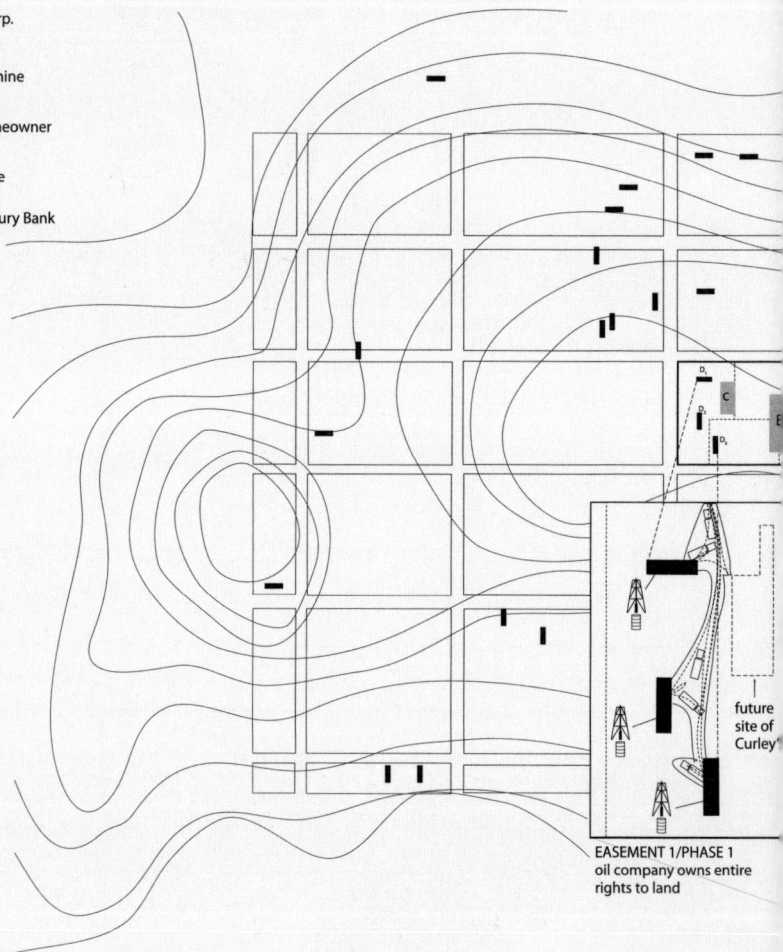

EASEMENT 1/PHASE 1
oil company owns entire
rights to land

22

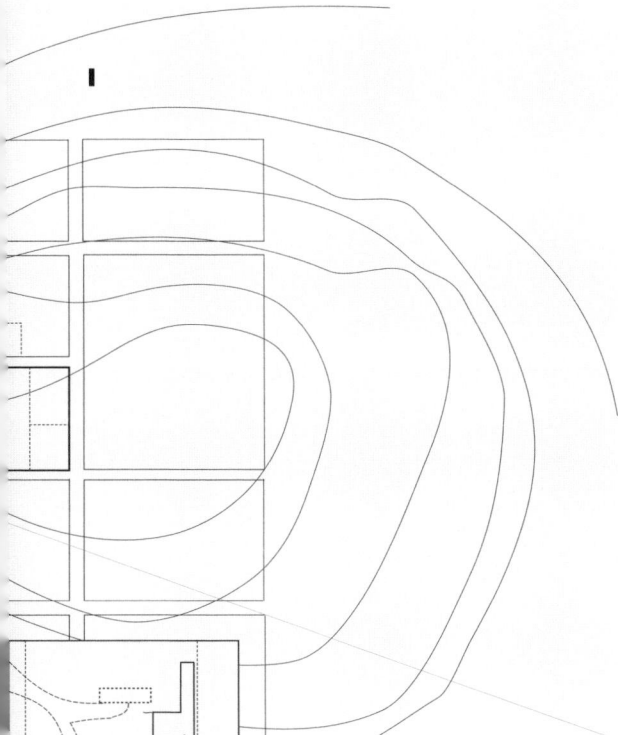

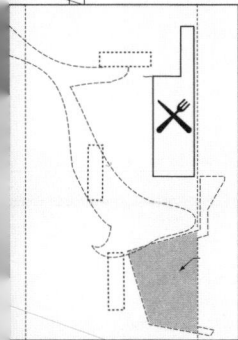

future
easement
from Curley's
to bank

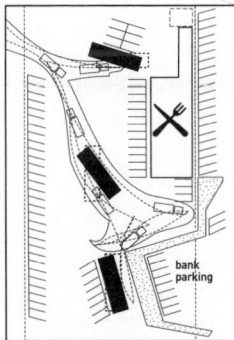

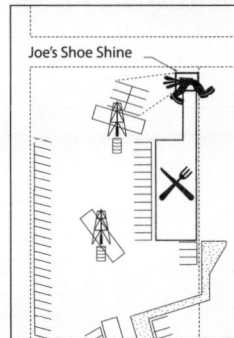

Joe's Shoe Shine

EASEMENT 2/PHASE 2
Surface rights are sold to Curley's, Oil
company maintains an easement for
truck access to rigs.

bank
parking

EASEMENT2
an easement granted by Curley's
to Joe's Shoeshine

EASEMENT 1/PHASE 3
Oil derricks are rotated to maximize
parking for Curley's Cafe Oil company's
easement and Curley's parking layout
are adjusted accordingly:
mutual accomodation

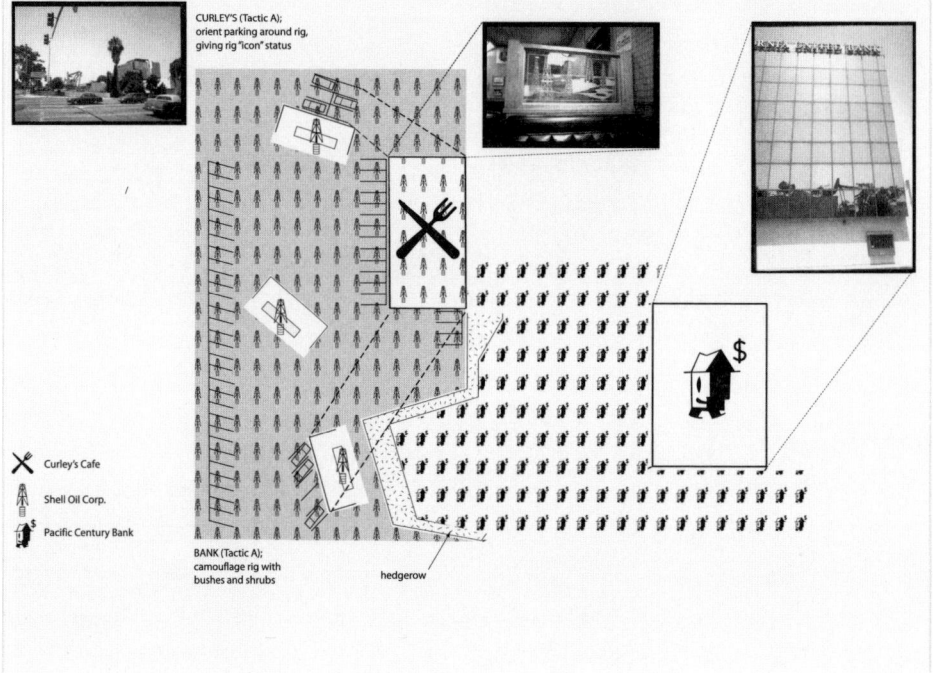

Spheres of Influence (Shell Oil/Curley's Cafe/Pacific Century Bank)

CURLEY'S (Tactic A);
orient parking around rig,
giving rig "icon" status

Curley's Cafe

Shell Oil Corp.

Pacific Century Bank

BANK (Tactic A);
camouflage rig with
bushes and shrubs

hedgerow

23

for a customer parking lot and drop-off area. However, this layout did not correspond to the existing orientations and servicing patterns of the wells. In order to accommodate the new owner of the ground rights it had just sold off, it was necessary for Shell to rotate its pumps in such a way as would minimize the loss of parking spaces and obstruction of vehicular circulation. Beyond this, however—what many rightsholders would have considered a nuisance or eyesore—the presence of the rigs has ironically had just the opposite effect: namely, that of distinguishing Curley's as a veritable L. A. landmark; and a critical component of its financial success. In fact, Curley's own behavior reflects this: 1) like the pumps, it operates twenty-four hours a day; 2) it makes no effort to conceal the two rigs; 3) the image of the derrick is celebrated throughout the Cafe interior in etched glass, and even figures prominently in its own logo (figure 23). So long as the derricks remain (probably even after there is oil left to pump), Curley's will prosper. Like an ecosystem, it thrives on the presence of the derricks, just as Joe the Shoeshine Man relies in turn upon Curley's customers for its subsistence.

Meanwhile, both Shell's and Curley's interests are spatially entangled with Home Bank, a portion of whose property (also the site of the third derrick), is actually ground-leased from Curley's. Given the overlap of rights in this location, it is not surprising that it is the most visually complicated area of the entire site, a product of the move-countermove structure

2600 Block, Cherry Ave. (Signal Hill)

**Negotiated Access
(Pacific Century Bank:
Denny/Hockenbrocht)**

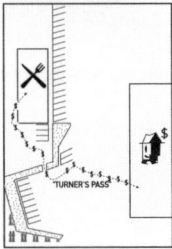

hidden Rod Shop

Denny & Hockenbrocht

Gardenia Alley

EASEMENT 4/Phase 2
pedestrian walkway negotiated with
Denny family across lot immediately
adjacent to bank

EASEMENT 4/Phase 1
Hockenbrocht property is acquired by
bank for bank customer parking

EASEMENT 3
A.K.A. "Turner's Pass"
makeshift passage from bank
to restaurant

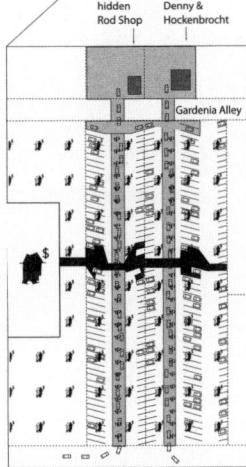

"TURNER'S PASS"

EASEMENT 4/Phase 3
private residences adopt drive aisle through bank
parking lot as extended driveway

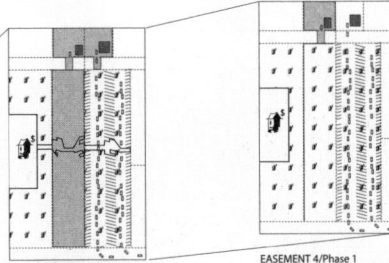

private homeowner

Curley's Cafe

Pacific Century Bank

24

of their co-evolution (figure 24). In an effort to camouflage what it considers the unsightly presence of a rightsholder (Shell) whose long-term presence on the site was long ago legally secured, the Bank screens the rig with a berm and hedgerow. This attitude is in obvious contrast to the other two pumps, which stand as de facto advertisements for Curley's. At the same time, the aforementioned entanglement between bank and cafe is emblematized by "Turner's Pass"—a hand-built, bridge-like passageway through the hedgerow which provides a shortcut between the two (figure 24, 25, 27). The owner of Curley's built it to facilitate the flow of goods and people between the two businesses (Curley's banks with Home, while the bank's employees and patrons frequent the café).

The bank's north parking lot is the subject of a similarly complex set of circumstances (figure 24). Emerging from the building and crossing through the lot is a serpentine land-scaped path which inexplicably ends halfway across its width (figure 26). This oddity is explained by the history of the bank's development. When it first needed to expand from its original lot (on which the building is located), the adjacent northern parcel was not available. Home Bank instead acquired the next one to the north, having succeeded in negotiating with the neighboring property owner to obtain an easement allowing customer access across that property from the new remote parking area to the bank itself, which the landscaped path

25

26

was built to demarcate. When the same neighbor eventually agreed to sell the intervening parcel to the bank in order to accommodate yet more parking, the path was preserved as a site amenity, its inexplicable termination halfway across the parking lot a record of the bank property's complicated evolution. In a final, ironic twist, the Hockenbrocht family, the homeowners to whom the first property purchased by the bank belonged, requested that upon the sale of their property to the bank, they be granted an easement that would entitle them to use the bank's parking lot as a de facto driveway and parking area.

Like the children's string game of Cat's Cradle, the back-and-forth process associated with bargaining successively builds formal and organizational complexity—and interest—into the outcome as a direct result of its response to contingency. Through an aesthetic of apparent haphazardness, it can be read as a history of the property to that point, including the bargaining strategies and/or tactics of the contending parties; the disparity in strength between their material resources or symbolic power; and the exchange value of certain site attributes (each party's assessment of the terms of a given quid pro quo). Not unlike ecological communities, properties are functionally interconnected in networks that reflect such exchanges of energy, materials, and services. Rightsholders acquire energy from and help each other, but also compete with each other for the available resources.

That the logic of bargaining dictates an outcome that is by definition emergent challenges not only conventional forms of architectural production, such as that grounded in the *parti,* but equally those so-called "autonomous" methods that are so popularly explored and discussed today.[7] In contrast, negotiation offers a basis for form and organization that is grounded in the factors that precondition them. Design becomes a medium through which differences and conflicts can be worked out between interests, each with its own set of exclusive concerns, yet whose accommodation is necessary to the realization of the project-as-a-whole. As much as the above case studies symptomize change, they only do so post facto, rather than actually illustrating how form might be initially conceived so as to suggest how it may be shaped in a future situation. Their inclusion here is therefore not meant to suggest an interest in formalizing the notion of contingency, as if change needs to be legible in order to be operative. To the contrary: it is doubtful that design can ever "express" future change. Rather, all the architect can do instead is to look at design as a means of "setting a trap" to capture potential change—change that is waiting to be sprung or unleashed.

This means counting on change rather than simply looking for ways to spread it or buffer its effects. Architecture today needs design strategies that possess the ability not merely to maintain themselves in the face of change, but that actually realize the constructive role that anticipating change can play in opening the window for novelty. In order to do this, the architect must, like that of any good player in a game (like real estate) that deals with probability, provide or build in the "bait" that will tilt the odds ever so slightly in favor of his or her intent, without at the same time artificially limiting the outcomes or providing inferior alternatives. By "bait," I mean specific architectural and/or programmatic elements which have both a provisional immediate use, and at the same time sow the seeds for a variety of plausible futures—serving as attractors or nuisances which influence (encourage or deter) future choices and development in a non-prescriptive way. Game theory suggests that looser rather than tighter strategies are most instrumental in this regard, due to their capacity to be transformed and made more complex; they allow this bait to be placed within them

---

[7] Though this interest in so-called "authorless" or "autonomous" methods of formal and spatial organization has certainly been taken up by others over the last decade or so, the problem that often hobbles those arguments is that they are in actuality based upon an a priori rule set whose values belong to the architect, not to the marketplace. Largely because of this, those projects are unable to escape their own self-referentiality.

rather than attempting to incorporate it into the design of the trap itself. Like the children's game of chutes and ladders, the strategy is less an index of past change as it is a valve-like diagram of (numerous combinations of) possible choices or futures.

To do so hinges on the ability to operate at the cusp between control and disorganization. Heretofore, however, architects and planners have tended to dichotomize these two conditions—aligning themselves with the former and against the latter—artificially limiting themselves from exploring "fuzzier", more self-regulating design strategies.[8] What is needed is a shift to a type of thinking ahead in which, unlike scenario planning (in which form is a direct outgrowth of intricate scripting), form comes first, and becomes a conceit for the unfolding of different and unexpected futures.[9] Emblematized in the accidental landmark in Beverly Hills, this architecture does not exert one hundred percent control, a hundred percent of the time, but operates rather as a kind of preemptive infrastructure comprised of a few select elements or design features whose particularity is consciously but only incidentally—rather than performatively—related to possible (present or future) use. Unlike conventional infrastructure, it is strategized not merely to support, but to attract, leverage, and ultimately influence other scenarios that occur around and in connection with them, but which are less predictable.

Such an approach is especially pertinent to American cities today, where with the exception of a precious few publicly funded projects, most development, regardless of size, must provide public amenities of its own. The Bilbao-effect notwithstanding, this form of attraction is distinct from that lent by the cachet of a renowned architect, which can be fleeting at best. Instead, it requires a design which a) is singular enough in its imageability to lure the initial interest necessary to leverage future investments; b) whose formal characteristics are also encoded with an array of traits, initially hidden in plain sight, which will evidence themselves in response to differing audiences and contexts of use to which it may become subject over time; and c) at the same time is organized in such a way as to help shape those eventual transformations. Architecture can in this way renew its interest and relevance to the contemporary city not merely by virtue of its ability to sustain and adapt to change, but—as the enormity of popular attention accorded today to the culture of "the makeover" attests—by making change itself a spectacle and marketable asset in its own right.

In this "brave new city," architecture is a commodity—like everything else, tied first and foremost to speculation in future identity, and real estate values, rather than as a response to context. Rather than assessing what will work based upon past trends or current data, architects would do well to approach the problem of confronting risk more like entrepreneurs, who consider what could be—namely, by imagining how design can be conceived and strategized as a decoy to create a supply which creates its own demand, creating new and latent audiences in the process.

---

8 Stan Allen "The Logistics of Context," Stan Allen and Diana Agrest, eds. *Practice: Architecture, Technique and Representation* (Amsterdam: G+B Arts International, 2000), 159-60. Allen points out that the natural and man-made environment are, in their own ways, ecosystems whose evolution is a direct function of their ability to survive and adapt to change, in (the form of) land conversion, driven by institutional decisions, population growth and economic forces.

9 Here I am referring to what R.E. Somol refers to as "the Projective." See "Yes is More", his foreword to Sherman, *Under the Influence.*

Preceding pages: The 1.5-million-square-foot IKEA distribution center, Tejon Industrial Complex

Deborah Richmond

CONSUMERS GONE WILD

DISTRIBUTION

Descending out of the "Grapevine" north of Los Angeles, the I-5 is a river of asphalt traversing a mountainous landscape of suburban communities, day-trip ski areas, and crystalline reservoirs. As the freeway exits the mountain pass to make a four-hour beeline through California's Central Valley to San Francisco, the Tejon Ranch Industrial Center comes into view. Rows upon rows of shipping containers, lined up like nursing puppies along a linear array of loading docks, feed 1.7 million contiguous square feet of fully automated warehousing. Emblazoned with signs saying "IKEA," "Oneida," and "Petro," Tejon Ranch Industrial Center is the warehousing and distribution center of the future: a super-size box building and trucking "amenity" spread over cheap land like an unleavened pancake.

The Tejon Ranch Industrial Center marks the southernmost outpost of the latest territory to replace downtown Los Angeles as the container transfer hub linking the Ports of Los Angeles and Long Beach with the rest of the continent. The Ports of Los Angeles and Long Beach are monstrous, dominating North American shipping; together they receive more than three times the cargo volume of the next largest American port, the port of New York and New Jersey.[1] But this size is increasingly a liability making these ports potential targets of environmental regulations, labor demands, and terrorist attacks. By siting these new distribution centers outside of the city, shippers create a buffer of goods to hedge against

[1] United States Department of Transportation, "Freight Facts and Figures 2006," Figure 2-7. Top 25 U.S. Foreign Trade Freight Gateways by Value: 2005 ($ billions), 2006, http://ops.fhwa.dot.gov/freight/freight_analysis/nat_freight_stats/docs/06factsfigures/fig2_7.htm.

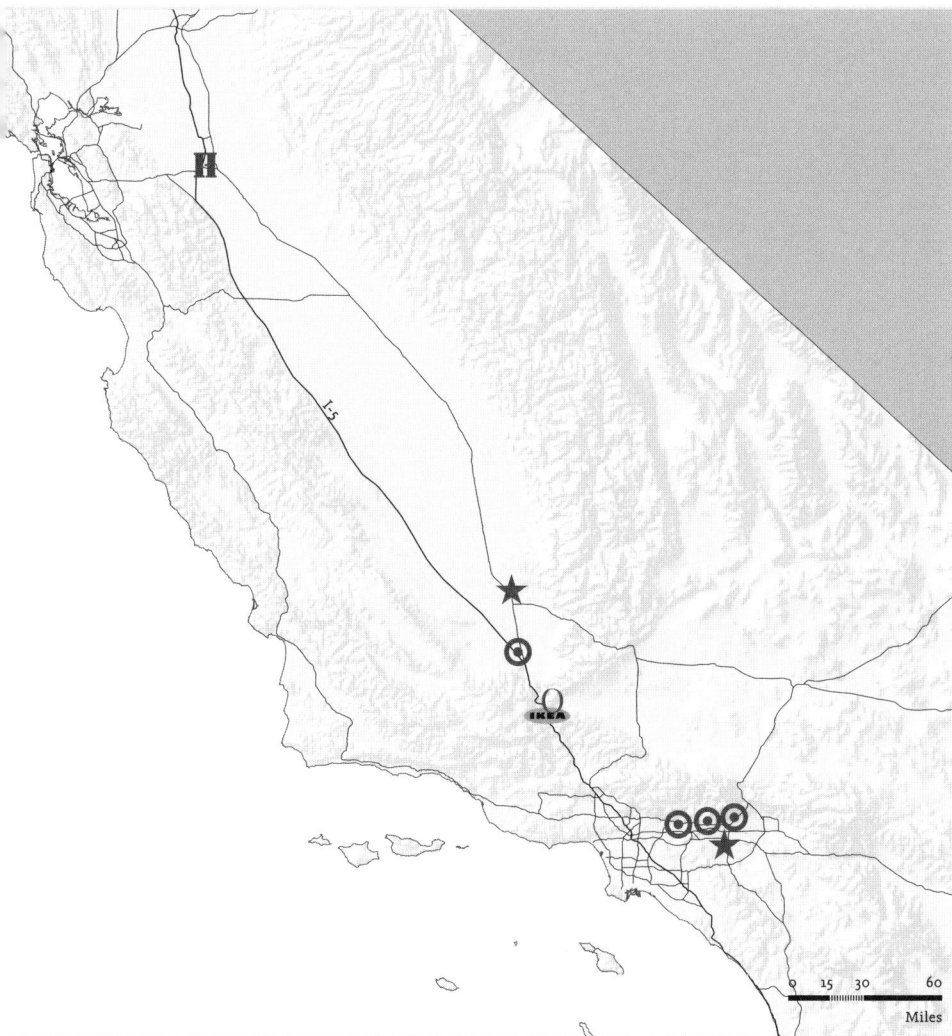

*Super-distribution
centers*

*Source: author and
companies' Web sites*

The Home Depot **H**
Ikea **IKEA**
Oneida ⭕
Target ◎
Wal-Mart ★
Interstate Highways ---
Major Water Bodies ▬

contingencies while reducing their reliance on the San Pedro ports, taking on shipments from ports in Seattle, Oakland, San Diego, and other points on the West Coast. These retailers, which include some of the biggest players in the American economy—giants like Wal-Mart, IKEA, Home Depot, and Target—array their distribution centers across the valley floor like so many tomato and alfalfa fields.

Oneida distribution center, Tejon Industrial Complex

Regardless of its desire to suppress the fact, Los Angeles has long been a port town. The ports of Los Angeles and Long Beach—together the largest in the nation and ranked in the top ten in the world in terms of container handling—feed the collective production of the Far East economies of China, Singapore, and Taiwan to the city, and beyond it, to the United States.[2] According to the online journal *Industrial Real Estate*, "the nation sucked in more than 120 million tons of containerized merchandise in 2004, up 140% from 50 million just a decade before."[3]

Slowly moving a giant, post-Panamax vessel carrying up to 12,000 shipping containers from one deep-water port in Hong Kong to another in Los Angeles is relatively uncomplicated and so cost-effective that for many years this has been enough to offset the costs of "drayage" (moving the containers off ships to warehouses and then to retail outlets) either by rail or by truck. Massive underwriting of the goods-handling infrastructure by local governments has kept the cost of shuttling goods rapidly through the Southern California metropolis low. Running adjacent to Alameda Boulevard, the $2 billion, 23-mile-long open trench of the Alameda Corridor conveys trains from the Ports of Los Angeles and Long Beach to rail yards near the city's downtown and on to points beyond in Kern County and the Inland Empire. Allowing double-height, stacked trains to pass while eliminating traffic conflicts at over 200 intersections between the ports and downtown, the corridor mitigates many drayage problems such as unfortunate collisions between passenger vehicles and trains full of televisions, blouses, and microcomputers. The corridor's effortless, below-grade flow through the city encourages the myth that consumer goods move freely around the world, benefiting everyone who gets their cut.

Roughly 60% of the goods coming through the Ports of Los Angeles and Long Beach are distributed to the Southern California region, while only one-third make their way onto local railroads (most notably via the Alameda Corridor) for distribution to the Midwest, South, and East Coast.

Tejon Industrial Complex

It is this character as a throughput city that has ultimately marked the landscape of Los Angeles more than water, more than cars, and more than movies. The transfer of shipping containers from ships to trains, trucks, container transfer buildings, retail outlets, and even homes, has been supported by a particularly voracious and narcissistic consumer whose ideal home is the city of Los Angeles itself, but whose influence radiates outward along truck routes and rail lines to the rest of the country. Shipping containers, the main actors in this supply chain logistics ballet, perform the task of squeezing the diverse material variety of the world's production—the global Play-Doh of consumer goods—through millions of 8' X 8' X 20' TEUs (Twenty-foot Equivalent Units). The appetites for material wealth known in the Middle Ages as gluttony, avarice, and covetousness— refigured today as super-sizing, consumer desire, and status consumption—have become smooth, featureless, and manageable through containerization.

---

[2] Port statistics compiled from the U. S. Department of Transportation's Bureau of Transportation Statistics for 2004.

[3] Matt Hudgins, "Rising Tide of Imports" in *Industrial Real Estate*, April 1, 2006, http://nreionline.com/mag/ real_estate_rising_tide_imports/index.html.

Containerization is brilliant at masking material disparity. The perfect foil, shipping containers represent the sterile latex barrier between the inequities of globalized industrialization (child labor, indentured servitude, subsistence living) and the fetishized individuality of the consumer—the belief that our possessions define our identity, indeed, that such an identity even exists.

The movement of consumer goods through the city creates an urban dialectic, as humans compete with their possessions for open space on roads and in the domestic interiors in which goods eventually accumulate. The physical impact of freight traffic on the city of Los Angeles has been to void out and genericize the externalized built environment while at the same time exerting an opposite force of hyper-internalization consisting of the construction of fantasy environments within the private realm, a force based almost exclusively on the accumulation of consumer goods. To walk down a street in Los Angeles is to become isolated in a public, transitory space of blind facades and low, blank walls where the only escape is to slip behind the line of private property, into the control space of consumer constructs. It is no surprise that the city that distributes such goods also fabricates the images of their desire. Hollywood may exist solely to excite the appetites of those that live outside the city, thereby feeding the city's true economy of relentless imports. Beyond the walls of the studio, much of the city is used as a film set, large quantities of empty enclosed space acting as stages for the production of images—a counterpart to the empty box buildings that warehouse and distribute the goods themselves—the talismans of consumer desire that accompany the image.

Any utopian image of Los Angeles's freeways is undone by the heaving eighteen-wheelers that shuffle goods from port to destination, posing serious risks to the safety of passenger vehicles, mere bulbs of metal gathering like small pinballs between troughs of container-laden trucks. Small vehicles are stung by sharp metal debris, bed-sheet-sized tire blowouts and a lack of visibility. The result is that the much-exalted experience of driving the area's freeways has been replaced by a kind of furtive stop-and-go along fortress-like walls of container-laden trucks bumper to bumper from Los Angeles to Seattle. Surface streets do not fare much better. Several transportation projects are on the boards today in Los Angeles to reshape roads, alleys, and driveways in older urban core areas to accommodate truck movements. Entire neighborhoods and interstate highways are sacrificed for the movement of goods. In part because of the purely spatial and physical strains placed on the city, the trend away from agglomerated infrastructural projects toward a more fragmented approach is well underway.

Too Late for Just-in-Time The new warehousing super-centers of Kern County represent a fundamental shift in shipping. The unprecedented rise in the volume of goods moving through container ports has negatively impacted port cities like Los Angeles, generating enormous amounts of pollution and traffic, and new laws—some already in place, some still being drafted—limit the rate and density of container movements throughout urban areas. In 2006, after the Southern California Air Quality Management District demonstrated that San Pedro (the city surrounding the Port of Los Angeles) has the highest rate of lung cancer in California, a new "Green Ports" plan was enacted, demanding that dock-side electricity be provided to ships so that they can turn off their diesel engines while in the port.[4] Rising costs of fuel have further degraded the efficiency of ground shipping. Demands by organized labor are impeding the relentless round-the-clock operation of the ports. On the West Coast, a longshore workers' strike in 2002 underlined the vulnerability of "just-in-time" goods movement through Los Angeles and other ports that closed over a five-week period.

---

[4] Janet Wilson "A Trade Boom's Unintended Costs," *Los Angeles Times*, April 23, 2006.

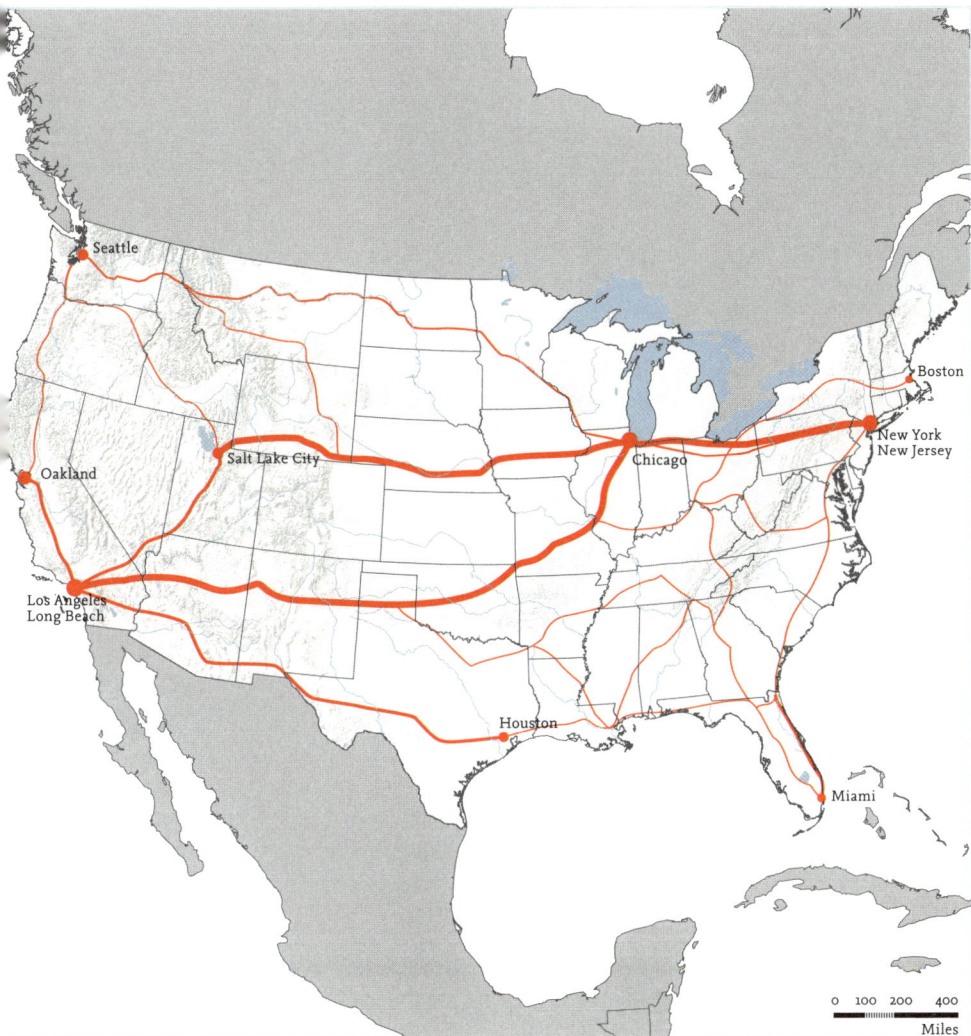

Seattle

Boston

New York
New Jersey

Chicago

Salt Lake City

Oakland

Los Angeles
Long Beach

Houston

Miami

0 100 200 400
Miles

*Diagram of Intermodal
Trade Flows through
the Ports of San Pedro
Bay, 1998*

Relative Levels of
Freight Density

*Source: author, derived
from Federal Highways
Administration Office
of Freight Manage-
ment and Operations,
"Multimodal Freight
Analysis, 2000"*

Faced by these threats to the cheap, reliable flow of products, importers are now considering other options, such as longer waterborne shipping routes to ports closer to final points of sale, outsourcing the port operations themselves to union-free land in Mexico, and a return to "traditional" warehousing strategies of storing goods over a longer term. The much-vaunted Alameda Corridor may soon be an infrastructural dinosaur.[5]

The future of goods infrastructure now lies far beyond any individual port and well into the hinterland where goods can be stockpiled in case of a "national emergency," such as a five-week delay in the arrival of Christmas merchandise.[6] In other words, the era of "just-in-time" shipping may be coming to an end in favor of a return to the age-old strategy of storing stuff nearby until it's needed. The significant difference from past strategies, however, lies in the Promethean scale of contemporary consumer demand, what one container historian refers to as "the bigness complex."[7]

Los Angeles-based shippers have traditionally moved goods out of the port to points east for warehousing and distribution. This is unlikely to change, given the 1% vacancy rate of industrial land around the port and the fact that even communities far from the ports, such as Ontario and Riverside, are now considered too expensive for warehouse construction. Moreover, the strategy on the West Coast, where 40% of the nation's consumer goods arrive (60% of which come from China), is to spread risk among several ports: Seattle, Oakland, Los Angeles/Long Beach, and San Diego. This is accomplished almost entirely through truck transport along the I-5 corridor as it barrels through California's Central Valley.

Only ten years ago, the largest warehouses enclosed approximately 500,000 square feet. Still, there was one prescient, notable exception: in 1991, Wal-Mart quietly constructed a 1.2-million-square-foot warehouse in the Central Valley, well before IKEA, Target and Home Depot followed suit. Variously called "container buildings" and "big box buildings," modern warehouses are intermodal buildings, fixed in place yet existing as links in a fluid supply chain of ships, trains, trucks and containers to which they must respond and adapt.

As William Mitchell observed, there exists in addition to all manner of "retail fronts," a corresponding "architectural back" consisting of the supply chain infrastructure that allows goods to arrive on demand at specific, physical locations around the world.[8] This architectural back has surpassed in cost and architectural importance any notion of a "front" for big box buildings. It is evident that more money is spent on the building envelope in terms of dock doors, special materials handling equipment, and site access to the rear of these buildings than is spent on the architecturally mediocre storefronts and office lobbies tacked onto the front of such buildings. One has only to pass along the loading-dock side of a warehouse or retail building to observe the subtle details that connect buildings to the supply chain. Attached by a weather-sealed gasket to the roll-up doors of the building, shipping containers come to rest.

The tractor cabs that hauled them long gone, containers sit idle, spanning between a retractable steel leg and the loading dock aperture. The interface is critical and proprietary: an individual retailer's materials handling strategy is often closely guarded. The IKEA facility at Tejon Ranch, for example, is sited behind high fences, locked gates and is

[5] Stephen P. Erie, *Globalizing L. A.: Trade, Infrastructure and Regional Development* (Stanford, CA: Stanford University Press, 2004).

[6] Jack Kyser, "A Huge Ripple Effect: Dockworkers' Strike Would Hurt the Economy." *Los Angeles Times*, September 13, 2002.

[7] Marc Levinson. *The Box* (Princeton: Princeton University Press, 2006), 231-245.

[8] William Mitchell, "Transarchitectures Symposium," (lecture, Getty Center, Los Angeles, June 6, 1998).

completely inaccessible to the public, even by appointment. Using techniques imported from Europe, IKEA's American warehouse is more closely guarded than the Port of Los Angeles in the age of terrorist attacks.

Signs of the emerging importance of warehousing came from an unlikely source. One week in 2001, the American Institute of Architects' newsletter announced the completion of a "large warehouse/distribution center" in Ontario by Bastien Architects, a California-based architecture firm, and Western Realco, a developer.[9] The A. I. A. is not known for promoting buildings on the fringe of design practice—apparently unless the building is very, very big. In this case, the warehouse covered some 1.1 million square feet of new, contiguous space. The same architect and developer team had recently completed an 818,000 square foot warehouse for the Home Shopping Network in Fontana. Since then, approximately a dozen such "super distribution centers" have been built each year in the U. S., each measuring a minimum of 1.5 million square feet of contiguous, single-story space.[10]

As Keller Easterling presciently observed in her 1999 article about containers and intermodal transport, "the containerization of goods has contributed to a new pattern of production and distribution that has not only altered the points of switching between highway and rail but has formatted the buildings that populate airport cities."[11] The formatted building—the intermodal

[9] "Bastien: Architect's Big Boxes Getting Bigger." *AIA Online*, April 17, 2001.

[10] Cory Restad, Tejon Ranch Company representative, interview with author, Tejon Ranch, September 1, 2006.

[11] Keller Easterling, "Interchange and Container: the New Orgman," *Perspecta* 30 (1999): 120.

building, in fact, continues to evolve and populate cheap real estate and good highways. The reliance on truck traffic is also a departure from the 1990s investment in true intermodality, between ship, rail, truck, and building, relying on trucks both for bringing goods to and from these distribution hubs. As a matter for architects to consider, the container itself is hardly interesting as an object retro-fitted for human habitation; rather, it is the extent to which more and more building types are being formatted with the specific aim of integrating fixed sites into the intermodal supply chain, or the extent to which buildings are already intermodal containers that pique our interest.

Containers lined up at a distribution center

A step down in size from the super distribution center and a degree more open to the public, the Big Box increasingly infiltrates the city. Formerly limited to the postsuburban periphery, according to a study prepared by the Public Law Research Institute of the University of California, for the purposes of defending municipalities in California against the incursion of forty new Wal-Mart supercenters cited a Columbia University study: "Big Box architecture [can be defined] as 'large windowless, rectangular single story buildings with 'standardized facades' that 'seem to be everywhere and unique to no place, be it rural town or urban neighborhood.'"[12]

The similarity of the Big Box to the super-distribution center prompts the question: where does the supply chain actually end? At what point do buildings stop being containers for goods and start becoming machines for defining consumer-driven identity? Once goods come into contact with the consumer, does the supply chain stop or does it continue?

Evidence suggests that finer grained shipping extends the goods supply chain right into the home. At the receiving end of the global supply chain, grossly distended McMansions have become little more than small-scale intermodal transit hubs, sites where goods are delivered on an almost daily basis by small trucks, SUVs and automobiles to reside until they become obsolete or undesirable, at which point they are stored indefinitely in public storage units, returned into a flow of recycled and second-hand goods distribution or, even more likely, shipped off to the growing, toxic mountains of the city's landfills.

Homebuilders have responded by reformatting the house into a warehouse. According to the National Association of Home Builders, the average home size in the United States was 2,330 square feet in 2004, up from 1,400 square feet in 1970 even as average family size decreased and real income remained stable. Today it is as important to house things as people. Walk-in closets, walk-in pantries, storage rooms, wine cellars, multi-car garages, entertainment rooms, and personal gyms proliferate. The existence of entire neighborhoods of 20,000-50,000 square-foot homes in major urban centers is not unusual anymore and at least one builder has introduced the classic, warehouse-building methodology of tilt-up slab construction to the home-building industry, constructing his own, 10,150-square-foot home and 4,300-square-foot garage using foam-filled concrete panels.[13]

Nor does it end there: with the proliferation of questionable home equity loans during the real estate boom in the first part of the decade, the house itself became a three-dimensional credit card, its insubstantial construction dematerialized further by speculative withdrawals to fund goods to fill its vast, waiting spaces.

---

[12] Columbia University, Graduate School of Architecture, Preservation, and Planning, "A Vision for New Rochelle: Plan for Revitalizing the City Park Neighborhood", May 2001 http://www.columbia.edu/itc/architecture/bass/newrochelle/extra/big_box.html quoted in Public Law Research Institute of the University of California, "California Responses to Supercenter Development A Survey of Ordinances, Cases and Elections," 2004, www.uchastings.edu/site_files/cslgl/plri_big_box_paper_04.pdf, 9-10.

[13] Ed Sauter, "Tilt-Up Construction: Not Just for Box Warehouses Anymore," *The Nation's Building News*, May 29, 2006, http://www.nbnnews.com/NBN/issues/2006-05-29/Building+Systems/index.html.

The End of the Supply Chain? Is there any hope in this relentless world of shuttling things? Under the continuous calculus of capital, the global distribution of wealth has not kept pace with efficiency of the global distribution of goods. As agglomeration strategies break down under pressures to diversify dependence on specific ports and to fragment warehousing, perhaps a similar breakdown in capital expenditures in the global shipping complex will enable small and medium-sized entrepreneurs to participate more directly in the requisition of labor and goods overseas at a smaller, more manageable scale. Until it does, containerization will remain the sinister embodiment of oppressive retail practices to depress prices and of a culture of "consumers gone wild."

Robert Sumrell

STORY OF THE EYE

PROP HOUSES

Four giant Maoi, or Easter Island Heads, line the otherwise blank facade of C. P. Three. Crafted for the 1995 Janet Jackson music video *Runaway*, these cast foam heads (stock numbers A4-1407A-D, $429.25/week per head) marked a transition away from the high-budget music videos of the early nineties, often shot over long periods of time at faraway locations to more economical, shorter shoots made in-studio. In *Runaway*, remote location footage and computer-generated backdrops were intermixed with close-up shots in which Jackson interacted with large, detailed set pieces. The result was a popular video that conveyed a global vision on a local budget. Omega/Cinema Props purchased the heads shortly after the video was completed and, since then, has rented them out for use in dozens of events, films, and television productions around the city.

C. P. Three, located on the corner of Santa Monica Boulevard and Bronson Avenue, is one of a quartet of prop houses comprising the Omega/Cinema props complex. In addition to the four Maoi, C. P. Three houses tens of thousands of additional props (an abbreviation of the term "properties") meant for outdoor use. These items include patio and garden furniture, Wild West artifacts, industrial goods, tools, packing crates, oil drums, and automotive parts. The largest building of the group, known simply by its symbolic name, Omega, is located just across the street. Omega's inventory spans the history of domestic goods including medieval, early American, Art Deco, neoclassical, traditional, and modern furnishings as well as drapes, linens, silk flowers, kitchenware, lamps, art, and small decorative accessories. Within the building one can find an authentic nineteenth-century Chinese opium bed (stock number F1-171, $862.25/week), a fourteen-arm, eighty-four-light "Maria Theresa" crystal

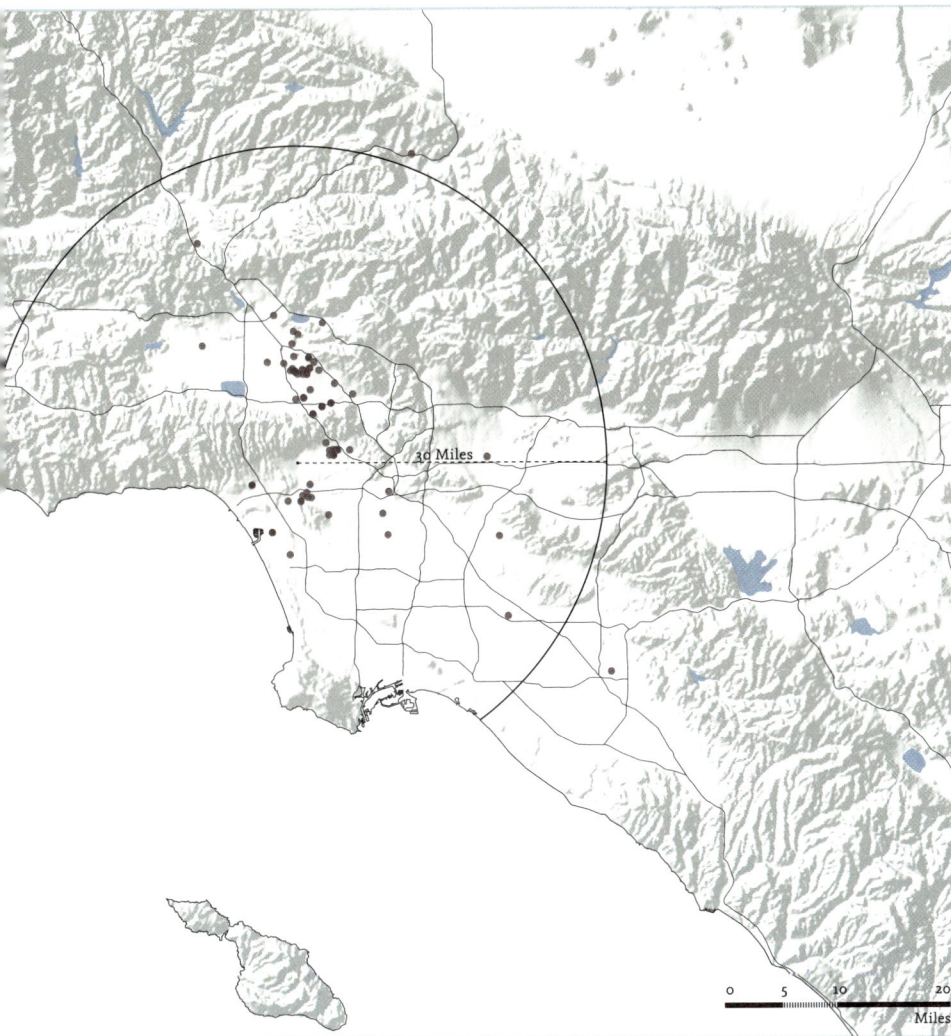

Prop Houses in
Los Angeles and
Thirty Mile Zone

Source: author

Prop Houses •
Thirty-Mile Zone —
Interstate Highways —
Major Water Bodies ▪

30 Miles

0   5   10   20
Miles

chandelier (stock number LA-1206, $795.75/week), and a complete, albeit non-functioning, Victorian pipe organ (stock number F1-1301, $1,647.25/week). Two additional buildings complete the facility: C. P. Two handles saloon, restaurant, gymnasium, store, and commercial fixtures including a mahogany back bar (stock numbers F-5501 A-Z, $2,897.25/week) and a stationary cardio bicycle (stock number G-265, $194.85/week), while C. P. Four rents computers, music instruments, electronic items, as well as institutional and office furniture. Here, a blue and grey iMac computer (stock number E-1303A, $217.00/week) and a black felt chalkboard eraser (stock number A-8707, $1.75/week) can be found.

Skulls and bones

Although Omega strives to be the last word in props, boasting "the largest selection of props anywhere in the Entertainment Industry," no single prop house can claim anything close to a complete material survey of the world.[1] Instead, a variety of prop houses offer highly specialized and themed fragmentary utopias, each catering to different needs and subject matters. The names of these shops often betray the secret passion of an obsessed collector: History for Hire specializes in obsolete militaria, hand-held antiques, and vintage film, radio, and television equipment; Air Hollywood provides airplane and airport elements; Dapper Cadaver stocks cinematic mortuaries; Major Medical supplies fictional hospitals. Other prop houses offer even more obscure goods: Sword & Stone outfits armies with medieval weaponry; Antenen Research rents working industrial robots; Cardboard People rents imitation audiences.

Prop houses like Omega supply material goods seen in films including both singular and exotic pieces as well as many banal items identical to those audiences have in their own lives. These goods serve many purposes, they provide contexts of both time and place allowing us to suspend disbelief while watching films, they create a seamless reality between actors and their environs, they articulate a specific mood or ambience that would otherwise not be apparent on stage or at a location, and they provide visual keys that establish spatial continuity between wide-angle scenes and close-ups, alleviating the discontinuity of montage.

There are no standard methods of operation or organization for prop houses. Some are rigorously organized, others are more haphazard. Nonetheless, all prop houses are logistics centers for the storage and circulation of objects. They allow art directors to compare a variety of similar goods to make selections, place the items on hold until final approvals are determined, let the objects out for an agreed upon rental period, and then retain the objects after the transaction is completed in case they should be required again. Many of the props cost more to rent for a week than they would if bought outright at a junk or re-sale store, but collecting such objects from a single location cuts labor and transportation costs, saving money and alleviating the problem of what to do with the item after the shoot is over.

Restaurant equipment

Prop houses and film locations are one of the many networks of entertainment support services essential to the survival of Hollywood. While films can be made in any city, the concentration of camera rental facilities, lighting companies, film stages, agents, entertainment lawyers, trained labor, and celebrity talent that are unique to Los Angeles ensure that the region maintains its dominance. If Hollywood specializes in the production of immaterial culture, prop houses and locations are its largest material substrate in the city, grounding it in a prosaic, if extreme, reality.

The industry's first official prop house began life as a pawnshop. Ellis Mercantile opened its doors in 1908, selling off the used personal and commercial goods of Angelenos who needed to make quick money (the boom and bust nature of the area's real estate has perennially forced Angelenos to downsize and sell off property). Early in Ellis's existence,

---

[1] Omega Cinema Props. "About Omega," Omega Cinema Props, http://www.omegacinemaprops.com/about.htm.

a studio employee came in to obtain a glass eye for one of the city's first film productions. Luckily, a down-on-his-luck Angeleno had recently brought in an eye to pawn. Since the studio had no need to keep the eye and there was always a chance that its cycloptic owner might come to reclaim his organ, it made sense to rent the eye rather than sell it. Within a short amount of time, Ellis Props was making all of its business from renting to the studios and shut down its pawn business.[2] Props became increasingly more important as film productions grew longer and more complex. In the early years of filmmaking, movie lengths were limited to a single roll of film for play at Nickelodeon theaters. Much like peep shows of later years, albeit without erotic content, these were generally short subjects that focused on a limited number of actions and little plot. By the time D. W. Griffith made his first Hollywood film, the industry had adopted the narrative qualities of the novel. Epics like *Birth of a Nation* and *Intolerance* established the need for realistic environments and set elements in order to convey a story. Through the 1920s Hollywood produced big-budget swashbuckling fantasies, historical extravaganzas, and melodramas for a cinema-mad public. Some twenty studios made more than eight hundred films a year in a ramped-up rate of production largely enabled by the implementation of Thomas Ince's "factory-studio system." Based on Fordist and Taylorist principles, the "factory-studio system" made productions cheaper and more efficient. Vertically integrated studios organized film crews as in-house departments, creating not only wardrobe and prop departments, but also in-studio wardrobe and prop houses specifically designed to store and manage the vast catalogues of material goods that were being used in multiple productions.[3] Studio prop houses kept these goods in circulation from film to film from the twenties through the Second World War, slowly growing and becoming more efficient.

As Europe lurched from economic crisis to economic crisis in the first half of the twentieth century, many formerly wealthy European noblemen and aristocrats were unable to maintain their estates and sold their most desirable properties and furnishings. Newly wealthy Americans like Jack Warner were eager to pick up the fragments of European culture and bring them back to the West Coast. Warner Brothers Studio properties obtained the majority of its valuable antiques and fine reproductions from such sources, putting them into play in their popular genre of historical epics.

But the most extravagant goods were purchased with the nearly inexhaustible resources of William Randolph Hearst for use both at San Simeon, his home in San Louis Obispo, and at his film company, Cosmopolitan Pictures. The most impressive film sets of this time were created at Cosmopolitan Pictures by one of Hollywood's earliest set designers, Joseph Urban. Urban, already famous for his theater set designs for the Metropolitan Opera House and the Ziegfeld Follies, was hired by Hearst to provide credibility for his mistress, the actress Marion Davies. Hearst spared no expense in these visual extravaganzas. Davies strived to be a major film star, demanding roles in historical films popular amongst members of high society. The luxurious sets and antique prop elements that Urban purchased lent credibility and refinement to Hollywood if not to Davies, inspiring envy and desire among society's elite as well as providing entertainment to the masses.[4]

The rest of the studios and the rest of America had to content themselves with less

[2] Ellis Props, "It All Started With A Glass Eye," Ellis Props, http://www.ellisprops.com/history.htm as archived by the Internet Archive Wayback Machine at http://web.archive.org/web/19990827224922/www.ellisprops. com/history.htm.

[3] Michael Storper, "The Transition to Flexible Specialization in the US Film Industry: External Economies, the Division of Labour and the Crossing of Industrial Divides," in *Post-Fordism: A Reader*, ed. Ash Amin (Oxford: Blackwell, 1994), 201-203.

[4] Juan Antonio Ramirez and John F. Moffitt, *Architecture for the Screen: A Critical Study of Set Design in Hollywood's Golden Age* (Jefferson: McFarland & Company, 2004).

valuable antiques and copies, many having been produced since the beginning of industrialization. New manufacturing techniques flooded the marketplace with cheaper consumer goods that sated the desire for previously unreachable products and spawned a romantic nostalgia for remakes of the pre-industrial past. Film sets were filled with real and imitation antiques as well as modern remakes of traditional handcrafted furniture styles. Regency furnishings were a perfect fit for the hyper-stylized movie sets of Hollywood's golden age, capable of being passed off as authentic antiques on film and generally in better condition, larger, and more dramatic than their prototypical forms. Late-eighteenth and early-nineteenth-century consumer goods suggested the aesthetics of Greek Neoclassicism, French Directorie, and Empire Styles, all of which were influenced by the romance of Europe's colonial holdings to be made more severe, more fantastic, and more exotic.[5]

By the late 1920s, the procession of revivalisms evolved into a more historically rigorous period of mass eclecticism. Equating culture with knowledge of the Old World, and having only a short history of their own to draw from, Americans copied European aristocratic taste and tried to simulate generations of slow acquisition by obsessing over and copying historic styles.[6] Authenticity was of paramount importance to eclectic environments. Experts who understood the history of architectural styles and had knowledge of how the rooms within them should be furnished fell into great demand, quickly establishing two glamorous new professions. Hollywood art directors became nearly as famous and important as film stars, while interior decorators took over clients' homes.[7] In Los Angeles, the best worked in both fields, showing mass audiences how to bring props into their own homes through film sets as they moonlighted as decorators for the Hollywood élite, creating moods and atmospheres inspired by the good taste and glamour conveyed in film.

In this new environment, young American socialites such as Woolworth heiress Barbara Hutton would take on the ultimate prop, marrying destitute "princes" or minor nobility to give their *nouveau riche* wealth an air of permanence and importance.[8] The lives of such young socialites and actresses confused the distinction between acting and personal life, creating media celebrities whose behavior a growing audience sought to copy.

More than just serving as an infrastructure for Hollywood, the world of prop houses is a mirror for our own world of surplus goods, providing insight and instruction into how we relate to property and how we use objects to create structure in our own lives. Sociologist Erving Goffman likened consumer goods to props used by actors performing on a stage. In his view, settings and props support the performance of daily life: "those who would use a particular setting as part of their performance cannot begin their act until they have brought themselves to the appropriate place and must terminate their performance when they leave it." In particular, Goffman observed how individuals used such settings to navigate through the class system at social clubs, where "a large number of luxurious settings are available for hire to anyone of the right kind who can afford them."[9]

But a newly perfected media was changing the structure of prop houses by changing the way audiences related to objects. The postwar rise of television introduced a new relationship between media, objects, and consumers that bore little resemblance to live theater performances. Television encouraged privatized entertainment, replacing social interaction

[5] John Pile, *A History of Interior Design* (London: Laurence King Publishing Ltd, 2005), 229-231.

[6] Pile, *A History of Interior Design*, 301-306

[7] Russell Lynes, *The Tastemakers* (New York: Dover Publications, 1980), 229 and Pile, *A History of Interior Design*, 310.

[8] C. David Heymann, *Poor Little Rich Girl: The Life and Legend of Barbara Hutton* (New York: Lyle Stuart, 1984).

[9] Erving Goffman, *The Presentation of Self in Everyday Life* (New York: Doubleday, 1959), 22-23.

with passive amusement. As Robert Putnam observes in *Bowling Alone*, his study of postwar social changes in America, "the artifice of canned laughter [often heard in TV programs] reflected both the enduring fact that mirth is enhanced by companionship and the novel fact that companionship could now be simulated electronically."[10] The social model based on participation in group theater was replaced by membership in a mass audience whose participants often viewed everything on the screen with equal credulity and enthusiasm. Since television shows were freely given away, producers embraced advertising, sought out sponsors, and utilized product placement, merging corporate interests with public entertainment. Game shows introduced consumers to new consumer goods, while soap operas and sitcoms showed audiences how to live among products, suggesting that viewers compare the lifestyles and goods that appeared on the screen with the domestic environment surrounding the family television. Since sets created for television shows were stocked with goods rented from prop houses, prop houses thrived, increasing the range of their inventory.

Television commercials were more influential than television programs, appealing directly to the consumer to make new purchases. Conceived of by marketers and filmed by independent production companies, television ads were largely independent endeavors that relied exclusively on renting equipment, stages, and props from outside sources. Renting these props and sets saved time and labor while keeping costs down on commercial jobs where the bottom line was always maximizing profits.

When they appear in television ads commercial goods become props, objects presented as pure image with an entirely symbolic use value. Once purchased and taken home, the consumer good has to serve both as the symbolic prop that seduced us on television while also performing the function it was ostensibly purchased to accomplish. Early television audiences were keenly aware that commercials played on their emotions and maintained an intense skepticism towards the goods they saw presented there. As a result, the majority of ads created during the 1950s were not sold through fictional narratives, but rather through sales pitches based on a technique known as the Unique Selling Proposition, a non-creative pitch that relied on showing an "expert" or a cartoon "advertising character" that advocated the merits of products directly to consumers.[11] The results were rampant consumption of novelty goods that promised to do more and be better than the old consumer goods and a mass celebration of the affluence of a consumer society that could support these claims.

Television ads quickly became the measure by which society determined its needs and values, replacing traditional standards of function and necessity. The effect was felt across all social classes and disciplines. Literary critic Roland Barthes in his book *Mythologies* and architects Peter and Alison Smithson in their article "But Today We Collect Ads" grappled with the implications of these social changes, declaring that the goods we buy are not the objects themselves, but the objects as they are presented—mythologically and semiotically— and that these images are the new measure of what consumers demanded from the material world. If intellectuals collected advertisements, it was because consumers collected and lived among props, the images of the commodity portrayed in the ad manifested as the mythological consumer object itself.[12]

Interior, self-storage unit

Non-functional television cameras and assorted Christmas toys

[10] Robert D. Putnam, *Bowling Alone: The Collapse and Revival of American Community* (New York: Simon & Schuster, 2000), 217.

[11] Jackson Lears, *Fables of Abundance: A Cultural History of Advertising in America* (New York: Basic Books, 1994), 256.

[12] Roland Barthes, *Mythologies* (New York: Hill and Wang, 1972) and Alison and Peter Smithson, "But Today We Collect Ads," *Ark* 18 (November 1956), 49.

The shock of new commodities portrayed on television and the deluge of cheap imports flown in from overseas manufacturers underscores consumers' powerlessness and bewilderment at material goods. This reaction is akin to the wonderment and confusion felt by natives of the Pacific Rim nations like New Guinea and Melanesia during World War II when foreign armies airdropped war materials onto the islands and set up temporary base camps and occupation zones. At the end of the war, foreign influence disappeared as abruptly as it arrived, ending the cargo drops. The natives, who had no prior exposure to—or understanding of—Western or Japanese culture, assumed that the goods were gifts called down by the foreigners from the gods, and they copied the "ritual activity" and practices that they observed the soldiers making, in order to reinstate the sacred delivery of cargo. Natives wore headphones carved from wood, built control towers, waved landing signals, and constructed runways complete with giant straw airplanes all to no avail. Cargo remained elusive and no amount of imitation seemed to appease the gods. Most of the world's traditional cargo cults have since vanished as globalization has spread into the islands and incorporated them into the international market economy or as the natives simply gave up, determining that the gods would never smile upon them. Only a few islanders continue to maintain faith, patiently waiting for cargo.[13]

Unlike New Guinea, cargo never stopped descending upon the Western world. America's passive consumption, ritualized work practices, and reliance on the construction of environmental contexts strangely relates more closely to the practices of cargo cults than Goffman's analogy to theater only a few years before. Mass-media celebrities and television personalities are now transformed into telematic presences, taking on the role of divine spirits presenting the strange cargo that is flown in and dropped from mysterious locations like Japan and China, magically appearing on retail shelves. The inference is that consumers can only draw in the power from these goods if they deserve them and that they will only deserve them if they imitate the rituals as seen on televisions, enacting lifestyles to attract future cargo.

Audiences assembled settings in their own homes to reflect the sets they saw in films and on television in order to make their environments equally worthy of attracting additional goods. It is these contexts and rituals that are essential to cargo cults, whose members understand that such gestures are more important to objects than ownership. Television lamps belong with the television (as do TV trays, recliners, and remote controls) much more than they belong to us. Similarly, a proper bed requires matching bedside tables, a dresser and vanity in order to become a complete bedroom set, even if it is put into a spare room to only rarely or even never be used. Mass-marketed goods suggest the perfect world of media images and department store displays, a world whose artificial, geometric order is ambivalent to human occupation.

Once consumer demand for functional cargo such as dishwashers, refrigerators, televisions, and stereos was satiated, boredom with mass-produced, mass-marketed goods of the 1950s set in. Responding to this condition, marketers sought new ways to appeal to consumers, stimulating demand by suggesting that products could act as emotional and symbolic props, providing context and significance to individuals as they sought out meaningful lives. In turn, the mass market broke into smaller, focused markets. Older, wealthy consumers practiced cultural elitism, purchasing conspicuously expensive and rarified avant-garde art and antiques, while teenagers and college students who had grown up in the materialist fifties sought out lifestyles that denounced mass consumption by shopping in junk and thrift

[13] For an introduction to cargo cults see Lamont Lindstrom, *Cargo Cult: Strange Stories of Desire from Melanesia and Beyond* (Honolulu: University of Hawaii Press, 1993).

stores, engaging in alternative lifestyles, and embracing hand-made items.[14] Norma Sakura, an editor for the *New York Times* Home Section, brought attention to the alternative spaces these individuals lived in with her 1972 book *Underground Interiors*. In it, she states:

> The commercialism of everyday existence, the bombardment of our senses by advertisements on TV, radio, and billboards, has caused many of us to feel a revulsion for the collecting of material things…Finally there is a need for people today to live in an environment of their own making, one that they have influence in some way, to counter their feeling of impotence in other faces of their daily existence.[15]

Sakura backs this statement by presenting images of apartments and lofts given over to personal fantasy, where strange collections and personal goods are displayed to provide a personal ambience and sense of emotional security. Other books like Karen Fisher's 1972 *Living for Today* celebrated the disposable, temporary decor of the apartment lease, while Adele Williams's 1976 *Thrift Shop Decorating* repackaged the practice of scouring thrift shops and junk bins to make it acceptable and fashionable to mainstream audiences.[16]

Commercials, television, and film embraced this carnivalesque aesthetic, suggesting that consumption was not a way to achieve permanent satisfaction but rather a never-ending process of self-realization. Television ads and commercial goods often used a negative appeal, making soft sells and multi-media spectacles that played to the emotions and suggested that the consumer was wise to marketers' ploys.[17] The result, ultimately, was that a tremendous number of different styles were conveyed in rapid succession, each validating the other and expanding the acceptable range of desirable goods.[18] Because none of these goods had any absolute value, everything had the potential to be seen as valuable. The business of media became the business of providing contexts to create the conditions by which temporary value could be established.

Throughout the decade consumers purchased more and held on to everything. Even unnecessary and outdated goods were something to hold on to, because their potential value exceeded the typical market value of a consignment shop or yard sale. The postwar houses many consumers lived in bulged under the strain of these excess commodities. Older houses had little storage, possessing small closets, dank basements, and overheated attics, while newer houses often had no basements or attic space at all. To keep all their props, families had to move their excess goods into offsite storage.

Self-storage facilities first appeared in Texas in the 1960s, but quickly spread through the Sunbelt just as a great migration of families arrived from the North and East with tons of extra stuff. In California, another bust economy forced many families into smaller houses.[19] Unwilling to give up their possessions, these families stored them in self-storage warehouses. These were nothing less than personal prop houses, not so much places to store sentimental goods, but rather miniature prop houses to keep objects that could be called on again during holidays, for example, or re-sold at a moment of heightened value. The excess of goods created from the "crisis of accumulation" and the continuous need for modulating

---

[14] Jean Baudrillard, *Revenge of the Crystal. Selected Writings on the Modern Object and Its Destiny: 1968-1983* (London: Pluto Press, 1990), 42-43.

[15] Norma Sakura and Oberto Gili, *Underground Interiors* (New York: Quadrangle Books, 1972), 1.

[16] Karen Fisher, *Living For Today* (New York: Viking Press, 1972) and Adele Williams, *Thrift Shop Decorating: How to Decorate Your House To Suit Your Taste and Purpose* (New York: Arbor House, 1976).

[17] Thomas Frank, *The Conquest of Cool* (Chicago: University of Chicago Press, 1997), 230-233.

[18] Baudrillard, *Revenge of the Crystal*, 87-91.

[19] See Rob D'Amico, "What's In Store: Has Mini-Storage Become Mega-Storage?" *The Austin Chronicle*, September 1, 2000, Home Section and Tom Vanderbilt, "Self Storage Nation: Americans are Storing More Stuff Than Ever." *Slate* (July 2005), http://www.slate.com/id/2122832/.

and articulating the domestic environment has made prop masters and art directors of us all, storing and hiding as many goods in reserve as we place in public view–just in case they might become necessary again.

United Parcel Service transfer facility

In response to changing media needs, throughout the seventies, studio prop houses were re-filled, re-imagined, and re-constructed. In 1971, responding to a study that showed that advertisers were more inclined to spend money for spots reaching younger, more urban demographics, CBS executive Fred Silverman canceled a number of the network's long-running television shows, many of which had rural themes, in a sweeping move known as the "Rural Purge." *The Beverly Hillbillies, Green Acres, Hee Haw, The Ed Sullivan Show*, and *Hogan's Heroes* all met the axe. Silverman replaced these shows with more contemporary, often gritty programs like *All in the Family, The Mary Tyler Moore Show, The Bob Newhart Show*, and *M*A*S*H*.[20] As other networks followed suit, a deluge of everyday commercial goods poured in to serve the new productions. With space at a premium and Hollywood's gold and silver ages seeming contrived and outdated, many prop houses threw out their old, overly stylized props, replacing them with new consumer goods that supported cultural criticism as well as pop and youth culture.

The eccentric collections of the handful of new, independent prop houses that emerged in the 1970s embodied the focus on self-realization through collecting. Similarly, the emergence of nostalgia films such as *Chinatown* or *The Godfather* and science fiction epics such as *2001: A Space Odyssey* and *Star Wars*, together with the raft of imitators that these film spawned, called for authoritative prop houses that could deliver and construct not just one object but a rigorous, self-consistent grouping of objects. The Fordist, vertically oriented in-studio prop house gave way to specialized prop houses focusing on individual themes, each one its own collection of objects, realizing its owner's dream. Frequently these prop houses emerged from idiosyncratic private collections and the personal favorites of art directors culled from the liquidation of major studio prop houses like MGM and Twentieth-Century Fox, which increasingly out-sourced as much of each production as possible.[21]

The new range of prop goods demanded for entertainment made the job of sourcing props that much more difficult. The first truly searchable guide to the network of props and prop houses started as a personal three-ring binder of notes and phone numbers assembled by Deborah Hemela while she was working on Norman Lear's sitcoms about everyday life. Originally published in 1978 as the *Prop & Set Yellow Pages*, *Debbie's Book*, as it is known today, remains the authoritative guide for props, sets, events, and themed environments. The 2007 edition lists more than 2,200 separate film businesses providing over 1,600 categories of hyper-specialized resources including trash, road kill, taco carts, dirt skins, taxidermy, and artificial food.[22]

Modern Props

Debbie's Book moved to the Internet in 1997, only two years after GEMM networked used record stores and eBay introduced the world to almost unlimited online auctions. The text-based searching common to such databases allows consumers to find goods as concepts, independent of their actual arrangements and location, linking potential consumers with a huge number of potential distributors, many of whom are hyper-specialized collectors them-selves, on a transaction-by-transaction basis. These items are then shipped through giant distribution centers operated by companies like United Parcel Service and Federal Express

---

[20] Paul Farhi, "Network TV, Ensconced in a Blue Period: Election Result May Signal Rebuff off Show's Locales" *The Washington Post*, November 28, 2004, N1.

[21] Joel Waldo Finler, *The Hollywood Story* (London: Wallflower Press, 2003), 17

[22] Debora Anne Hemela, *Debbie's Book: The Source Book for All Entertainment Industries* (Pasadena: Debbie's Book Inc, 2007)

to any location around the globe in a nearly instantaneous process. Chris Anderson refers to this process as "the Long Tail," a condition in which everything becomes available to everyone and, taken in aggregate, combines the most abject goods with the most unexpected buyers to generate an enormous amount of income.[23]

As a result, art directors can now use retail stores and online resources as prop houses. Nearly everything in Los Angeles is for rent and can be leveraged for a profit. Even exclusive department stores and antique galleries in Beverly Hills make money by renting their merchandise. Barney's, Neiman Marcus, and Saks Fifth Avenue all have studio services that allow stylists to take out a loan of clothing on the promise of a 20% purchase upon return.

But it isn't just products that are for rent, stores are as well and so are homes, churches, offices, empty warehouses, and government buildings such as Los Angeles City Hall and the Municipal Court. As an anonymous city without any special character of its own, Los Angeles can be easily altered to simulate distant locations. Many seemingly failed buildings downtown and throughout the city remain derelict in order to generate revenue as film locations. Similarly, the city makes use of its outdated and inoperative correctional facilities: both the County Sheriff's Sybil Brand Institute in City Terrace and the Los Angeles County Jail in Lincoln Heights are regularly rented out as film jails and prisons, finding a purpose in film even though they are legally unfit for the confinement of anyone other than actors.[24]

A labor agreement struck between the film and television unions in the 1960s produced the "thirty-mile zone" (TMZ) or "studio zone," a radius spreading thirty miles from the intersection of Beverly and La Cienega Boulevards, understood as an acceptable travel distance for union members to work in under prevailing normal "studio rates and working conditions." Any locations falling outside of this area, with the exception of a piece of parkland once owned by MGM, are billed at higher "distant location" rates and travel fees. Nearly all of Los Angeles's prop houses are located within this zone, as are most of its locations. To keep budgets low, the distant corners of the world as well as many places that fall just across the border, are re-created within this perimeter.[25] For example, the FOX Network's television show *The O. C.* was filmed at simulated locations within the TMZ even though the real "O. C." was only miles away.[26] Such locations are another form of prop, making the city into a giant prop house of buildings and outdoor spaces available for rent.

While the inability to distinguish between real-world locations and film locations may be baffling, the inability to distinguish real-world objects and movie props can be far more problematic. Both prop currency and prop guns are regulated by federal guidelines in an effort to limit their free circulation, while branded goods are protected under tight legal restraints when used on a set. The Secret Service was relatively lax in enforcing counterfeit laws regarding movie money (which has become increasingly more realistic since originally legalized in 1958) until recently, when large amounts of movie money were released into the general population during the filming of the film *Rush Hour 2* (2001). In the film, about $1 billion of fake currency designed by Independent Studio Services was blown up in a gag that sent bills flying all over the film set. Bills were subsequently found in circulation in the general economy, allegedly pushed through strip clubs and small, dark nightclubs, triggering

[23] Chris Anderson, *The Long Tail: Why the Future of Business is Selling Less of More* (New York: Hyperion, 2006), 1-26.

[24] Center For Land Use Interpretation, "On Locations: Exhibit About Film Locations At CLUI Los Angeles," *The Lay of the Land: the Center for Land Use Interpretation Newsletter* (Spring-Summer 2001).

[25] Christopher Grove, "Small-screen scouts eye underexposed corners: Dressing the Town for International Looks," *Variety*, November 26, 2001.

[26] The O. C. Insider, "Backstage Pass Insider Commentary: France Myung Fagin: Locating the O. C.," *The O. C. Insider*, http://www.theocinsider.com/backstage/insidercommentary/archive/06.html.

a crackdown by the Secret Service who immediately went in and confiscated not only the rest of the run of bills that ISS had sold to other prop houses, but the plates as well to prevent more bills from being produced.[27]

Current regulations for prop money are strict. The Counterfeit Detection Act of 1992 permits color illustrations of U. S. currency only under the conditions that the illustration is either less than three-fourths or more than one and one-half, in linear dimension, of each part of the item illustrated and that the illustration is one-sided.[28] Prop houses that continue to defy these rules run the risk of facing very real counterfeiting charges.

Functioning weapons, like currency, are often demanded for use in extreme close-ups, and are often required to "work" on screen. On May 12, 1984, television actor Jon-Eric Hexum was laying on a bed at the Twentieth Century Fox lot in Century City, resting between takes for his CBS series *Cover Up* when he pointed a prop .44 Magnum revolver to his forehead and pulled the trigger, accidentally killing himself. Hexum, ironically playing the part of an undercover weapons expert posing as a fashion photographer, was unaware that the revolver, although loaded only with empty cartridges and blanks (a cartridge filled only with paper wadding and gunpowder) was still capable of harm. The force of air drove the wadding from the blank into his right temple, forcing bits of his skull into his brain.[29] Less than a decade later, on March 31, 1993 film actor Brandon Lee was similarly shot and killed on set while filming the Goth action thriller film, *The Crow*.[30]

In response to these on-set incidents, both state and federal laws concerning the handling of firearms on set have tightened, as have union guidelines that determine who may handle munitions and how they are inspected.

In addition to actors, irresponsibly handled props can kill companies too. It is illegal to use the reputation and presence of a branded good in order to sell another product or film without explicit permission of the owner of the brand. When permitted, this practice is referred to as product placement. Since the 1890s, commercial goods have been introduced into film narratives as product placements, merging fiction and reality into a seamless network of property, but it wasn't until Steven Spielberg's 1982 film, *E. T.: the Extra-Terrestrial*, that products became integral to the narratives of feature film plots. Steven Spielberg first approached Mars Candies with the idea of placing M&Ms prominently into the movie as E. T.'s favorite candy. Spielberg hoped that using an established, real-world candy would help suspend audience's disbelief in his science-fiction film and make his filmic plea for world peace more realistic. Mars declined, but Spielberg cemented a deal with rival candy company Hershey's, which had recently developed a competitor to M&Ms, Reese's Pieces. While Reese's Pieces was not the only branded promotional object featured in the film, its prominent position in the film's narrative brought it great attention. The promotional campaign developed by Hershey's launched the new candy to the marketing limelight, temporarily tripling the candy's sales, reducing Paramount's promotional budget, and establishing a permanent place for product placement in Hollywood.[31]

[27] Richard Fausset and Andrew Blankstein, "Films' Fake Cash Can't Look Too Real; Props: After Bogus Bills Get Into Circulation, Secret Service Turns Them into Money Losers for Two Valley Firms," *Los Angeles Times*, June 6, 2001, Home Edition, B1.

[28] *The Counterfeit Deterrence Act of 1992*, Public Law 102-550.

[29] The Internet Movie Database, "Biography for Jon-Eric Hexum." *The Internet Movie Database*. http://www.imdb.com/name/nm0382149/bio.

[30] The Internet Movie Database, "Biography for Brandon Lee (I)." *The Internet Movie Database*. http://www.imdb.com/name/nm0000488/.

[31] Jay Newell Charles T. Salmon, and Susan Chang, "The Hidden History of Product Placement," *Journal of Broadcasting & Electronic Media* Vol. 50, No.4 (2006): 575-594 and Patti Summerfield with files from Lisa

By 2005, product placement in film and television generated $2.25 billion annually. Increasingly, products play more prominently into scripts as "hero props" whose deals are negotiated and optioned by lawyers and accountants rather than scriptwriters. In the 1995 brand-filled James Bond film, *Golden Eye*, Bond's classic Aston Martin was replaced with a real-world BMW Z3. A decade later, Bond was downgraded again to a Ford Mondeo for the 2006 film, *Casino Royale*. Ford allegedly spent $24.5 million dollars, or seven times lead actor Daniel Craig's salary, to make the switch happen.[32]

The Protestant ethic of thrift and production that Max Weber observed in American culture is long gone. Instead, we have radical abundance propped up by massive debt. Even though consumption is still rampant, we have passed the point of needing to produce more things as a society. Our homes are prop houses, filled with useless consumer goods that exist primarily to create a context that we can react to. Our growing relationship to our objects, or props, is that of a programmer to bits of code.[33] As programmers, we assemble these pieces of code into a context, or language, that builds a program to execute a series of actions. Network systems are the infrastructure on which these programs run and interact. No network is essential, just as no single node is vital—all that matters is movement within the network. What we are left with is a constant circulation of bits, like the elements and molecules in chemistry that create a living ecosystem—it is this constant cycle of change that keeps the system vital.

Prop houses provide a utopia for this condition. Not only do they suggest that our Long Tail desires might one day be valuable, they promise that objects can endlessly circulate in an infrastructural condition, provide context and meaning to produce momentarily perfect settings.

In 1999, Ellis Props closed its doors and put its inventory up for auction in both live auctions at the Universal Hilton and on the Internet through eBay and Amazon.com. Unable to compete with too great a surplus of commercial goods and faced with a decline in revenue from fleeing productions to any of the growing media cities around the globe, the company simply could not longer support its expenses.[34]

As the fallout from the recent real-estate and dot-com booms continues to settle, we may soon turn against our goods, feeding upon them as sources of income to leverage as well as to enjoy. Online marketplaces like craigslist.org and iRent2u now make banal items ranging from hammers to houses available for rent.[35] We cannot escape our property; we are tied to it forever, as part of its history of circulation. We have become little more than the context for the things that own us, remaining connected to them as incidental players in the stories they tell while circulating.

Pharmaceutical supplies

Human torso, body parts, and circus props

D'Innocenzo, "So Your Brand's a TV Star. What's it Worth?'" *Strategy Magazine*, February 2006. http://www.strategymag.com/articles/magazine/20060201/media.html.

[32] Lara Magzan, "The Business of Bond...James Bond: 'Buy a Ford Today' is Just One Part of the Latest Bond (Marketing) Adventure," *CNNMoney*, November 12, 2002. http://money.cnn.com/2002/11/21/news/james_bond/index.htm and Ford Muscle, "James Bond Will Drive a Ford..." *Ford Muscle*, March 3, 2006. http://www.fordmuscle.com/blog/james-bond-will-drive-a-ford/11266.

[33] Baudrillard, *Revenge of the Crystal*, 91-95.

[34] Paul Clinton, "The Stuff of Dreams: Auction of Film Props Signals Sale of a Century," *CNN.com*, http://archives.cnn.com/2000/SHOWBIZ/Movies/06/07/prop.house/index.html.

[35] Brad Stone, "Rent Anything From Neighbors," *The New York Times*, February 18, 2008, http://query.nytimes.com/gst/fullpage.html?res=940DE4DB1E30F93BA25751C0A96E9C8B63.

Lane Barden

THE TRENCH
THE ALAMEDA CORRIDOR
PICTURING LOS ANGELES:
CONDUITS, CORRIDORS,
AND THE LINEAR CITY, PART 3

The rail system and trench in the Southern California landscape created by the Alameda Corridor Transportation Authority is a concrete groove inscribed so neatly and discreetly into the city's surface that it appears to be a secret. That a cut, ten miles long, fifty feet wide, and thirty-three feet deep could exist in a metropolis without anyone noticing, is difficult to comprehend. This is a vast, exceedingly ambitious piece of infrastructure, which eliminated traffic problems at two hundred former at-grade railroad crossings, reduced locomotive emissions and emissions from trucks idling at crossings, cut noise pollution, and dramatically increased the speed of the movement of more than $200 billion in cargo each year.[1] The Alameda Corridor and the trench have secured Los Angeles' future as the primary gateway for cargo from the Pacific Rim into the United States. Its importance to the city's existence cannot be overstated, yet even the most informed citizens of the city are mostly unaware of its existence because it is almost invisible. You could be driving next to it and never know it is there, much less know that millions of dollars in freight move through it on a daily basis.

The Alameda Corridor is a main artery in the flow of imports from the Pacific, especially China, that have created our current trade imbalance and made it possible for Wal-Mart, Home Depot, Target, and dozens of other major and minor franchise retailers to remain fully stocked with uninterrupted precision and abundance. It would be realistic to argue that the trench is central to the everyday efficiency of global capitalism.

1 Alameda Corridor Transportation Authority, "News Room-Fact Sheet," Alameda Corridor Transportation Authority, http://www.acta.org/newsroom_factsheet.htm.

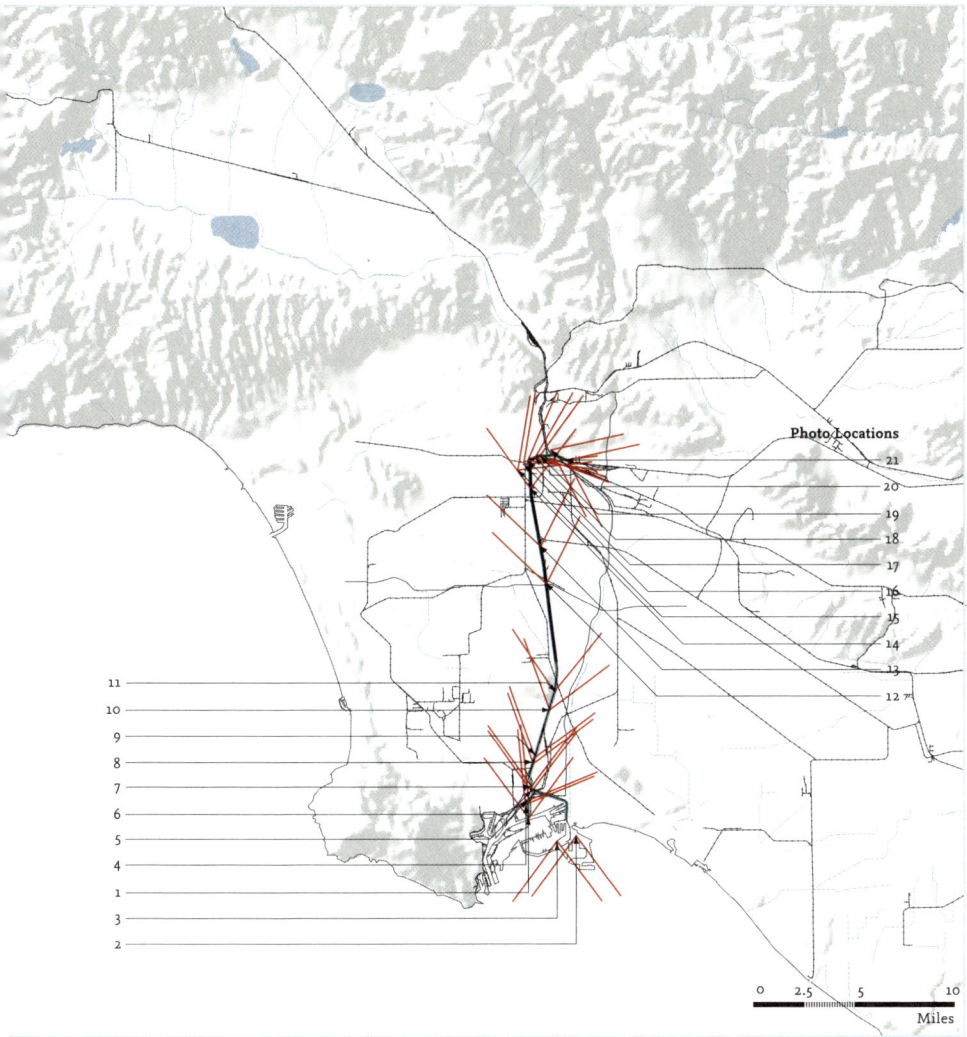

Photo Locations

21
20
19
18
17
16
15
14
13
12

11
10
9
8
7
6
5
4
1
3
2

| 0 | 2.5 | 5 | 10 |

Miles

Numbers correspond to plate numbers of photographs in this chapter

Photograph Viewshed
BNSF
Alameda Mid-corridor Trench
Alameda Corridor South
Railroads

The trench is a reminder that the street level surface we normally think of as the ground, is not the ground at all; but merely a datum line between what is visible and what is not in a city. One of the few distinguishing landmarks among the sea of shining white warehouses in the photographs of the Alameda Corridor is a relatively large tract of land that looks like a park, but was actually an urban farm (see plate 15). This was the South Central Farm (now destroyed by the property owner), a collective of gardens maintained by Latino families living in South Los Angeles who produced food there not for sale, but for their own sustenance. Above ground, there were dozens of little gardens. Below ground, mega-tons of merchandise and food were passing by daily only a few yards from the farm. No one saw the irony. It was simply part of the everyday routine. Neither the farm nor the Alameda Corridor was aware of the other nor did it care. Yet from the air, the intricacies of the urban surface suggest that nothing can exist by itself—that warehouses, gardens and imports are all interdependent components in the same sphere of activity.

Immediately after passing by the farm, the trench emerges from the subsurface and turns east toward the Los Angeles River (see plate 19) where the Alameda Corridor crosses and merges with rail lines that run north and south. Here, the Corridor approaches its final destination, the Burlington Northern and Santa Fe Rail Yard and Intermodal Terminal (see plates 20 and 21), through a convoluted splash of infrastructure implanted and interwoven into the city's surface like an artificial heart. Rail lines, bridges, the river, and city streets all twist into a massive web of irreducible pathways, splayed out so densely across the surface that any activity other than its own is thoroughly excluded.

3

At this point, the trench has brought the cargo from the Port, twenty miles to the South, to a location large enough to deal with it all and function as a staging area for distribution to points north, east, and south. The Los Angeles city limits at the port contains only the port and the rail lines. This facility, if installed at the port, would consume a significant chunk of the city of Long Beach; instead all the cargo travels up the corridor to the Los Angeles metro area. When the rail lines fan out into the terminal, the trench has completed its job.

Symbolically embedded in this job so well done—this unprecedented, and uninterrupted gusher of incoming consumer goods moving through the trench—are troubling issues. The economy, the environment, and our life experiences are at this moment, out of balance. Reflected in the lack of outflow of goods along with a precariously posed, exaggerated idea of what we will demand to have in order to carry on, this activity is a form of trade that can just barely be called trade, in which we hold our breath while our wants and needs become so conflated that the distinction between them disappears entirely. The trench is a secret only on the surface. Beneath the surface, everyone intuitively knows what is sustainable and what is not. In the end, it is not the efficiency of the trench and its successes that are so astonishing, but the profound ironies of its invisibility.

5

7

9

11

13

15

17

19

21

ACKNOWLEDGEMENTS

This book was produced with support from the Graham Foundation for Advanced Studies in the Fine Arts. Without the hard work of Forum board members Frank Escher and Jack Burnett-Stuart, this project would not have been possible. At Columbia, Dean Mark Wigley of Graduate School of Architecture, Planning and Preservation generously supported the Netlab throughout this project. Also at GSAPP, Evan Allen, Benedict Clouette, Derek Lindner, and Sarah Williams made key contributions. Michael Kubo's work preparing the book for publication was crucial. At SCI_Arc, Neil Denari, Gary Paige, Margaret Crawford, and Kevin McMahon encouraged me to pursue all matters urban and infrastructural. In Los Angeles, Matt Coolidge was an inspiration without equal while Paulette Singley, John Southern, Alan Loomis, Steve Rowell and Greg Goldin gave much-needed encouragement and prodded me on deeper into infrastructure. Aaron Betsky and Mark Jarzombek lent their support for my vision for an earlier version of this project. Robert Sumrell was closest of friends and best of critics. At the Netlab, Leah Meisterlin and Susan Surface's brought the project to entirely new levels. Most of all, at home, Jenny, Liam, and Viltis put up with another crazy project of mine and made it all worthwhile.

IMAGE CREDITS

4-11: Kazys Varnelis
13: Steve Rowell
18-19: Kazys Varnelis
20-29: Barry Lehrman
31-35: Kazys Varnelis
45-47: David Fletcher
49-65: Kazys Varnelis
66-73: Matthew Coolidge/CLUI
76-99: Lane Barden
100-101: Kazys Varnelis
102-111: Steve Rowell
112-113: Sean Dockray
115: Steve Rowell
118-119: Kazys Varnelis
123: City of Los Angeles Department of Building and Safety
125: Kazys Varnelis
127 (TOP): Kazys Varnelis
127 (BOTTOM): Steve Rowell
128-131: Kazys Varnelis
134-135: Ed Ruscha
139: Kazys Varnelis
141-143: Warren Techentin
145: David Burns, Matias Viegener, Austin Young
146-151: Kazys Varnelis
156-175: Lane Barden
176-177: Robert Sumrell
178-189: Roger Sherman
193: Kazys Varnelis
194-203: Roger Sherman
206-217: Kazys Varnelis
218-223: Robert Sumrell
227 (TOP): Kazys Varnelis
227 (BOTTOM): Robert Sumrell
231 (TOP): Kazys Varnelis
231 (BOTTOM): Robert Sumrell
235: Robert Sumrell
236-251: Lane Barden

ABOUT THE MAPS

Leah Meisterlin of the Network Architecture Lab at Columbia University's Graduate School of Architecture, Planning, and Preservation produced the maps in this publication using ArcGIS.

Initial inspiration for the maps came from Frank Ruchala's *OiLA* thesis at the Harvard Graduate School of Design. The Network Architecture Lab refined that vision. Our intent has been to lend consistency to the essays with twenty-first century counterparts to Mary Banham's maps for *Los Angeles: The Architecture of Four Ecologies*.

ABOUT THE AUTHORS

LANE BARDEN (http://www.lanebarden.com) is a photographer, teacher, and writer based in Los Angeles. He has taught photography at SCI_Arc and the Art Center College of Design, exhibited nationally, and has published numerous articles on photography and contemporary art.

MATTHEW COOLIDGE is the director of the Center for Land Use Interpretation (http://www.clui.org), a not for profit educational research organization based in Los Angeles.

SEAN DOCKRAY (http://spd.e-rat.org) is an artist and writer living in Los Angeles. His publications include *Bidoun, Cabinet, X-TRA,* and *Volume.*

DAVID FLETCHER is principal of the San Francisco based firm, Terrain Urban Design + Landscape Architecture (http://www.terrainla.com). He has taught at Harvard Design School, the University of Southern California, Otis College of Art and Design and Centre d'Etude d'Architecture et d'Urbanisme in Saintes, France. He is the author of *VOID City,* a book of his research and studio projects on the industrial city of Vernon, California. His work on the Los Angeles River Revitalization Master Plan won an A. I. A. award for Regional and Urban Planning.

TED KANE is an architect, photographer, and writer based in Los Angeles. He is the founder and editor of *Polar Inertia,* a journal devoted to urban and nomadic and research (http://www.polarinertia.com). He is a board member of the Los Angeles Forum for Architecture and Urban Design.

BARRY LEHRMAN lives in Minneapolis and practices landscape urbanism internationally. His photographs are in the collection of the Architectural Archive at the University of Pennsylvania and the Kent-Lucas Foundation.

LEAH MEISTERLIN holds an M. S. in Urban Planning and is pursuing an M. Arch. at the Columbia University Graduate School of Architecture, Planning, and Preservation. She is a GIS specialist, map designer, and a researcher at the Network Architecture Lab.

RICK MILLER is a Los Angeles-based researcher studying how nomads at the suburban edge of Ulaanbaatar, Mongolia settle the vernacular landscape. He was trained as an architect and worked on photography and documentation of the built heritage in the Field Projects section of the Getty Conservation Institute. He is a board member of the Los Angeles Forum for Architecture and Urban Design.

DEBORAH RICHMOND is a principal of Touraine Richmond Architects (http://www.touraine-richmond.com) in Venice, California and has taught architectural design and theory at the Art Center of Pasadena and SCI_Arc. She is a former board member of the Los Angeles Forum for Architecture and Urban Design.

STEVE ROWELL (http://www.steverowell.com) is an artist and designer currently working in Los Angeles and Berlin. He is an associate director at the Center for Land Use Interpretation. He is a former board member of the Los Angeles Forum for Architecture and Urban Design.

FRANK RUCHALA JR. is an associate city planner in New York's Department of City Planning. His work has been published and exhibited in the U. S. and internationally.

ROGER SHERMAN is principal of Roger Sherman Architecture and Urban Design (http://www.rsaud.com) in Santa Monica. He is author of *Re: American Dream* (Princeton Architectural Press, 1995), and *Under the Influence: Negotiating the Complex Logic of Urban Property* (University of Minnesota Press, 2008). He is Co-Director of cityLAB, an urban design thinktank at UCLA, where he also teaches.

ROBERT SUMRELL (http://www.robertsumrell.com) is co-director of AUDC, which published *Blue Monday: Stories of Absurd Realities and Natural Histories* in 2007. He works internationally in both production design and architecture.

WARREN TECHENTIN is co-principal of Techentin Buckingham Architecture in Los Angeles (http://www.techbuckarch.com). He has taught at the University of Southern California, Arizona State University, and the University of British Columbia. He is a former board member and president of the Los Angeles Forum for Architecture and Urban Design where he coordinated a competition on the redesign, reuse, and repackaging of dead malls and compiled the results into a pamphlet, *Dead Malls.*

FIONA WHITTON is an architectural designer and currently the Executive Director of TELIC Arts Exchange (http://www.telic.info) in Los Angeles. She is a former board member of the Los Angeles Forum for Architecture and Urban Design.

KAZYS VARNELIS (http://kazys.varnelis.net) is the
Director of the Network Architecture Lab at the Columbia
University Graduate School of Architecture, Planning,
and Preservation. Based in New York, he holds a Ph.D. in
the history of architecture and urban development from
Cornell University. Varnelis is on the architecture faculty
at Columbia and is a member of the founding faculty of
the School of Architecture at the University of Limerick,
Ireland. He was formerly on the faculty of the Southern
California Institute of Architecture where he was also co-
ordinator of the History and Theory program. Varnelis has
been a visiting lecturer at the University of Southern California, University of Pennsylvania, and the Massachusetts
Institute of Technology. He has worked with the Center
for Land Use Interpretation and is a co-founder of AUDC,
which published *Blue Monday: Absurd Realities and Natural
Philosophies* in 2007 and editor of *Networked Publics* and *The
Philip Johnson Tapes: Interviews by Robert A.M. Stern*, both
published in 2008. He was President of the Los Angeles
Forum for Architecture and Urban Design in 2004 and 2005
and Vice-President for Publications in 2003 and 2006.

THE NETWORK ARCHITECTURE LAB [NETLAB]
is a research unit in Columbia University's Graduate School
of Architecture, Planning, and Preservation. The Netlab
investigates how computation, communications, and
changing social networks impact architecture and the city.

THE LOS ANGELES FORUM FOR ARCHITECTURE
AND URBAN DESIGN is a non-profit organization
dedicated to supporting innovative art, architecture, design,
and urbanism. The Forum generates events, initiates publications, and instigates discussion to engage both design
professionals and the broader community in Los Angeles
and beyond.

EDITED BY
Kazys Varnelis

with
Michael Kubo (Actar)

MAPS BY
Leah Meisterlin (Netlab)

PUBLISHED BY
Actar
http://www.actar.com
info@actar.com

A PUBLICATION OF
The Network Architecture Lab,
Graduate School of Architecture,
Planning and Preservation
Columbia University
http://www.networkarchitecturelab.org

AND
The Los Angeles Forum for
Architecture and Urban Design
http://www.laforum.org

GRAPHIC DESIGN
Marieke Bielas (Actar Pro)
Susan Surface (Netlab)

DIGITAL PRODUCTION
Carmen Galán, Oriol Rigat (Actar Pro)

PRINTING
Ingoprint S.A.

DISTRIBUTION
Actar D
Roca i Batlle 2
08023 Barcelona
Tel +34 934174993
Fax +34934186707
office@actar-d.com
http://www.actar-d.com

DISTRIBUTION IN THE UNITED STATES
Actar Distribution Inc
158 Lafayette St. 5th Floor
New York, NY 10013
Tel +1 212 966 2207
Fax +1 212 966 2214
officeusa@actar-d.com
http://www.actar-d.com

ISBN 978-84-96954-25-0
DL B-47819-08

Printed and bound in the European Union